Camera Obscura   100

Feminism, Culture, and Media Studies

On Chantal Akerman
Guest Editor: Patricia White
for the *Camera Obscura* Editorial Collective

Editors: Lalitha Gopalan, Lynne Joyrich, Homay King, Bliss Cua Lim, Constance Penley, Tess Takahashi, Patricia White, and Sharon Willis

Advisory Editors: Paula Amad, Aubrey Anable, Joanne Bernardi, Shohini Chaudhuri, Michelle Cho, Rey Chow, Wendy Hui Kyong Chun, Mary Desjardins, Mary Ann Doane, Rosa-Linda Fregoso, Bishnupriya Ghosh, Jennifer González, Elena Gorfinkel, Roger Hallas, Amelie Hastie, Jennifer Horne, Dina Iordanova, Ana López, Yosefa Loshitzky, Kathleen McHugh, Mandy Merck, Meaghan Morris, Frances Negrón-Muntaner, Kathleen Newman, Lisa Parks, B. Ruby Rich, Ella Shohat, Beretta Smith-Shomade, Janet Staiger, Jacqueline Stewart, Sasha Torres, and Mimi White

Managing Editor: Chip Badley

Editorial Assistants: Rachael Ball, Brian Huser, and Sarah Lerner

Camera Obscura is published three times a year by Duke University Press, 905 W. Main St., Suite 18B, Durham, NC 27701.

Thanks to the University of California, Santa Barbara, College of Letters and Science and Department of Film and Media Studies for their generous support of the editorial office. *Camera Obscura* also benefits from the generous support of the following institutions: the University of Rochester, Brown University, Bryn Mawr College, Swarthmore College, the University of Texas at Austin, and the University of California, Irvine.

Send correspondence to *Camera Obscura*, Department of Film and Media Studies, University of California, Santa Barbara, CA 93106-4010.

Visit Duke University Press Journals at www.dukeupress.edu/journals.

Direct all orders to Duke University Press, Journals Customer Relations, 905 W. Main St., Suite 18B, Durham, NC 27701. Volume 34 of *Camera Obscura* corresponds to issues 100–102. Annual subscription rates: print-plus-electronic institutions, $267; print-only institutions, $247; e-only institutions, $201; e-only individuals, $15; individuals, $30; students, $20. For information on subscriptions to the e-Duke Journals Scholarly Collections, contact libraryrelations@dukeupress.edu.

Print subscriptions: add $11 postage and applicable HST (including 5% GST) for Canada; add $14 postage outside the US and Canada. Back volumes (institutions): $247. Single issues: institutions, $82; individuals, $12. For more information, contact Duke University Press Journals at 888-651-0122 (toll-free in the US and Canada) or 919-688-5134; subscriptions@dukeupress.edu.

Photocopies for course or research use that are supplied to the end user at no cost may be made without explicit permission or fee. Photocopies that are provided to the end user for a fee may not be made without payment of permission fees to Duke University Press. Address requests for permission to republish copyrighted material to Rights and Permissions Manager, permissions@dukeupress.edu.

Direct inquiries about advertising to Journals Advertising Coordinator, journals_advertising@dukeupress.edu.

Camera Obscura provides a forum for scholarship and debate on feminism, culture, and media studies. The journal encourages contributions in areas such as the conjunctions of gender, race, class, and sexuality with audiovisual culture; new histories and theories of film, television, video, and digital media; and politically engaged approaches to a range of media practices.

Contributor Information

Camera Obscura seeks substantial essays (approximately 6,500–9,000 words, including endnotes and references) that engage with current academic and popular debates in feminism, culture, and media studies. We encourage potential contributors to browse recent issues of the journal for examples of the types of scholarship we currently seek.

Camera Obscura is also interested in short pieces (750–2,500 words) on current media practices, practitioners, resources, events, or issues for the section "In Practice: Feminism/Culture/Media." The editors encourage authors to use the short format to experiment with form in a critical context. The section includes solicited contributions and open submissions, with the intention of enriching dialogue between feminist media scholarship and the practices—production, distribution, exhibition, organizing, curating, archiving, research, and so on—that sustain it.

Please submit one electronic copy (as a Microsoft Word email attachment to cameraobscura@filmandmedia.ucsb.edu) of the manuscript with a cover letter. Manuscripts should be double-spaced and use endnotes. *Camera Obscura*'s documentation style follows *The Chicago Manual of Style*, 17th ed., chap. 14.

Camera Obscura, Department of Film and Media Studies, University of California, Santa Barbara, CA 93106-4010; fax: 805-893-8630; email: cameraobscura@filmandmedia.ucsb.edu.

Indexing and Abstract Listings

For a list of sources in which *Camera Obscura* is indexed and abstracted, see www.dukeupress.edu/camera-obscura.

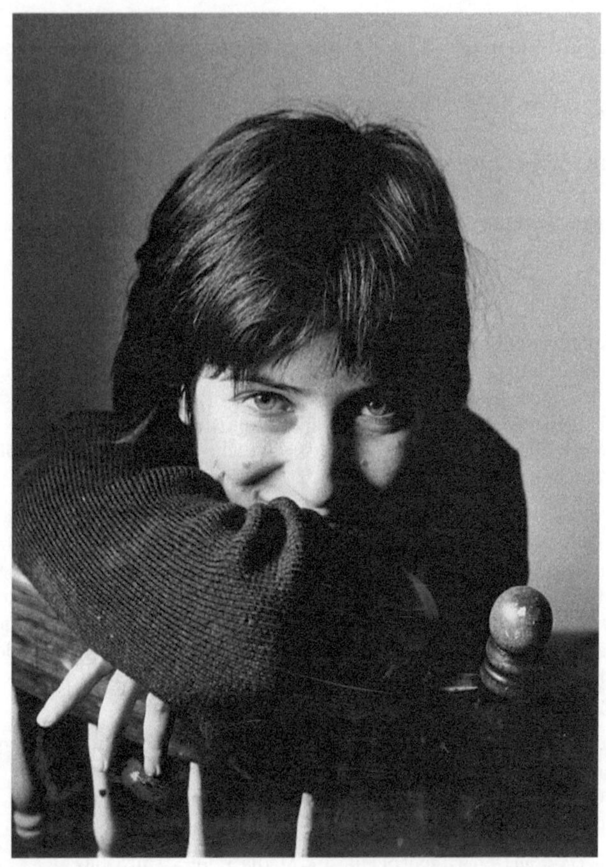

Figure 1. Chantal Akerman, New York City (ca. 1976).
© Jane Stein

Camera Obscura
and Chantal Akerman

Patricia White

The first issue of *Camera Obscura*, published in 1976, opened with an unsigned editorial. In "Feminism and Film: Critical Approaches," the collective's founding members Janet Bergstrom, Sandy Flitterman-Lewis, Elisabeth Lyon, and Constance Penley—identified only in the journal's front matter—introduced readers to what Penley would later characterize as a "distinct and insistently polemical strain of feminist film criticism."[1] The issue was dedicated to French theoretical perspectives and to "films made by women . . . that offer a critique of the representation of woman in classical cinema. They contribute to the development of a feminist counter-cinema both by having as their central concern a feminist problematic, and by operating specific challenges to cinematic codes and narrative conventions of illusionist cinema."[2]

In the same issue, Christina Creveling profiled filmmakers committed to such practices under the heading "Women Working," Chantal Akerman among them. Creveling documented each of the director's films to date, as well as the work in progress that would become *News from Home* (Belgium/France, 1976). Of *Jeanne Dielman, 23 quai du Commerce, 1080 Bruxelles* (Belgium/France, 1975),

Camera Obscura 100, Volume 34, Number 1
DOI 10.1215/02705346-7264064   © 2019 by *Camera Obscura*
Published by Duke University Press

1

she wrote with anticipation: "I have not seen this film and it has no distributor in this country. My hopes are not high that it will find one: it is unusually long, it can be considered a non-narrative film, and it is clearly made from a feminist perspective."[3]

Later that year, the *Camera Obscura* collective had the opportunity to see *Jeanne Dielman* and to interview Akerman about it at the Pacific Film Archive. The filmmaker's words, and a critical essay written by "Janet Bergstrom for the *Camera Obscura* collective," both notable for the thrilling precision of their language, appeared in the second issue. Akerman: "I *do* think it is a feminist film because I give space to images that are never, almost never, shown in that way, like the daily gestures of a woman"; Bergstrom: "It is the quality and interest of the controlling look that makes *Jeanne Dielman* stand out formally as feminist, and not any particular formal feature."[4] The film and the journal were thus entwined and ensconced in an originary moment of transatlantic feminist film studies.

This, the hundredth issue of *Camera Obscura*, returns to Chantal Akerman to mark the journal's ongoing commitment to such dialogic encounters between feminist criticism and moving image practices. The journal's polemics have softened; its feminisms are transnational, queer, and intersectional; and its scope has expanded to encompass other forms of media, as well as contributions from many fields, schools of thought, and locations. With the exception of Constance Penley, who oversees the journal's production and editorial staff at the University of California, Santa Barbara, the membership of the editorial collective has changed. Certainly, a focus on a single filmmaker in a special issue cannot encapsulate all that the journal has become. But as Akerman herself declared: "I have thought that the more particular I am, the more I address the general."[5] The history of Akerman's films and the responses they have excited are significant measures of the intellectual and affective intensity of feminist film culture—a *living* history, made by women, with the help of others, whose labor is as enduring as the image of Jeanne Dielman's.

Filmmaker, writer, installation artist, teacher, daughter, sister, lover, friend, Akerman was a restless soul whose death by suicide on 5 October 2015 has occasioned numerous eloquent tributes and critical assessments, both heartbreaking and inspiring. Bérénice Reynaud compiled a powerful memorial collection of writings by women who knew Akerman that appeared in *Senses of Cinema* in December 2015. She was motivated in part by "the outpouring of emails, testimonies, letters even, from *women* from all over the world, some of them very young, saying, 'I never knew Chantal Akerman, but her cinema speaks to me, so profoundly, so intimately.'"[6] (Recall Teresa de Lauretis's account of *Jeanne Dielman* in "Rethinking Women's Cinema" as a film that "*addresses its spectator as a woman*, regardless of the gender of the viewers.")[7] Appearing a year later, Ivone Margulies and B. Ruby Rich's collection of essays in *Film Quarterly* highlighted the transnational community of Akerman scholars and friends who are going on living and working in the wake of her passing.[8] *Camera Obscura*'s editors have found Akerman's work—its intertwining of emotion and aesthetics, of the epiphany and the *longue durée*—of central importance to their own. This special issue is then a necessary contribution to and acknowledgment of the creative production, curation, scholarship, and forms of sociality constituting this global response.

The issue opens with an account by one of Akerman's key collaborators. In her interview with Ivone Margulies, Claire Atherton details the synchronies and exchanges that characterized her work as editor of Akerman's films and installations over thirty years. Returning to *Camera Obscura* are two of the journal's cofounders whose work has been crucial to Akerman scholarship. Janet Bergstrom contributes a fascinating conversation with cinematographer Babette Mangolte about working with Akerman in New York in the 1970s. Their exchange is also a return, as Mangolte was first profiled in that same "Women Working" column in *Camera Obscura* in 1977 and featured in the subsequent issue.[9] Loaded with detail and previously unpublished in English, this 1998 interview has been updated and supplemented by the participants. Mangolte's collaboration with Akerman is vividly documented in photographs by Jane Stein of the shoot of *Hanging Out Yonkers* (Belgium, 1973), Akerman's first, uncompleted, docu-

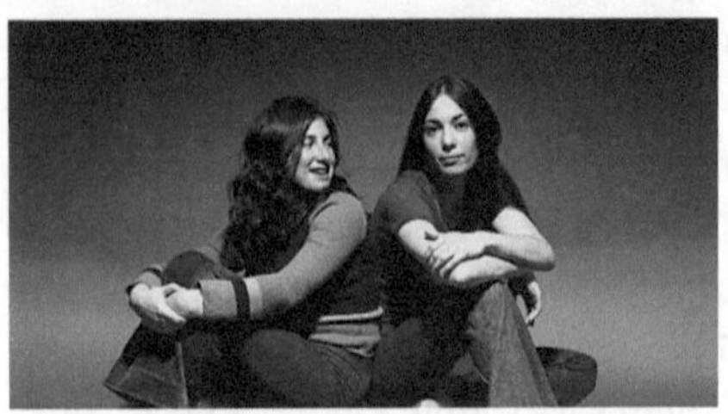

Figure 2. Chantal Akerman and her friend Jane Stein, whom she met in New York City in 1971. Courtesy of Jane Stein

mentary. Stein's original offering of a couch in New York in 1971 launched the filmmaker on this decisive period of her career; her photos offer a rare glimpse of Akerman's creative process and the community around her at the time. And Mangolte's precise eye and exuberant intelligence are as evident in her account of Akerman's final work, the five-screen and soundscape installation *NOW* (2015), as they are in the stories she tells of introducing Akerman to the avant-garde forty years earlier.

Sandy Flitterman-Lewis, another founding editor of *Camera Obscura*, contributes a moving testimony in the form of a memory chain modeled after French writer and Holocaust survivor Georges Perec's *I Remember*. In this intersubjective chronicle of her work on and alongside Akerman, Flitterman-Lewis conveys both the centrality of Akerman's family history and Jewish identity to the filmmaker's work and, in her associative style, something of Akerman's own delight in combining the fortuitous with the formalist. Complementing this piece is the affecting tribute Claire Atherton contributed to Akerman's memorial. The biographical, the embodied, the anecdotal—perspectives and topics that were approached gingerly in early feminist film criticism—have proved essential in analyzing the "particular generality" of Akerman's achievement. With Akerman's background as a Belgian child of Holocaust survivors, a lesbian, and an artist who suffered from bipolar disorder, she makes no claims to universality but inhabits her time and place and practice against a distinct historical horizon.

Memory is a central concern of Akerman's oeuvre—the ways bodies are imprinted by routines, the stories and silences that run through generations, the way films are reinterpreted in gallery-based work—and it is theorized and enacted in several contributions to this issue. Maureen Turim interprets the transmission of generational legacies in Akerman's work through the key installation *Marcher à côté de ses lacets dans un frigidaire vide* (*Walking Next to One's Shoelaces in an Empty Fridge*, 2004), which combines the diary of the filmmaker's grandmother, who perished in Auschwitz, with filmed conversations with Natalia Liebel-Akerman, the daughter who survived. Akerman grapples with her mother Natalia (Nelly)'s experiences in film after film and in autobiographical works like this installation and the memoirs *Une famille à Bruxelles* (*A Family in Brussels*, 1998) and *Ma mère rit* (*My Mother Laughs*, 2013).[10] Turim's compelling framing of this multigenerational maternal legacy is complemented by Brenda Longfellow's deft and poignant reading of *No Home Movie* (France/Belgium, 2015) through the framework of Bracha Ettinger's concept of the matrixial. Filmed in the months before Natalia's death and premiering only weeks before Akerman's own, the film is a tender rendering of the elderly widow's quotidian existence in her Brussels apartment and of her daughter's attempts to connect. While much thoughtful criticism about *No Home Movie* has appeared since its release, the perspectives of these prominent North American feminist scholars in the context of this special issue meaningfully connect this last film to Akerman's oeuvre while enlivening psychoanalytic approaches to her work.

Akerman's passion has always been an antidote to melancholy in her work, and the joy of song is the subject of Kelley Conway's essay, which chronicles women's singing (often off-key) and its disruption to normative images of femininity and female desire across Akerman's films. Eroticism and gender identity inform Akerman's recurrent themes of ambivalence, exile, and empathy as much as do familial ties, although these subjects have been overshadowed by, or folded into, the topics of mourning and the maternal in recent Akerman criticism. Conway's is one of few essays in this issue to address lesbian desire in Akerman's films, and it is striking that it connects desire to music, a topic that returns in the pieces collected in the "In Practice" portfolio.

In 2008, the *Camera Obscura* collective reinstated the journal's short-form coverage of feminist media practices, both within and outside the academy; the "Women Working" feature of the journal's inaugural issues was revived as "In Practice." Feminist scholarly attention to public feelings, so germane to cinema itself (and to Akerman's fluency in that medium, as I have been suggesting), informed this decision. For this issue's "In Practice" we asked organizers to share accounts of Akerman memorial events both to document the events and to evoke the sense of discovery and common cause that characterized this work. We extended invitations to Eva Kuhn and Ute Holl, organizers of a symposium in Basel in 2016, and to curators Michael Mazière in London and Sandra Percival in Portland, Oregon. The events and accounts produced by this generation of scholars and curators reach out to new publics for Akerman's work.

"The Difficulty of Forgetting," as the Basel memorial symposium was named, is the theme of ten short contributions from Akerman specialists on wide-ranging topics—food, trains, genre, and more—in the filmmaker's oeuvre. The polyvocal form of this conference report aspires to capture the rhythm and reflection provoked by its public screenings and presentations. Kuhn speaks of film as a membrane that holds inside and outside, memory and history, in tension in Akerman's attention to the everyday; Holl evokes the protagonist's feeling of being haunted by Germany's recent past as she travels with her films in *Les Rendez-vous d'Anna* (*The Meetings of Anna*, Belgium/France/Germany, 1978); Eva Meyer describes how the vector of song and an ensemble cast redistribute memory in *Golden Eighties* (France/Belgium/Switzerland, 1986).

Mazière, in turn, describes the curation of *Chantal Akerman: NOW*, a 2015 retrospective of Akerman's gallery-based work that complemented a complete season of Akerman's films programmed by A Nos Amours (Adam Roberts and Joanna Hogg) in London, events that were shockingly disrupted by Akerman's death. Percival's year-long artist season in Portland, Oregon, was curated in memoriam and included screenings, lectures, and live events. The season culminated in a performance by world-renowned cellist

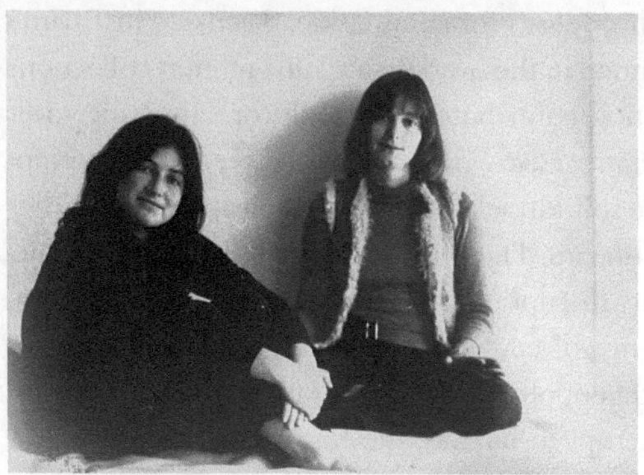

Figure 3. Chantal Akerman and Marilyn Watelet,
her lifelong friend and producer from Brussels, 1972.
© Jane Stein

Sonia Wieder-Atherton of *CHANTAL?* (2018), a piece that incorporates Akerman's first film, *Saute ma ville* (*Blow Up My Town*, Belgium, 1968), and the filmmaker's voice reading from *A Family in Brussels*. Percival's framing of her onstage conversation and correspondence with Wieder-Atherton captures the pathos and intensity of this tribute by Akerman's longtime companion and collaborator. These events, and others not documented here, strive to connect Akerman's work across media—writing, film, video, installation, and live performance—evoking her abiding interest in the play of presence, absence, and the idea of an elsewhere.

The editors of *Camera Obscura* extend our gratitude to sisters Sonia Wieder-Atherton and Claire Atherton, who are working with Akerman's sister Sylviane and her lifelong friend and producer Marilyn Watelet through the Chantal Akerman Foundation, Cinematek in Brussels, and the Marian Goodman Gallery to preserve Akerman's work and produce research materials, such as the filmography and list of installations we include here.[11] Their generosity helps communicate the scope of Akerman's accomplishment to a readership most familiar with her films, and their intimacy with the filmmaker brings a sense of her loyalty, charm, and humor to these pages.

Akerman's propensity for rumination, discussed in Turim's essay, is perhaps echoed in the overlaps and divergent recollections gathered here: multiple contributors invoke the opening voice-over from *Histoires d'Amérique: Food, Family, and Philosophy* (1988), attempt to make sense of the soundtrack of *NOW*, and spiral back on earlier claims and commentaries. These inconsistencies reflect the structure of memory—its disruptions, its consolations, and its generativeness. Much is unresolved, as it was for Akerman: questions of desire, identity, and geopolitics. Memory's lapses and unexpected links shape any attempt to narrate the history of this journal as well. Setting issue 100 beside issue 1 of *Camera Obscura* marks four decades of public thinking and feeling about feminism, media, and culture—and it marks a return. Akerman's career reflects the unimaginable changes produced in this interval by feminist cultural inquiry, and also its most basic, ongoing provocations. In *Lettre d'une cinéaste* (1984), Akerman says, only half joking, "In order to make films, you have to get out of bed." *Pour faire un film, il faut se lever. Levons-nous.* Let's rise.

Notes

My thanks to Myra Alfreds, Nicola Mazzanti, Sandra Percival, B. Ruby Rich, Jane Stein, Marilyn Watelet, and Andrea Weiss for help with dates, photos, and contacts. Special thanks to Ivone Margulies, the members of the *Camera Obscura* editorial collective, and managing editor Chip Badley for their generous assistance with the conceptualization and editing of this special issue.

1. Constance Penley, "Introduction—The Lady Doesn't Vanish: Feminism and Film Theory," *Feminism and Film Theory*, ed. Constance Penley (New York: Routledge, 1988), 1. For further reflection on the journal's history, see *Camera Obscura* Collective, "*Camera Obscura* at Thirty: Archiving the Past, Imagining the Future," *Camera Obscura*, no. 61 (2006): 1–25.

2. "Feminism and Film: Critical Approaches," *Camera Obscura*, no. 1 (1976): 4.

3. Cristina Creveling, "Chantal Akerman," *Camera Obscura*, no. 1 (1976): 137.

4. Janet Bergstrom for the *Camera Obscura* collective, "*Jeanne Dielman: 23 quai du Commerce, 1080 Bruxelles*," *Camera Obscura*, no. 2 (1977): 118.

5. Quoted as the epigraph to the introduction in Ivone Margulies, *Nothing Happens: Chantal Akerman's Hyperrealist Everyday* (Durham, NC: Duke University Press, 1996), 1.

6. Bérénice Reynaud, "In Memoriam—Chantal Akerman: La Passion de l'intime/An Intimate Passion," *Senses of Cinema* 77 (2015), sensesofcinema.com/2015/chantal-akerman/introduction -chantal-akerman-an-intimate-passion/.

7. Teresa de Lauretis, "Aesthetic and Feminist Theory: Rethinking Women's Cinema," *New German Critique* 34 (1985): 161.

8. Ivone Margulies and B. Ruby Rich, eds., "Dossier: Chantal Akerman," *Film Quarterly* 70, no. 1 (2016): 11–84. See also Margulies's account of the event "Chantal Akerman: New York Remembers" in her article "Remembering Chantal Akerman: A Dry and Moving Intensity," *Criterion Current*, 23 March 2016, www.criterion.com/current/posts/3986-remembering -chantal-akerman-a-dry-and-moving-intensity. Andrea Weiss, an organizer of the New York event presented by City College and the Film Society of Lincoln Center on 19 March 2016, produced a video record, available online at vimeo.com /162304275.

9. "*Camera Obscura* interview with Babette Mangolte," *Camera Obscura*, nos. 3–4 (1979), 198–210.

10. Chantal Akerman, *Une famille à Bruxelles* (Paris: L'Arche, 1998), *A Family in Brussels* (New York: Dia Art Foundation, 2003); Chantal Akerman, *Ma mère rit* (Paris: Mercure de France, 2013). Two English translations of the latter work are forthcoming, by Corina Copp for the Song Cave in the US and by Daniella Shrier for Silver Press in the UK.

11. The filmography and list of installations included here are not definitive. Cinematek conservator Nicola Mazzanti notes that the establishment of an authoritative filmography of Akerman's works will be one of the first endeavors of the collaboration with the Chantal Akerman Foundation, whose preliminary website launched in May 2018, www.chantal-akerman.foundation.

Patricia White is Eugene Lang Research Professor and chair of the Department of Film and Media Studies at Swarthmore College. She is the author of *Women's Cinema/World Cinema: Projecting Contemporary Feminisms* (2015) and *Uninvited: Classical Hollywood Cinema and Lesbian Representability* (1999), and her work in feminist and queer film studies has been published in *Camera Obscura, Cinema Journal, Film Quarterly, GLQ,* and *Screen* and in such edited collections as *Sisters in the Life* (2018), *Indie Reframed* (2016), *A Feminist Reader in Early Cinema* (2002), and *Out in Culture* (1995). She is coauthor with Timothy Corrigan of *The Film Experience* (5th ed., 2017) and coeditor with Corrigan and Meta Mazaj of *Critical Visions in Film Theory* (2011). White serves on the board of the nonprofit feminist media arts organization Women Make Movies and has been a member of the editorial collective of *Camera Obscura* since 1997.

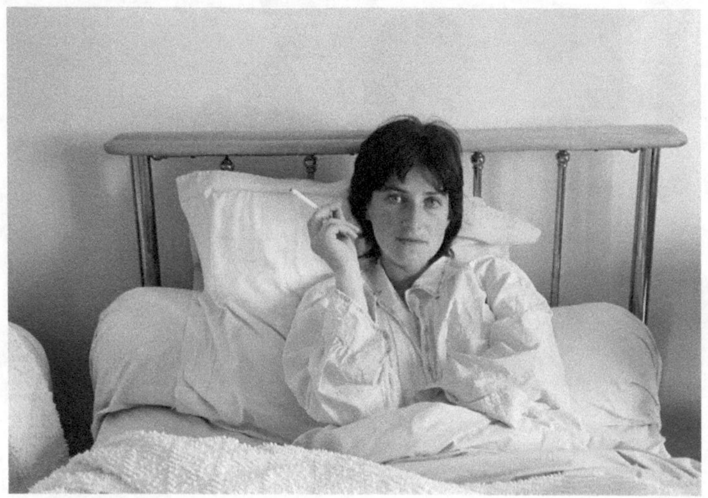

Figure 4. Chantal Akerman in Cannes, 1977.
© Elizabeth Lennard

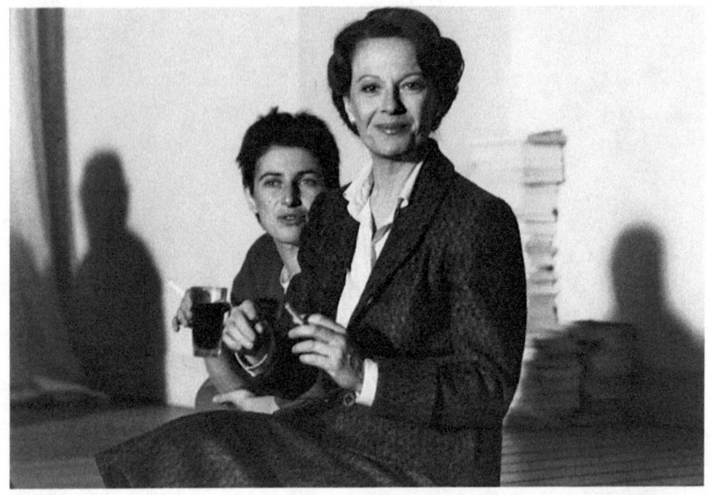

Figure 1. Chantal Akerman and Delphine Seyrig, 1984.
© Catherine Deudon

Our Way of Working:
A Conversation with
Claire Atherton about
Chantal Akerman

Ivone Margulies

Claire Atherton worked closely with Chantal Akerman for thirty years, editing numerous fiction films and documentaries. She also worked on all of Akerman's installations. At the invitation of *Camera Obscura*, Ivone Margulies interviewed Atherton in Paris in December 2017. The interview has been edited for publication.

Ivone Margulies: *Claire, tell me a little bit about you and Chantal at the beginning.*

Claire Atherton: It was in 1984. I was working at the Centre Audio-visuel Simone de Beauvoir, whose purpose was archiving and producing women's films. I did technical work—I went to shoots, carried the gear, prepared the camera, sometimes did sound. One morning, I remember it was a Sunday, Delphine Seyrig, who was the president of the center, called me. She and her niece Coralie Seyrig were performing in *Letters Home* at the time, a play based

Camera Obscura 100, Volume 34, Number 1
DOI 10.1215/02705346-7264074   © 2019 by *Camera Obscura*
Published by Duke University Press

on Sylvia Plath's diary. French TV wanted to film it. Delphine didn't trust French TV; she wanted Chantal. So Delphine asked me to go with Chantal to record it on video. Two days later, I took the camera—the gear was very heavy gear at that point, not light like the video equipment we have now, you know—and I went with Chantal to a little theater in Paris in Rue Blanche. It was an actual . . .

Performance.

Yes, with an audience and everything. I put the camera on the tripod and set up the microphone, did a little sound check, and I told Chantal she could start filming, I would focus. Then the play began, and after a while, Chantal told me, "You hold the camera, I will focus!" So, I filmed. l didn't even have time to feel fear. Everything seemed so simple. We didn't speak much, but every time I moved to one direction or zoomed a little to get closer to Delphine or Coralie, Chantal was about to tell me to do so. It was like a dream, you know. The presence of Delphine and Coralie, and Chantal next to me—it was a very deep feeling. After the shoot, she said, "It's incredible, we feel exactly the same way!" Then she ran to Delphine and said, "Who is this young girl? I want to work with her!"

This story means a great deal to me. Of course, because it's the beginning of our collaboration—but also because it says something about how Chantal worked and how she chose people to work with. She didn't ask for degrees or anything. She just trusted her feelings. She did not decide with her head, but with her heart and with her whole body.

By the way, the footage wasn't in focus. But we just forgot French TV!

After that, we worked together on short movies that are quite unknown, such as *Autour d'un marteau* (*The Hammer,* France, 1986) about artist Jean-Luc Vilmouth, or *Rue Mallet Stevens* (Belgium, 1986). It was like Chantal's underground French period. She was also preparing *Golden Eighties* (France/Belgium/Switzerland, 1986) and *Les Années 80* (*The Eighties,* France/Belgium, 1983). But she liked very much doing those little bricolages in video, trying things. When I look at that period now, with distance, I think that's what led us to work on the installations. We were inventing a way of working. In 1986 Chantal made a film of *Letters Home* with a new mise-en-scène. It wasn't a filmed performance anymore—it was a shoot of several weeks. That was the first important film we edited together.

Claire, I remember that the editing is very worked through, isn't it?

Yes. We were editing in video. The principle of video editing is to copy the rushes from one cassette to another. But each time you copy, you lose image and sound quality. For that film, since we had very little money, we were working with U-matic video, without time code. So we had to edit the final version directly. We couldn't go backwards to change a take or correct the length of a shot or anything. We edited totally chronologically with no possibility of changing. We liked that. It was like working without a net. Sometimes we looked at several takes of a scene, and when we felt it was a good one, we stopped looking. It seems incredible not to have seen all the takes. But we trusted our feelings, and we shaped the film like that.

In fact, it's important for me to begin to build a film from the first shots as if it were the foundation of a house. The more the film grows, the more it exists on its own terms, and the more it rejects some scenes and accepts other ones. It leads you, and it builds its own chronology. The beginning is like a choice you make, sometimes without knowing why. Then you work with this choice, and little by little you begin to understand the reasons for it. Some people say that in editing you have to concentrate first on the structure and the meaning and then work on rhythm. For me, that's impossible, because the rhythm is part of the narration. I can almost say it's the rhythm that creates the narration.

The connection you make with the technical aspect of U-matic—the fact that you can't go back, that you associate that with a method that you and Chantal created of accumulating from the first image—that's very interesting.

Yes, this first collaboration editing in U-matic was very important. I was very lucky to edit that film so young, because when you are young, you don't ask yourself that many questions—you just go. You know, I have always loved Chinese language and civilization, and I was studying it at that time. In Chinese thinking, particularly for the Taoists, you don't force things. You let them come. You create a movement, and life is this movement. Movement is linked to another important concept in Taoism, which is emptiness. Emptiness is the place where the links between different things can be made and meaning can emerge. I don't know if Chantal and I really had a method, but if we did, it was linked to that way of thinking. We both needed to discover while doing. We were not closing the film in a particular meaning. We were creating a space for the film to grow.

I have a question about No Home Movie *(France/Belgium, 2015)— about deciding to include the images of the desert in the film. Was it because she was making those desert images at the same time as she was making* No Home Movie?

Well, more or less yes. But the story of *No Home Movie* is particular. It's a film that wasn't "premeditated." What I mean is that Chantal had not decided to make a film before shooting. In April 2014, we were supposed to work together on an installation based on images she had shot in the desert. And that was when Chantal's mother died.

A few weeks later, when we met in the editing room, which was in Chantal's living room, Chantal told me: "You know, for the past two years I have been filming my mother a lot. I don't remember what I filmed, but I would like us to look at all those images together and see if we can make something." I remember she said "something"—she didn't say "a film" or "an installation." So that's what we did. We looked at all the images. It was like spending time with Chantal's mother, keeping her with us. For almost two weeks, we looked and edited a little bit. We were not really editing—just putting moments together. The first version we made was almost four hours long and was only images of Chantal and her mother.

During this period, we were also working on the other images—the ones Chantal had shot in the desert. We usually looked at them at the end of the day after having spent a lot of time with Chantal's mother. We began to edit a three-screen installation.

Little by little, it became obvious that we would mix the images of the desert with the images of Chantal's mother. It was as if we felt it from the beginning, but we hadn't said it with words [because] we hadn't realized it really. We put in the tree, and the bench, and Natalia walking in the corridor. At that moment, we knew a film was possible. The real process of editing could begin.

At first we named the film *Home Movie*, then Chantal changed it to *No Home Movie*. The images of the desert became an installation that we called *From the Mother to the Desert* (*De la mèr(e) au desert*, 2014). It was shown a few months later in Jerusalem. So everything was linked. That's how we worked, and that's why I like to say that Chantal knew how to welcome what we call in French *hasard*.

Chance.

Yes, chance. All of a sudden it was so clear that the two *matières* would mix and that the film would appear. I don't know how to translate the French word *matières*.

Material?

Yes, something like material, but more alive. The images of the desert created a distance, which is always so important in Chantal's work, not to be stuck to the emotion. The images of the desert are an elsewhere—they are not linked to a particular location. We didn't know at that moment that this film would be so concerned with questions about what it is to be close and to be far. Chantal always wanted to give space to viewers to build their own relationship to the film, to raise questions by themselves, to work. . . . She wanted to be at the same level as the viewers. She didn't want to know more.

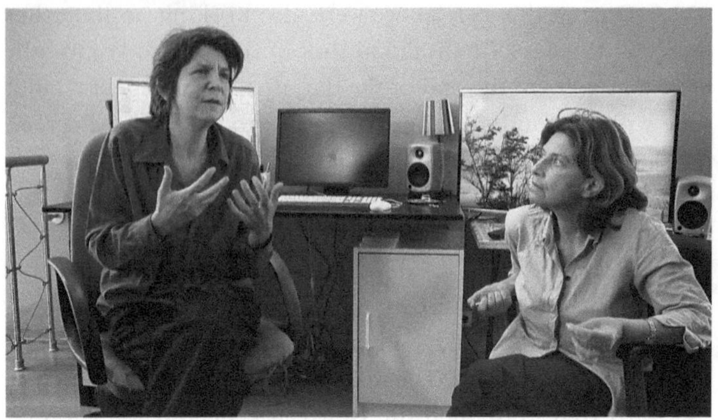

Figure 2. Claire Atherton and Chantal Akerman, 2014.
© Artémis Productions

I am curious about a couple of shots inside the apartment in No Home Movie, *when Chantal was walking towards the balcony at night, using a subjective camera that I find very unusual for her. These shots are very abstract. They feel markedly more urgent, and they start from within the apartment, ending with a look out of the balcony into the garden. The shots are dark, and one simply senses their repeated movement towards the outside. I don't remember ever seeing such dramatic, subjective shots. I'm not saying that everything is not subjective—I know that everything has her behind it, even though it may look static or very symmetrical. But those shots are expressive, almost expressionistic, in a way that I had never seen in her work. Did you talk about that? Were you surprised by those shots?*

No, we didn't talk about that. You know, the whole film was a surprise! In the rushes I could see how Chantal was building the frame. It was completely instinctive. She didn't have a tripod, of course, so she put the camera on a table, then moved the table to get the right angle. Then she pushed the camera to the right, then to the left, then backwards, then again to the right. All that was very noisy and messy. You thought the camera would fall. And all of the sudden a frame appeared, as if it had been scientifically composed, completely symmetrical, and so strong.

It's true, the images you are talking about are almost expressionistic. But they don't show anxiety. They are full of anxiety by themselves. It was different each time with Chantal. She was always inventing—everything was possible, she had no rules. She had a very physical and organic relationship to images. In one shot at the end of the film she goes out on the balcony, and the frame becomes completely white. It's shot with a different camera, a Nikon. Chantal wanted to try out the light. I thought the light was so dramatic that I just put the shot in, and it stayed there. It immediately became part of the story of the film.

Yes, that way of working is there in the use of light in the film—the mother sometimes blocks the light, sometimes is silhouetted, and sometimes the entire place is dark, and then there is that white by the balcony. There is an arc connected to the disappearance of Chantal from the film physically, and of the mother too. Sometimes the mother is there; sometimes she is not there. There is a balance. I thought of the films of [Yasujirō] Ozu. There is something so calm—bittersweet, dramatic, but calm.

Yes. I think it's because her images carry that dramatic intensity in themselves. You know, images are alive. They have their own secrets. In editing, if you are receptive to light, to lines, to colors— if you don't close images in a particular meaning—they talk to you and lead you. That's very Taoist! Though we didn't really talk about Taoism.

You never talked to Chantal about Taoism?

Sometimes, but not in a way that was linked to our editing process. I don't think we wanted to understand what it was that was so deep between us. We probably liked the mystery! But I've always thought that there was a link between my passion for Taoism, the importance of emptiness and movement, suggesting more than showing, et cetera, and our way of working. For example, in *D'Est* (*From the East*, France/Belgium, 1993), the images of people waiting—

Different groups think of different histories there.

Yes. It's not simply information about a particular situation at a particular time. It's a way of looking at the present so deeply that something more profound appears. Something that is beyond what you see and recalls other situations, other times.

As you were speaking, I was thinking of D'Est. *When you look at those lines of people, you think about displacement. Chantal made allusions to Jewish history, of course, but in later films she was thinking about parallels with other histories. In an interview, she talks about her mother watching* South (Sud, *France/Belgium, 1999), or maybe* From the Other Side (De l'autre côté, *Belgium, 2000), and remembering how her family always moved close to the walls, afraid. I think that she started making more explicit parallels.*

Yes, but the parallels only became explicit at the end of the editing process. The work on *D'Est* was very important. I think it was the beginning of something. We worked on the editing as if it were a composition. This word has to be understood in both its plastic and musical meanings. We were sculpting images and sounds in time and space, searching for the right rhythm. We edited the same way Chantal had shot—following our intuitions without trying to understand. We used very simple words, talking about colors, lights, contrasts, rhythm breaks or rhythm continuity, night and day, exteriors and interiors, violence and softness. When we looked at the long tracking shots over the faces of people waiting, or at the images of people walking, we talked about their eyes, their looks, their movements, their smiles, their beauty, and sometimes their sadness. I think we felt that those images referred back to other people waiting or walking, to other queues, but we didn't talk about it. That consciousness came at the end of the editing process. I think if we had been more conscious at the beginning, we would have been paralyzed.

It was the same kind of movement for *South,* and also for *From the Other Side,* and *Là-bas* (*Down There,* Belgium/France, 2006). Each time Chantal left to shoot, she followed an intuition, a desire,

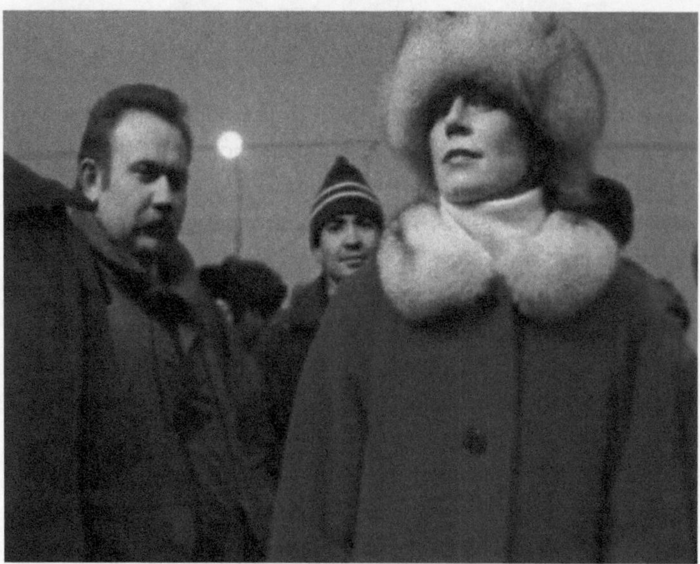

Figure 3. *D'Est* (1993). Courtesy of Fondation Chantal
Akerman and Marian Goodman Gallery

but she didn't know exactly what she would find, or even what she
was looking for. Before leaving to make *South*, Chantal talked about
the silence, the frightening silence of the South of the United
States. She wanted to film the landscape and to feel how history is
encrypted in it. It's not that landscape explains history—it's that
landscape is inhabited by history. So she went there with a small
crew. They drove all around, and each time she felt there was something to film, they would go out and film. When they arrived in Jasper, there was a commemoration ceremony for James Byrd Jr., who
had been murdered the year before, so she filmed the ceremony in
the church. She didn't go there knowing there would be this commemoration. She was open to the present, and the present evokes
the past. That's the film's strength, and it only appeared to us at the
end of the editing. The past is not shown. It is hardly described, but
it is evoked by the present.

Can you talk a little bit about the installation NOW *(2015)? I know that for a long time Chantal wanted to make a film about the Middle East.*

Yes, that's true, and she wrote a beautiful text about that. But *NOW* is not really linked to this project, at least not directly. I mean it's not about the Middle East. It's about our world, about our world moving toward its end. *NOW* originated in sound. Chantal said she wanted us to experience fear, war, flight, imminent disaster, through the entanglement of soundtracks in space. She wanted us to experience chaos, to feel the extent to which our world is unhinged by violence. As always in Chantal's works, there is violence, there is suffering, but there is also a very deep humanity.

Five screens are suspended, showing tracking shots in a desert with different rhythms. It's not a particular desert; it's a desert. And there are also two projections on the ground that make it move and vibrate. The viewer can walk [through] the space and discover the different layers of sound. The first layer is what we called "fear." You hear the sounds of footsteps, gravel and stones, and animals screaming and running. The second layer is what we called "war." Sounds of bombing, of helicopters and planes, but also songs, music, voices in different languages, whispering, explosions. Sounds of war, and also human presence. Disaster and hope. The third layer is divided between the left side and the right side: the sea on the left channel and the town on the right channel. In the second and the third layers, we added audio from Chantal's other films. For example, there is the scene from the church in *South* and also the scene of the migrants talking in *From the Other Side.*

At the table—I love that scene.

I've been thinking that Chantal always used something as counterpoint. No Home Movie *has the counterpoint of the desert and the mother; in* News From Home *(Belgium/France, 1976), of course, she has the counterpoint of the soundtrack and the place.*

Yes, in *No Home Movie,* the desert is a kind of counterpoint. It creates a distance. And the distance is what makes the look possible, I think. The distance creates—

—perspective, exactly. It is as if No Home Movie *had only the mother material. A lot of people pushed aside the images of the desert and just talked about the home movie, because, I think, they only wanted to focus on Chantal's relationship with her mother. But for me, it's not a home movie. For me, it's a movie. I think she was very proud of the film. She was very proud of the film as a film. A lot of people use the intimacy of their personal lives as a sort of support. Chantal was not like that. It wasn't about exposing. It wasn't about confession.*

Yes, she was very proud of this film as a film. She used to say it was her most immediately accessible film, and she was hoping it would reach everyone. You know, Chantal's cinema is not psychological. It doesn't explain anything. It doesn't give any reasons. When you explain, you stop the movement, you stop the transformation, and that's where you begin to lie. Chantal's cinema makes us move and think. *No Home Movie* raises the question of how to be inside and outside, close and far, with and without. It's a film about life and about loss. When Chantal Skypes with her mother, she says, "I want to do something about the fact that there is no distance anymore in the world." These words were like a little jewel that showed us the way in the editing. Sometimes you find little moments like this in the rushes, which help you to understand what the film is about. And you build the film around them.

The blue chair in No Home Movie *left a big impression on me. And then I found in her novel* Ma mère rit *(My Mother Laughs, 2013) a description of the chair, the overturned chair in her garden. There was something very moving about the chair. It's a very human thing, really. A chair doesn't exist if someone hasn't sat on it. So, an empty chair and a chair that's turned around because of the wind is quite resonant. Just the fact that Chantal was writing novels, too, and how good everything was—it's amazing.*

Oh yes, she was an extraordinary writer. Her writing is full of images. What we liked about the chair was the blue, the blue on the green. The blue jumped out, and it was so moving. What you say about the chair that was turned over and empty, that came later. I remember when we showed the film to a friend for the first time, he said that when he saw the chair, he knew it would come back later in the film. But *we* didn't know! That's how we worked. If Chantal had known that she would film the chair to show this and that, the shot of the chair wouldn't have the same strength. Chantal never made an image with the editing in mind. She made an image because the image came to her—

Said something to her.

And that's a magnificent present to receive as an editor, when the images are free, and still have their . . .

Energy?

And secret.

That image has a secret because no one knows exactly what is drawing her to it. We did an event around A Family in Brussels *in Brazil, a reading of the translation Flora Süssekind and I published as* Uma família em Bruxelas. *People who had never seen an Akerman film were incredibly moved by it. I would have loved to tell Chantal about the reception of the performance—how members of my family, people who don't have any aesthetic sensibility, were just so moved. Because it's almost universal—the fact [that] she doesn't use names.*

Yes, and the way *je* becomes *elle* and becomes *je* again.

It's so precise, but at the same time, it's . . . maybe abstract *is not the word, but* impersonal. *More human because it's impersonal.*

Yes. Precise but not fixed, always in motion. You know we made an installation out of this book in 1998 called *Selfportrait/Autobiography: A Work in Progress.* It's an installation with six monitors: three monitors in the first row with images from *D'Est;* two monitors in the second row with images from *Jeanne Dielman;* and a sixth monitor in the third row which we called "apparitions": a black screen that from time to time showed images from *Toute une nuit* (*All Night Long,* Belgium/France, 1982), *Hotel Monterey* (Belgium, 1972), and *Jeanne Dielman, 23 quai du Commerce, 1080 Bru-xelles* (Belgium/France, 1975). All over the space, Chantal's voice is reading *A Family in Brussels*. It's a very strong piece.

I want to ask you about something else. You edited Almayer's Folly (La Folie Almayer, *France/Belgium, 2011), right? Another great film. I was curious about how you edited the ending, when Almayer (Stanislas Merhar) does his rambling monologue about forgetting his daughter. Maybe I'm crazy, but I thought it was a continuous shot!*

Yes, it is one shot!

Amazing. I understand his chair was pushed so he gradually moves closer to the camera, out of the veranda, and into the sun. His expression is desperate, melancholic, and we are unsure about what he says. How did you decide where to cut?

It's so difficult to explain this decision. It's a question of feeling. I feel in my whole body when it's the right moment to cut. Chantal and I almost always felt the same way, and when we didn't, we knew there was a problem. For that shot, the sound was the difficult part. We had done a very simple sound edit. It was beautiful and full of tension. Then the sound crew put in more sound, and it became too—

Naturalistic.

Yes. And it seemed too long. So we took out all the added sounds, we left only Stanislas's voice and the little noises, and we rediscovered the feeling of the shot—its tension and its proper length.

I don't even know how to describe that shot. It's psychological, but because it's a monologue, it's not psychological. It's like internal and external.

Yes. He is inside and outside. He is in his head and in the river. He is in the past and in the present. And there is the sun and the boat, going by.

I didn't like the film right away. There's something disjunctive—the parts don't seem to go together. Chantal said there were two endings. They couldn't be put together, so she put one ending (the murder of Dain at the karaoke performance) at the beginning. Brilliant. Did you realize that the ending of Jeanne Dielman *and the ending of this film have almost the same duration?*

Oh really?

Yes, the sitting—it's seven minutes and a bit.

I don't know whether Chantal realized this. I don't think she did. She always worked with her intuitions. And at the same time, everything is so *juste*.

Yes, precise. She shapes it so it gets a certain charge, a weight.

I like this image of shaping. Editing is physical. It has a lot to do with weight and lightness. I like comparing editing to sculpture.

I think that with Chantal's films, time and flow matter as much as the content. I mean the drama.

Yes. It's part of the drama.

*I was thinking of another film that I adore more and more—*Portrait d'une jeune fille de la fin des années 60 à Bruxelles *(Portrait of a Young Girl at the End of the 1960s in Brussels,* France*, 1993). I don't know if it's directly autobiographical or not, but the protagonist talks about the father always wanting to change the furniture. It's the kind of detail that just gives life to a film.*

Like the "double curtains case" in *Tomorrow We Move* (*Demain on déménage*, France/Belgium, 2004), an everyday matter that's called an *affaire* as if it was a court case. So it's ordinary and extraordinary, and it takes on many meanings throughout the film.

Doesn't she say in A Family in Brussels *that her father was always buying paintings?*

Yes, yes.

So there's something there, a thread, in her attention to detail and how she describes people. Because I don't imagine she herself worried about curtains or furniture.

She could be worried about curtains and furniture! You know, she had no rules about what was or was not important. Every detail could become important.

Well, in that fantastic little film of hers called Dis-moi *(Tell Me,* France, *1982), she visits three older ladies who lost their mothers in the Holocaust and listens to their memories of their mothers and grandmothers. She has tea and eats with them. At the same time, offscreen, she asks her own mother about her grandmother who perished in the camps and her great-grandmother who took her mother in when she came back. Chantal asks the last woman, the one who talks about her mother sewing, to sing the songs that her mother used to sing. In a way, she has the woman embody, incarnate the mother, the same way that Chantal behaves like a compliant granddaughter, eating all the food offered. I'm also Jewish, and when I went to my grandmother's I had to eat no matter what time of the day it was. It's a very moving film. Do you remember in the end, the woman asks her to stay for dinner and she falls asleep?*

Yes! But again, that just happened. She didn't plan it.

No? She just fell asleep.

Claire Atherton is a film editor, born in San Francisco in 1963. She studied Chinese philosophy, language, and culture before turning toward cinema. In 1986 she started working with Chantal Akerman on *Letters Home*, which triggered a thirty-year collaboration until Akerman's last film, *No Home Movie*, and last installation, *NOW*. She also works with a wide range of directors, artists, and young filmmakers.

Ivone Margulies is professor of film studies in the Film and Media Studies Department at Hunter College, City University of New York. She is author of *Nothing Happens: Chantal Akerman's Hyperrealist Everyday* (1996), coeditor with B. Ruby Rich of a dossier on Akerman for *Film Quarterly* (Fall 2016), cotranslator with Flora Süssekind of *Uma família em Bruxelas* (2017), editor of *Rites of Realism: Essays on Corporeal Cinema* (2003), and author of *In Person: Reenactment in Postwar and Contemporary Cinema* (2019).

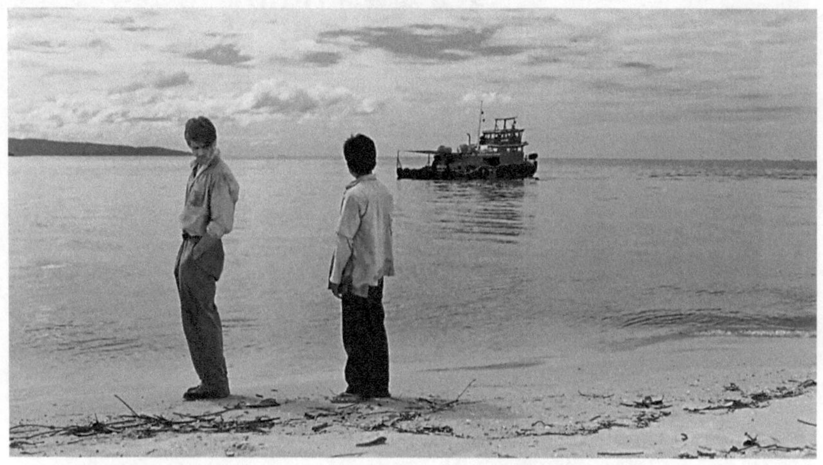

Figure 4. *La Folie Almayer* (2011). © Liaison Cinématographique/
Paradise Films/Artémis Productions

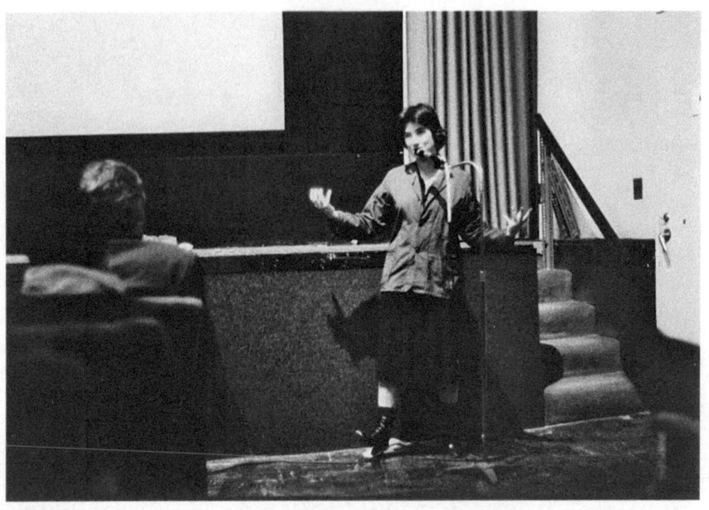

Figure 1. Chantal Akerman at her first Museum of Modern Art screening of *Jeanne Dielman* in November 1976. © Babette Mangolte (All Rights of Reproduction Reserved)

With Chantal in New York in the 1970s: An Interview with Babette Mangolte

Janet Bergstrom

Chantal Akerman never forgot the shock of seeing *Pierrot le fou* (France/Italy, 1965) when she was fifteen: Jean-Luc Godard's film spoke to her directly, privately. It was a conversion experience. Now she had a calling: she needed to make her own films with that sense of immediacy. When she was eighteen she attended the Brussels film school INSAS briefly.[1] In 1968 she made her first movie, *Saute ma ville,* a thirteen-minute masterpiece with a unique first-person presence. With no backing, no money, she managed to make the film in 35mm with the help of a few film students.

She played the film's only character herself, and almost entirely inside her own tiny kitchen. Luck and talent led to funding for a second film, one with a budget, shot in June 1971: *L'Enfant aimé ou Je joue à être une femme mariée.* But Chantal wasn't happy with it and left the film unfinished. In October 1971 she went to New York for the first time. There she met Babette Mangolte, the photographer and cinematographer who would become her friend

Camera Obscura 100, Volume 34, Number 1

DOI 10.1215/02705346-7264084   Interview responses © 2019 Babette Mangolte; all other new text © 2019 Janet Bergstrom

Published by Duke University Press

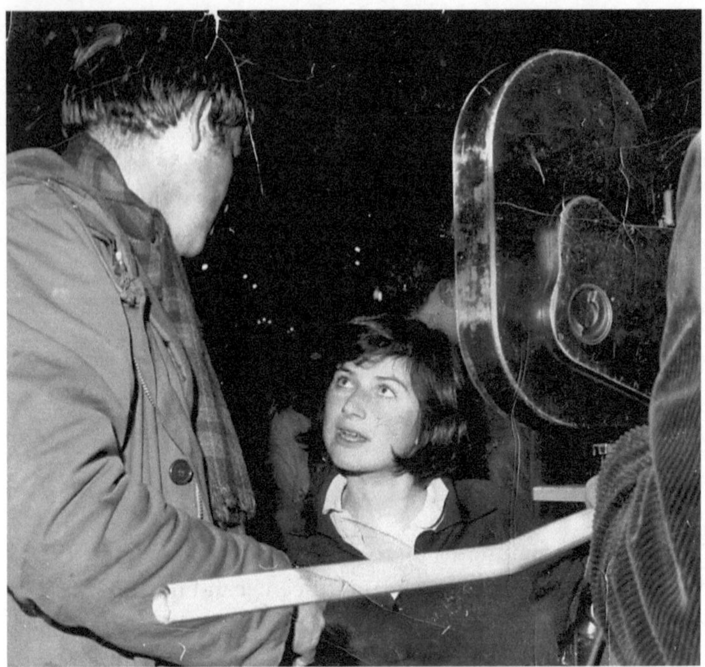

Figure 2. Cameraman René Fruchter, Chantal Akerman, and the 35mm Cameflex camera they used to shoot *Saute ma ville*, ca. 1967 or 1968. Photographer unknown

and guide to the mélange of avant-gardes of the day: film, dance, performance art, music, theater. With Babette, Chantal experienced Michael Snow's *La Région centrale* (Canada, 1971) over and over again until the theater closed. That was the next shock that changed her conception of what cinema could be.

I knew Babette quite well by the time I recorded this discussion on 29 June 1995 in Los Angeles. (The edited interview was originally published in Italian translation in 1997 for the Pesaro Film Festival, without an introduction; we revised and expanded it in May 2018.)[2] In the early 1970s I had admired her beautiful photographs of performance art in the pages of *Artforum* and her cinematography for Yvonne Rainer's *Lives of Performers* (US, 1972) and *Film about a Woman Who . . .* (US, 1974). Then I saw the films she shot for Chantal: *La Chambre* and *Hotel Monterey* (both shot in New York in 1972),[3] *Jeanne Dielman, 23 quai du Commerce, 1080 Bruxelles* (Belgium/France, 1975), and *News from Home* (France/ Belgium, 1976). And I knew films that Babette had directed and photographed herself, such as *What Maisie Knew* (US, 1975) and *The Camera: Je* (US, 1977). We crossed paths in different cities, sometimes by chance, sometimes with purpose (Paris, San Diego/La Jolla where she was teaching, Los Angeles, and elsewhere). Trying to research Chantal's career, I kept running into different chronologies, with gaps, in Chantal's interviews about that early period in New York.

In those days, I found that asking Chantal directly did not help much, particularly regarding the many things she considered unimportant. Babette, on the other hand, loved talking about the specifics of what she had done, Chantal's films, and any of the work she had seen and/or been involved with, including equipment she used, technical possibilities she wanted to try and why, and the people who helped, sketching broader and broader networks of influence.

For this interview, I asked Babette if we could focus on her collaboration with Chantal on her 1970s New York films. Besides Jonas Mekas and Anthology Film Archives, Babette brought in the art scene—Richard Foreman, Robert Wilson, Annette Michelson, Yvonne Rainer, Philip Glass—and some people who were not in New York, such as Marcel Hanoun, Antoinette Fouque, and Jean-Pierre Gorin. Sometimes she pointed out connections with films that Chantal made later. She was happy to talk about how they were able to make no-budget films in New York compared to the constraints facing a new filmmaker in France or Belgium at the time. I think Babette would have talked at length about everything she mentioned, but we didn't have the time then for an oral history. Maybe someone could do that now.

In addition to Akerman's 1970s films as discussed in the interview, Mangolte also shot Akerman's *Un jour Pina a demandé . . .* in 1983 for French television, Antenne 2. The film is considered one of the best ever made with the late Pina Bausch and her Wuppertal Dance Theater, and one of the best films ever made on dance. Mangolte contributed not only as the cinematographer but

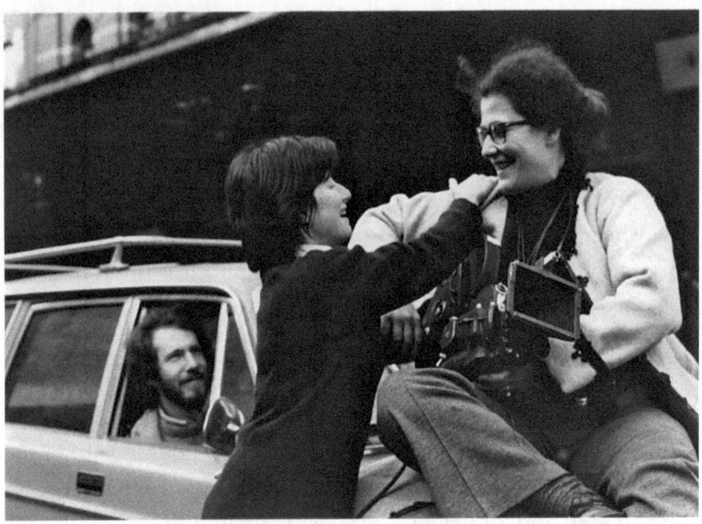

Figure 3. Chantal Akerman and Babette Mangolte shooting
Mangolte's film *The Camera: Je* in New York in 1976.
© Epp Kotkas (All Rights of Reproduction Reserved)

also through her extensive knowledge of experimental theater and
dance.

Janet Bergstrom: *I'd like to ask you about your work with Chantal Akerman. When did you meet?*

Babette Mangolte: I was in New York City. She had gotten my
name and phone number from Marcel Hanoun. She had met him
at the Jerusalem Film Festival in July 1971. We met in October
1971, so she was twenty-one, very young, and I was twenty-nine.
She had left INSAS, she had made *Saute ma ville* and had just
made *L'Enfant aimé ou Je joue à être une femme mariée*, that aborted
film. I think she had gone to Israel shortly before, where she had
family. In any case, she had decided to come to New York, and she
called me. We saw each other on and off, and I dragged her to
see movies. I must say we saw some memorable films together. In
late January 1972 we saw *La Région centrale* at the Elgin Theater. It
was a real event. At that time, you could go into the theater in the

middle of a movie if you wanted and stay until the place closed. The film played for two weeks to sold-out audiences, from ten in the morning until midnight or something. I remember we were sitting next to each other watching it. We stayed all day. The film is over three hours and has a very hypnotic image. That experience was very important because we kind of thought it was the best film ever made. I think I'm the one who introduced her to Snow's films, because one of the reasons I came to New York was to see them. She wanted to come to New York because it's where movies are made. She had family in New York, too—an uncle or a cousin—so she had also come because of that sense of diaspora, to see them. Chantal lived in New York continuously from October 1971 until March 1973, so there was a year-and-a-half period when she was very invested in that city. But by the end of 1972, she felt that her life had to be in Paris. She left permanently to go back to Europe to do *Je tu il elle* in 1974 and then *Jeanne Dielman*. She returned in April 1976 to make *News from Home*—we shot in late June for one week—and she went back to Paris and Brussels to finish the film. She came back to New York for the screening at the Museum of Modern Art in November 1976.

I had arrived in October 1970, so I had been in New York for a year before I met her. I was working for Klaus Moser. He had a custom darkroom and did printing for clients like Richard Avedon, the *New York Times*, *Harper's Bazaar*, and Condé Nast. I had darkroom skills—I had a darkroom at home in Paris—and you don't need to speak English to work in a darkroom, so that was a real advantage. The way I got that job is very interesting: I had taken photographs of Richard Foreman's third play, *Total Recall*. I had brought my camera from France, and I had borrowed twenty bucks from Annette Michelson to buy the film. I told her I wanted to take pictures because it was really a great play and nobody was seeing it—there were five people in the audience. The play had been running like that for two months, and it was an incredible play. Easy to photograph, too. I could not ask her to pay for the processing and so on. So I said, I just have to find a darkroom. The chemicals are not going to cost that much if I do the labor.

I was in an elevator talking to Veronica Silver in French

about this—Veronica was an American film editor who was married to Marcel Hanoun—and there was another woman in the elevator, a German photographer who understood some French, and she invited us for coffee. Veronica explained a little more to her. She thought I was Jewish. Veronica is Jewish, and she was Jewish, so she decided to help me and told me to go and see Klaus Moser. She gave me his phone number and address. Klaus had come from East Berlin in the mid-1950s. This was fifteen years later, and he was married to an American. I think he had sympathy for the fact that I did not understand a word of English, because when he arrived he did not understand a word of English either. He trusted me and said, "Yes, you can stay," and "When I do my bookkeeping at the end of the day, you can use the darkroom." He did not ask me to pay for anything. So I came back the next day to develop my contact sheets. I kept hanging around, helping him out. In return, I could use the darkroom after hours, and then later it became a real job.

In 1972 I was working with Yvonne Rainer on *Lives of Performers*, and I had the use of Robert Rauschenberg's 16mm Arriflex S camera for Yvonne's film. It's a nonsync camera; I postsynchronized the very short lines that needed it during the editing, which I did as well. The camera was stored at Yvonne's loft, but before and after *Lives of Performers* I could use it when I wanted to. I would go to Yvonne's, pick it up, and return it.

I shot *La Chambre* with that camera. I had access to film equipment, and so I could provide it for Chantal's films. I think that at the time her work was in opposition to the structured filmmaking she had tried to do in that film which had failed, *L'Enfant aimé*. She had made it with a regular crew and a cameraman who bossed her around. She had not been able to express what she wanted. The New York context was Michael Snow, Stan Brakhage, people working totally against the film industry. I think that using cameras owned by friends and making films when you didn't know exactly where they would be shown was very liberating for Chantal. She certainly had the ambition to make narrative film, because a year later she realized she would not be able to do it in the US and she would be much better off going back to Brussels where she knew there was a financial support system she could tap—"l'avance sur recettes" [advance on ticket sales]. I think the looseness of the independent film scene and the optimism of that period in New York were very important for her psychologically—more important than the films she made, though I thought they were very nice. The one I was most involved in, conceptually, was *La Chambre*.

Let me ask you first, how did you get involved with Richard Foreman's plays?

The person who made it possible for me to get to New York was Annette Michelson, who was a friend of Marcel Hanoun and had just seen his most recent film, *Le Printemps* (France, 1971), that she greatly admired and for which I had been an assistant cinematographer. It is a stunning film visually and very intelligent. Marcel told her I had worked on it and on *L'Été* (France, 1969) and *L'Hiver* (France/Belgium, 1969) before that, and I had edited a film Marcel had shot on [Antoni] Gaudí. I had started to work with him in 1967, so I knew him very well. I would be one of the first names he would give to Chantal. For me, Chantal was interesting because she was a young woman who wanted to live in the US, and that was my own experience, although I was older. That was the bond that made us hook up. Annette was very influential. She introduced me to Brakhage three days after I arrived in New York and Snow two days later, and a month later she told me I had to see that theater piece by Richard Foreman. I fell in love with Richard's theater. Annette later also introduced me to Yvonne Rainer and recommended me to be the cinematographer for *Lives of Performers*. Without Annette, nothing really would have happened. For me, her influence has been very positive.

In Richard's plays text is important, but it's also so visual. I understood little or none of the English, but I could understand the play, which is what was so interesting. It was not like Robert Wilson, whose plays I also saw at that time, in which the text is really removed. For Foreman, the text is important, but I could understand the play without understanding the text, and it was important for me at the time to focus visually. Chantal went to these plays, but I don't think she was as interested in Foreman as I was. She definitely saw whatever was available. She could have seen two or three of his plays.

In *Histoires d'Amérique: Food, Family, and Philosophy* (Belgium/France, 1988), shot in New York City, some of the actors, including George Bartenieff and Crystal Field, are from a New York experimental theater group. They were in Richard's movie *Strong Medicine* (US, 1981) and were also the producers of the Theater for a New City, on Jane Street, the theater where Yvonne did the performance piece *story about a woman who . . .* , and Richard did one play there, a great play, *Classical Therapy*. Some of the actors Chantal used in *Histoires d'Amérique* she had seen in Richard's plays or in other plays I was shooting photographs for.

A close friend of Chantal's, Jane Stein, was working for the New York Shakespeare Company, designing masks and puppets, and worked on Broadway theater productions and also off-Broadway. In fact, Chantal arrived in New York with Jane's phone number from someone in Israel. She went straight from the airport to Jane's loft and became her roommate for a while when she first came to New York. They always remained in contact.[4]

So Chantal had contacts outside of my own in New York, and she had the desire to investigate the city in a world that was not necessarily mine—I was very located downtown in the art world, in Anthology Film Archives and the people around what in the early

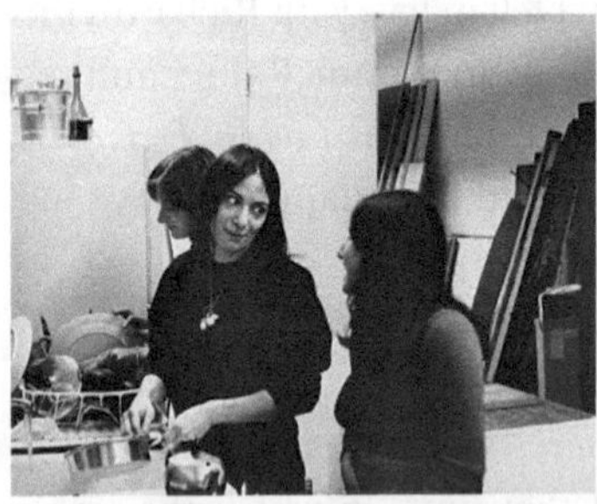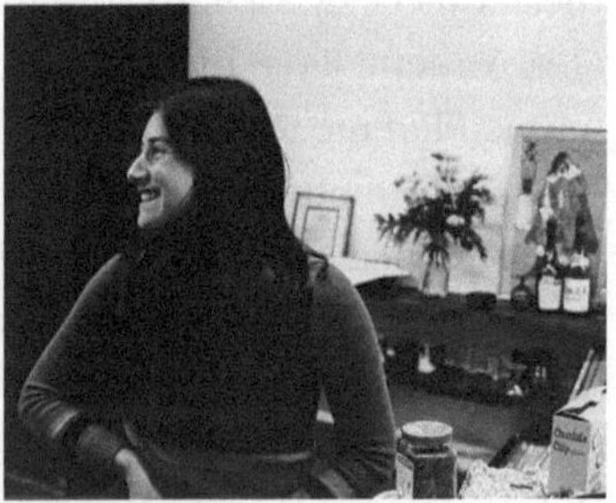

Figure 4. (left) Marilyn Watelet, Jane Stein, and Chantal Akerman, looking at Jane, in Jane's kitchen, October 1972. (right) Chantal Akerman in Jane Stein's loft, October 1972. © 1972 Babette Mangolte (All Rights of Reproduction Reserved)

1960s was called "the underground." I think she had contacts not only with the underground but with theater and performance art that was Broadway or off-Broadway oriented. Richard was really off-off-Broadway. Chantal did not speak English well, but she could manage, whereas I could not manage until the end of my second year in New York. When Chantal arrived, she had English that was serviceable. Obviously it changes the way you enter a city a lot when you can speak the language.

Do you think she wanted to meet filmmakers in New York, like Snow or Brakhage?

Not really, no. Not that I know of. That makes me think about a photo I took that I think is interesting. One evening a week Richard and Kate [Manheim] were at home for friends. There was plenty to eat and drink, so people always came. I have a picture from 1973, with Richard and Kate and other people, where Chantal looks like a little girl. She is very short, and she's sitting on the ground; the others are on the sofa. Somehow I was part of that group because I had known them longer than she did, and she was much younger than they were. I was thirty, she was twenty-two, and those people were thirty-five or thirty-eight. That was a big difference, when you're twenty years old and you're with people who aren't exactly famous but who already do work that is reviewed in the *Village Voice* and the *New York Times*. It's not quite the same when you approach them. The fact that she was young was interesting. She absorbed a lot because of it.

Another thing we did together was to go to a loft on Elizabeth Street where Philip Glass performed *Music in Six Parts*. The first picture I shot of Glass was taken there; probably they were some of the first pictures ever done of Glass with this group because the group was just starting at that time. That was important for Chantal. In France, people were still going to music in concert halls. Of course, nobody knew Glass would have the career he has had. She loved the music. I loved the music. The room was full, with eighty people and fifteen musicians. It wasn't an enormous room, just a regular loft. At some point in 1973 she stayed with a friend who lived on 15th Street between Broadway and 6th on the outskirts of Union Square. I could walk to her apartment from St. Mark's Place. It was very near. It was really downtown, too. We saw a lot more of each other when she lived there because I could call her and say, "Do you want to go? I'm going to go tonight."

Later in the 1970s, it was relatively easy for us to be in touch with each other even though I was living in New York and she was living in Paris because I was moving a lot and she was too. We were always in contact. She came back to New York to do *News from Home* in April 1976. I had asked Annette Michelson for information about an inexpensive hotel where you could cook, because Chantal wanted to be in a place where she could write. That was the Hotel Excelsior, on 81st Street, off Columbus. Chantal was there at least six weeks thinking about the script, taking subways and thinking about what she could do. We saw each other three or four times a week, talked on the phone. We were in contact, but I wasn't really working on the project. She was writing the script, thinking about what to do. It's in the middle of that period of gestation that she mentioned her idea for the voice-over.

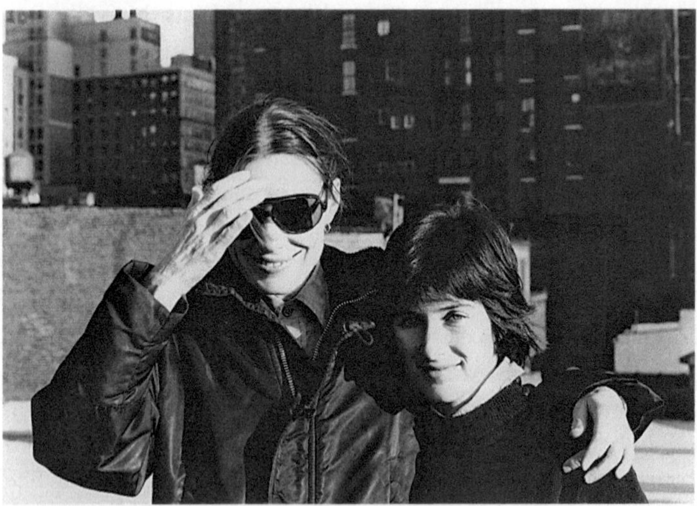

Figure 5. Choreographer Lucinda Childs with Chantal Akerman on a roof in New York for Mangolte's *The Camera: Je*, shot in 1976. © 1976 Babette Mangolte (All Rights of Reproduction Reserved)

German TV funded *News from Home* as part of a series of portraits of cities by independent filmmakers. They got to know Chantal because of *Jeanne Dielman* at Cannes. *Jeanne Dielman* cost hardly anything considering the quality of the film, because the crew was not well paid, and it was shot and edited quickly. I finished mixing my first film, *What Maisie Knew*, on 3 January 1975 and worked on the release print with the DuArt lab for three weeks. I flew from New York to Brussels at the end of the third week of January to prepare and shoot *Jeanne Dielman*. We had two full weeks of preproduction for makeup tests, costumes, storyboards, and lighting in the rented apartment that was our set.

I decided to drill holes in the ceiling so that all the electrical cabling would be off the floor and attached to the ceiling because the apartment was small, and stepping on cables would have been dangerous and cumbersome. Delphine [Seyrig] had enormous respect for me because I was able to put all the electrical connections for each light switch in the apartment on a relay system so that when she turned a light switch on or off, all the movie light sources for reproducing the effect of the lamp in the room were turned on or off at the same time. I had asked a friend of mine while I was preparing how to solve the problem of the constant use of light switches in the script. I was told about relays, where you patch all the lights to one bank and have a bank of cables triggered on and off by the actor using the light switch that was part of the set.

We shot from mid-February to mid-March 1975, and *Jeanne Dielman* was shown at the Cannes Film Festival in May.[5] It was a five-week shoot, seven weeks in editing—a simple mix. In late April I came back from New York to Paris to work one week at LTC, the Paris lab that had processed the dailies, to work with the timer for the release print. It was a very economical film, but there were enormous debts because of it. Chantal used some of the funding for *News from Home* to pay *Jeanne Dielman*'s debts.

When I was at the lab doing the timing for *Jeanne Dielman*, I never had a screening of all the reels in story order. I didn't see the entire film until December 1976 at the Museum of Modern Art in New York. I had no clear idea of how powerful it was when I worked on it in 1975. It was only when I saw the film projected at MoMA in the presence of an audience that I knew it was a masterpiece. My admiration for Chantal was there to stay—a powerful source of intellectual stimulation for my life to come. Projection of what I shoot is very important because I framed for a large screen. I learned that from Marcel Hanoun in France when we worked together between 1966 and 1970.

News from Home was made for only $20,000. I spent half of the money for the shoot in New York, and the rest went to Chantal for editing and finishing the film in Brussels.

And you shot it?

Yes. Absolutely. And I handled the money, in the sense that I had an account at the lab I had used for *The Camera: Je* that was still active. I completed *The Camera: Je* after *News from Home*, but I had finished shooting it before Chantal's film. *News from Home* was shot in that heavy, smoggy June yellow light you get in California and New York. I think my work on it was done over a period of three weeks altogether, two weeks of preparation and one week shooting. Actually, I had taken care of the insurance earlier, because we needed it for the subway and the midtown area, like Fifth Avenue. The biggest hurdle in preparation was to get the okay from the subway system, and for that we needed liability insurance. Now I realize it wasn't that expensive. Today [1995] it costs $2,000, but then it was only $300 or $400. It took more than two weeks to get the shooting authorizations. I handled the money with the lab and the production, working with the same assistant I had used for *The Camera: Je* and the same setup. It was done very cheaply.

I had one assistant, his car, and the rented equipment, the same equipment I had used on my own film. That's the reason I know how much money was spent. I knew we had to be economical. It was not difficult. Once Chantal had the idea to keep the camera rolling and maintaining duration in the subway waiting for the train to come in (which is obviously a Michael Snow idea), the film was shot relatively quickly.

Agnès Varda was very impressed by *News from Home* because it was shot at night. That was only possible because a film stock had

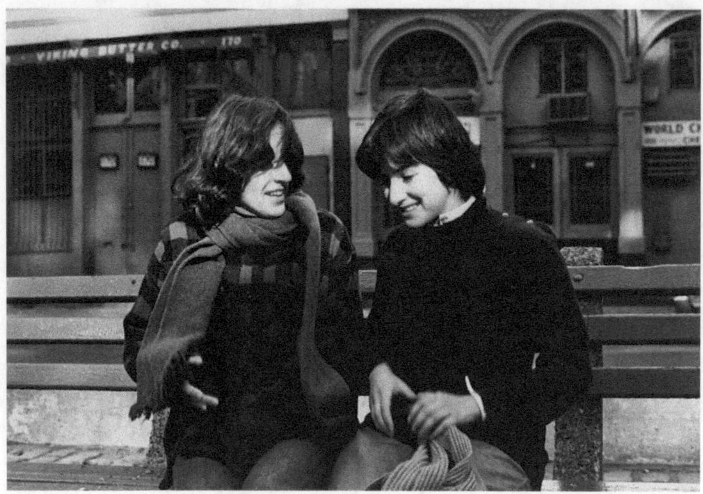

Figure 6. Epp Kotkas and Chantal Akerman in Duane Park, 1976. Epp Kotkas was an assistant on *News from Home* at the time. © 1976 Babette Mangolte (All Rights of Reproduction Reserved)

become available that you could push and a lab that could do that pushing, my lab, TVC. It couldn't be done in France because of the copyright on the Chemtone process. The pushing they could do with Kodak chemistry was not really that good. *News from Home* has a very specific Chemtone look. The sensibility is totally European, but I think the pastel look comes from the Chemtone process owned by TVC. I don't know exactly when TVC started using it, in 1975 or 1976. Shortly before that I knew of its existence, and I said to Chantal, "Let's test it." And we did. Before that, no filmmaker in their right mind would think they could get an image inside a subway station using available light only. It's too dark. At 500 ASA, you have to be at 1/15 of a second for a still photograph. We were shooting 500 ASA . . . and, in 1976, negative color film was not manufactured at 500 ASA, only at 100 ASA.

You have to realize that for somebody like Chantal to do *L'Enfant aimé* in Belgium, she had to have a production company. She could not rent equipment under her own name.

Why was that?

I could not have rented professional equipment, at least then, as a camera person in France. I would have to ask a production company—a place I had already worked for as a camera person or camera assistant or editor—to underwrite the rental equipment, and I would have to repay the production company for it. It was a very different system. One of the reasons I was in New York was because as long as I had the cash, I could rent a camera under my own name and use it, and nobody would ask me anything. That's a very important element about the possibility of making *News from Home.* Belgian television also paid for part of it, but that money was given to Paradise Films, Chantal's production company. Marilyn Watelet, her friend since high school, was head of production, working mostly pro bono. The production system she implemented with Paradise Films is modeled on the American system. It's not at all what they do in France. There was no independent . . . I suppose you could find the equivalent of a [Georges de] Beauregard, the producer Godard found. There have always been production companies that have helped independent filmmakers in France. But for a young woman (Chantal was twenty-six then), that is much more difficult to do than for someone who has already found a way into the system.

In America, it was different. You had no problem. In March 1972 I needed to set up an account at Cameramart to get equipment for Yvonne's film, *Lives of Performers.* To rent the lighting gear and a dolly, I had to tell them what I had done in France. There was no VHS at the time (which became common later), so I could not give them a cassette. They believed me because, even though my English was very bad, it was obvious I knew the equipment. I knew what I needed. I could give them an equipment list. They didn't review my technical qualifications as long as I paid for the insurance. I think it was important for Chantal to see that films were being made in the US with no production company behind them, no funding outside of the personal money of the filmmaker. And at the same time, this gave her the sense that she could go back to Brussels and import that method. I think she did that with Paradise Films. The name came from the Living Theater's famous production *Paradise Now* that I saw in Avignon in 1968. That was one of the first reasons I wanted to go to New York—to see new theater.

Chantal went back to France after about a year and a half. What happened during this period?

She went back to France in 1973. We had a long discussion. She decided then she didn't want to live in New York, not because she didn't like New York—she loves New York still—but because she thought she had a better chance to make films and to get funding in France than in the US. I think she didn't want to keep on making films like *Hotel Monterey* or to be the next Michael Snow. She definitely wanted to go back to narrative film. So it was a very conscious decision for her to go back to France to try to make a film. The first film was *Je tu il elle*, but she made it because she had a script for a different film that Delphine Seyrig had agreed to shoot, and she felt she needed to show that she had already shot a feature to get funding.

It all started when *Hotel Monterey* was shown at the Festival de Nancy in November 1973, and Delphine saw it there. Nancy is a primarily a theater festival, but that year they had a small section of independent films. Delphine showed one of her feminist videos, made in collaboration, and Chantal had both *La Chambre* and *Hotel Monterey*. Delphine used to come to New York relatively regularly to visit her son and her former husband, Jack Youngerman, an abstract expressionist painter with whom she remained friendly. She knew the experimental film scene. She knew Jonas Mekas. She was also very interested in supporting women's work. She met Chantal at the festival in Nancy. That was really important because they stayed in touch, and Chantal probably told her, "I'm going to write a narrative film and if you like the script," or whatever . . . and Delphine said, "I will definitely read the script," or something like that. She was a feminist involved in shaping an organization in Paris in 1974 to produce video works, the Centre [Audiovisuel] Simone de Beauvoir.

Chantal wrote a script which had to do with two women and their friendship. The two women were supposed to be Bulle Ogier and Delphine Seyrig. The script was not very good. She applied for money from Belgium, but she felt she would never get the money with the portfolio she had. She had to do a film very quickly, so in 1974 she made *Je tu il elle* in 35mm black and white, shot in four or five days. She shot everything MOS [without sound] except the truck driver scene, which she shot in 16mm in one night and blew up to 35mm. I could not shoot it, unfortunately, although I was in Europe when she asked me if I wanted to. She could not pay anybody obviously, but that was not the problem—I had another job.

Chantal had the kind of smartness to say, "I have the opportunity to get Delphine Seyrig. She's known because of Alain Resnais all over the world, so my god I cannot miss it. I have to get the money from the Belgians." And to do that she did *Je tu il elle*. That takes guts. I think it's really interesting how pragmatic Chantal has been. She has made decisions that show that you can get something by investing in a certain way. She invested in *Je tu il elle*, which is a great film, but originally it was made to clench something else which she thought would be her first enormous career step—what would become *Jeanne Dielman*—and it ended up being that, too.

What was that script like for Bulle Ogier and Delphine?

She mailed me the script in New York in November 1974 and said, "Do you want to come and shoot my movie?" I was shooting *What Maisie Knew*. She had the Belgian money by then, and maybe she came to New York at Christmas. I said, "I don't like the script." She said, "I kind of agree with you, I don't like it," and she discarded the script. She could not get Bulle Ogier or else she decided it was too reminiscent of *Two or Three Things I Know about Her* (dir. Jean-Luc Godard, France, 1967) and not as good, and it was too sentimental. I really did not like the script. I told her it was too Godard. She must have agreed. She wrote a new script inspired by her aunt and mother (the prostitution is an invention) in just a couple of weeks, and that script became *Jeanne Dielman*.

There was an important work experience we had in common. It happened in the summer of 1973 when we worked for about two months on a film project with Antoinette Fouque, the psychoanalyst. I don't even remember the title of the film. It was never finished. Antoinette Fouque was one of the main organizers of the MLF [Mouvement de libération des femmes] in the aftermath of 1968. She did some interesting things like creating the bookstore *des femmes*. It was influential; they published good books. And she had cassettes made of women reading books by women. Later the idea was picked up by the big publishers, but it was original at the time, and the tapes have been very successful.

Chantal probably met Antoinette Fouque as soon as she came back from New York in April, and Chantal called me or wrote me about the project. A collective of women had decided to make a film, and they recruited me as a cameraperson and Chantal as a kind of technical adviser for direction. She would also participate, but really the subject matter was structured by Antoinette Fouque, and the collective of women had met and decided on the project a long time before we got involved. The money came from Sylvina Boissonnas, who is from the de Menil family. Chantal knew from me that the de Menil family had given money in the US to Philip Glass and Bob Wilson and so on. This was a link to a very old-fashioned system of patronage for the arts which has totally disappeared.

But it was the heyday of feminist thinking. In the US in 1971, I was introduced to Kate Millett, who wanted to make a movie. I never became involved. But Susan Sontag was making movies. It was a great period in the US when people were actually meeting from different areas. It was very pluridisciplinary. In France, that had not happened yet. People like Chantal imported that idea. Somebody else could have a different reading of that history, but I feel very strongly that the people who were younger, who came to New York just to get a sense of how it worked, imported that new way of doing things. After 1968, there was room for innovation because new people were in power. In France, the early seventies in many places was a very novel time because of that. I think that even though we failed in 1968, we succeeded in dislodging the people in power and a new generation came in.

I don't know how Antoinette met Chantal, but the idea to do an all-woman film was in the air.

Was the film a documentary?

It was fiction. Some of the women in the group acted in it. I forgot what the script was about. Anyway, it was never finished. We were shooting scenes hoping that the script could be finished. At that time, you were open. You could raise money without a script. And you could even shoot without a script. It's inconceivable now. In the month or six weeks of preproduction when I was working every day with the group, we met in Paris, so you had your own social life at night, and I felt I could breathe. But when the shooting began, we were in a suburb of Paris, maybe an hour and a half away by car. You could not go home at night, it was too far. I didn't have a car anyway. And you were supposed to work ten-hour days . . . even though actually we would only work three-hour days because somebody would stop because something was not ready, or Antoinette had decided something, or whatever. It was totally crazy.

Chantal knew them before me. I was involved with them for about two and a half months, and the only person I trusted was Chantal. When I left, I spoke to her about my decision, and she stayed another week and left after that. There was a kind of bond between us because we had gone through that horrifying experience with Antoinette Fouque in the summer of 1973.

Shooting *Jeanne Dielman* was done with the idea that the crew would only be female, so it was not the concept of an all-woman crew for the project that was the problem. It was Antoinette, who was an abusive personality. Chantal is very much involved in control, but she has more sensitivity to others. In the end, Antoinette did not get the film finished. I think that was an important experience for Chantal. The following year, she wrote the script about the two women. Many women were thinking of doing things just for women.

Chantal always says she knows where to put the camera, she's very sure of framing. What do you think about her visual style?

I took still photographs preparing for *Hotel Monterey* and *La Chambre* and *News from Home*. I used to do that for my own work, too. Not every filmmaker does. But I had a free darkroom, after all, and I had still cameras, so I went out and shot pictures. I think Chantal must have shot pictures too. I think we had some slides, and we also did black and white. I did the processing and the contact sheets for Chantal. Her framing is totally static. Chantal thinks beforehand about how it is going to look. In *Saute ma ville*, she's closer in terms of the framing; she acts in it. The tendency is always to have two or three axes, no more, in a little space, especially if you don't have the money to do complicated camera moves. In many ways I think that when she started wanting to do projects that were more complicated and rely on a crew, she decided to really control the visuals, because that's what I think she had felt the most betrayed by in *L'Enfant aimé*.

What was the idea behind Hanging Out Yonkers *[unfinished]? The rushes exist in Brussels, but I haven't been able to see them.*

There is nothing but rushes, and half of them have been lost. It's beautiful. It was shot on reversal film (which means there was no negative), so the rushes are the original footage. There was never any work print made that I know of. Chantal was given a little money to make a film involving kids between eleven and fourteen who were involved in drugs and came to a halfway house that was kind of a meeting place for them. Some of them lived there. They would come at night. Some of them came on drugs, but they were not supposed to. Chantal befriended them. The film was commissioned through a close friend of Jane Stein's, Myra Farhy, who worked there.[6] The money gave her a little income, but the film took a lot of it. I borrowed a Beaulieu camera to shoot it; it was a very small 16mm camera for amateurs. Chantal maybe made a little money, but I did not. I might have even paid for my own subway tokens. We did not have a car, and Yonkers is pretty far, an hour and fifteen minutes by subway. Then we had to walk. It was a bit of an ordeal to go there, but it was an important experience for both of us because we became genuinely interested in some of the kids and also in that sense of observing. It was indeed a documentary— the first documentary Chantal had ever done. Everything else was fiction. *News from Home* is a kind of documentary, too, but a borderline documentary. That was the only straight documentary before *Sud* (*South*, France/Belgium) in 1999.

Was it supposed to have voice-over narration?

I think the idea was to shoot footage and put it into a presentable form so it could be shown to a few people. It was not made to be shown on PBS or to show to Jonas Mekas for theatrical distribution. It was an in-house production. The first job you usually got when you left film school was a training film; this was the equivalent. The people who founded that program (which was not very well funded) decided it would be good to have some kind of visual material to show. In a way it was promotional, but it was meant to observe and be aware of tension. There was no script. We went there three times a week and shot whatever we saw. Chantal did not stage things, but she got to know the people, exactly like Jean-Pierre Gorin did in his documentary *My Crasy Life* (US/UK), about Samoan gangs in Long Beach, California, that I shot in 1991. It's the kind of documentary that's essay-like.

We shot some material; we had no work print, so we looked at the original as little as we could. We knew it was well exposed, we remembered what had been shot, we were collecting footage, we were waiting. The idea was that we would do something with it when more money was available. It was a project that was very dear to Chantal, and to me too. Our subjects were loving and pleased to be treated as adults by two young women who were sympathetic to their needs. I was very distressed when Chantal told me some of the footage had been forgotten on a subway train and lost. I don't know why the project got interrupted, but I think the funding dried up, and also, for whatever reason, Chantal decided to go back to France. But the warmth of what had happened between the adolescents and us didn't leave us for a long time. For me this unfinished project confirmed, after *Hotel Monterey*, that Chantal was a film director.

Which was made first, Hanging Out Yonkers *or* La Chambre? *Were you involved in* Le 15/8 *[dir. Chantal Akerman and Samy Szlingerbaum, Belgium/France, 1973]?*

La Chambre was made before *Hanging Out Yonkers. Le 15/8* is something she did in Brussels. I had nothing to do with it.

I found a list of credits that shows two versions of La Chambre *(1 and 2), with a different person in the second one, and, according to this, both versions have soundtracks. I have only seen one version, with Chantal in it, and it doesn't have sound.*

La Chambre—that's a film where I should be credited for some of the idea, because I told her, "Let's do a film like Michael Snow." It is one camera movement in eleven minutes using one entire magazine of film, four hundred feet at twenty-four frames per second. We got two magazines and shot twice. One version was better than the other, and for me that was the film. But if you tell me there's a *Chambre 1* and *Chambre 2*, it's actually take one and take two. I don't know which take was the best; it's probably the second take. The sound could have been done when she went back to Brussels. Chantal became friends with Jacques Ledoux, who was the head of the Brussels Cinémathèque, and he helped her a lot. I know nothing about the soundtrack, although Chantal could have had a tape recorder and recorded some sound at the location. *La Chambre* was shot in Soho in the apartment of a friend of Chantal's. I know I shot it twice.

It was the only film of Chantal's that was improvised. I suggested that we make one camera movement using the full magazine of film. I started to rehearse the speed of the 360-degree pan, and she improvised on the spot the movement she would make on the bed. I think it's a great film. I love the film. We decided to do it maybe two days before. I had spent some time in the apartment, so I knew the best light. I added the mirror for backlight to offset the sun. We had to shoot at the best time of the day, late in the morning when the sunlight was coming in and it would be brighter. The apartment was in a brownstone on Spring Street. The streets are narrow there, and it was pretty dark. We arrived an hour before. I positioned the camera on the tripod and made the pan. And I said to Chantal, "Okay, what do you want to do?" The fact that there are three revolutions, where we see her three times on the bed and she makes three different gestures, came that day. That was not planned. I told her I would do 360 degrees in eleven minutes, but it would have been much more difficult to execute a slow movement than going faster. I covered 360 degrees two and a half times, I think, but I saw Chantal on the bed three times.

We made *La Chambre* before *Hotel Monterey,* but when I wrote an essay for the catalog accompanying the big exhibition of her work at the Pompidou Center in Paris in 2004, Chantal asked me to reverse the chronology of *La Chambre* and *Hotel Monterey.*[7] Although I knew she was wrong, I let it be as she wanted and added an afterword to my original text. For her it was always a problem that Michael Snow's possible influence would be highlighted by the fact that *La Chambre* was her first film in New York. I feel that was her reason. And she repeated this incorrect chronology, which is unnecessarily confusing.

The relationship Chantal has with technique is interesting. With the early films in New York, we used hand-held equipment or very lightweight 16mm equipment on a tripod because there was no money. *News from Home* was feasible because we could shoot almost invisibly in the city of New York. It was like we were not there. There's that beautiful shot of the woman sitting on a chair on the sidewalk, looking at us. She had been sitting there every day. When we asked permission to shoot, she didn't care. There's that sort of glazed look that New Yorkers have. Chantal started *Je tu il elle* with the same kind of equipment, except that it was Arriflex 35mm instead of Arriflex 16mm: the camera was fifteen pounds instead of ten, not much heavier. But she wanted *Jeanne Dielman* to be like Godard in *Vivre sa vie* (France, 1962). Suddenly she wanted it to be shot with heavy equipment. It was a studio strategy, even though the film was shot on location in a real apartment. The first week shooting *Jeanne Dielman,* we changed to a heavier-weight camera, a Mitchell BNC. I think one of the reasons was that we wanted to have an absolutely steady image, and we were worried that the Eclair Cameflex we had at the beginning was not steady enough. When you project the image in a big auditorium with a huge screen, at high magnification, you get a certain waving with 16mm which is never as steady as 35mm. So if you were going to shoot in 35mm and you had Delphine Seyrig, you wanted to have something which was really perfect.

For *Jeanne Dielman*, the rehearsal in video was also very important. Sami Frey suggested it, and he brought his video equipment when he came the first week of shooting to visit Delphine.[8] I think Delphine's subsequent involvement with video work and making video herself came from this experience, because video hardly existed then. It was a reel-to-reel machine—this was before U-matic. Very few people had them. From 9:00 to 11:30 every morning, Chantal and Delphine—and me a little bit, but I was mostly preparing the camera and lights—rehearsed with video what was going to be shot in the afternoon. Then we shot with the crew from noon to 8 p.m. The mornings were just between Delphine and Chantal. It was their time to figure out Jeanne's gestures.

29 June 1995
augmented, revised, corrected June 2018

Afterword: Chantal Akerman, Our Shared Creative History
Babette Mangolte

When Chantal Akerman called me in October 1971, we became friends almost immediately. We had the same sense of exclusion from a film world controlled by men and the same fascination for New York City, with the discovery of experimentation in theater, films, and music. Our first important tie became working together with no clear aspiration: we didn't know if films like *La Chambre* and *Hotel Monterey* that we made in 1972 would lead anywhere. That tie was sealed by a project we did together in fall 1972 in Yonkers, New York (*Hanging Out Yonkers*) and another one, during the summer of 1973, outside Paris, working on a women's film project that was never finished, a disaster of an experience. But we discussed the reasons for the failure, and that helped us understand what feminist films could be.

During all the years of her life, Chantal could share her writing and her projects with me, and I gave her comments that could be direct and constructive. I remember that one of the strong regrets I had was when she gave me her script of *Toute une nuit* (Belgium/France, 1982) to read in 1981. I thought it was great, but I could not afford to go to Brussels when she finally got some funding. I would have loved to shoot that script. We always saw each other when I arrived in the same town where she was, and the same for her. We looked at each other's works all our lives. We shared a common history at the most important stage of our formation as filmmakers.

We were friends.

May 2018

Notes

1. INSAS stands for Institut National Supérieur des Arts du Spectacle et des Techniques de Diffusion.

2. The earlier version was published as Janet Bergstrom, "La femme à la caméra: Intervista di Janet Bergstrom à Babette Mangolte," in *Il cinema di Chantal Akerman*, ed. Adriano Aprà and Bruno Di Marino (Rome: Dino Audino Editore, 1997), 72–84.

3. It is important not to give a false impression of *La Chambre* and *Hotel Monterey* by stating the now-standard and seemingly obligatory country and date. These two films were experimental; they were shot with donated labor and money, and self-financed only to pay for the film stock and lab processing. Babette and Chantal had no idea how or if they could be shown anywhere. In other words, they were not made to be distributed.

    "For Chantal, those films were like a chronicle of her life because she lived in both places—the apartment on Spring Street (*La Chambre*) and later in May 1972, she lived for three weeks at the Hotel Monterey before and when we shot the film *Hotel Monterey*. Citing a country implies a production made with financing and distribution. While utopian intentions may have been part of those films, the production and dates found in sources like IMDB refer to the release and even for that, they are unreliable. These two films were released commercially only in the 1980s when Chantal started to have retrospectives. Before that, they had one screening each in 1973 in Nancy, France at a festival, as discussed in the interview. The editing and later the release were probably paid for through Jacques Ledoux at the Cinémathèque royale de Belgique, where Ledoux was director from the time of Chantal's *Saute ma ville* throughout all her

1970s films, maybe extending into the 1980s." Babette Mangolte, e-mail to the author, 8 August 2018.

4.   During the revision of this interview, Myra Alfreds (formerly Farhy) explained how both she and Jane Stein met Chantal in 1971. Someone Myra knew in Israel had given Chantal her phone number, and Myra would have told her about Jane, where she "was warmly welcomed, as only Jane can do." E-mail to Patricia White, 22 July 2018.

5.   *Jeanne Dielman* was selected for the section Quinzaine des Réalisateurs (Directors' Fortnight).

6.   According to Myra Alfreds, "Chantal came to visit me on her own in Yonkers and came up with the idea for doing the film. . . . She came back to Yonkers in May 2014 to see the programs and meet kids and families for a possible film idea." E-mail to White, 22 July 2018. Mangolte commented that Akerman's return to Yonkers "showed how she was concentrated on what she could do." Babette Mangolte, e-mail to the author, 23 July 2018.

7.   Babette Mangolte, "*La Chambre 1 et 2—Hanging Out Yonkers—Hotel Monterey—Jeanne Dielman, 23 quai du Commerce, 1080 Bruxelles*" in *Chantal Akerman, Autoportrait en cinéaste* (Paris: Editions du Centre Georges Pompidou/Editions Cahiers du cinéma, 2004), 174–76. Mangolte noted that in the article title *Hotel Monterey* should come before *Hanging Out Yonkers*, since that was the order in which the films were made. According to her calendar, she shot *La Chambre* in February 1972, Rainer's *Lives of Performers* in April, and *Hotel Monterey* in middle or late May. In her opinion, what is now known as the "silent version" of *La Chambre* is the best one. In the original interview, she didn't know that two versions existed—rather, that there were two single-shot, eleven-minute takes—and did not know about any soundtrack. Apparently Chantal added sound to one of the takes later, but originally it was shown silent.

8.   Parts of the video footage are included as a documentary, *Autour de Jeanne Dielman*, on most DVD and BluRay versions of *Jeanne Dielman*. The credits read: "Shot by Sami Frey, edited by Agnès Ravez and Akerman."

Janet Bergstrom is research professor of cinema and media studies at the University of California, Los Angeles. She followed Chantal Akerman's work since her first retrospective at Berkeley's Pacific Film Archive in November 1976. She is a founding coeditor of *Camera Obscura*, and her essay on *Jeanne Dielman* and excerpts from a group interview appeared in Fall 1977 in that journal. Other essays on Akerman include "Chantal Akerman: Splitting," published in her anthology *Endless Night: Cinema and Psychoanalysis, Parallel Histories* (1999), "Keeping a Distance: Chantal Akerman and the Spirit of the 1970s" in *Sight and Sound* (1999), and "Heartfelt," following Akerman's death, in *Senses of Cinema* (2016). Bergstrom specializes in archivally based, cross-national studies of émigré directors such as F. W. Murnau, Jean Renoir, Josef von Sternberg, Fritz Lang, and Alfred Hitchcock, as well as French/Francophone directors Chantal Akerman and Claire Denis. She has published five archivally based documentaries on DVD, most recently *Josef von Sternberg—Salvation Hunter* to accompany Sternberg's *The Salvation Hunters* (US, 1924) (Edition Filmmuseum, Austrian Film Museum, Vienna, 2016).

Babette Mangolte (US, born in France) is an internationally renowned experimental filmmaker and photographer who lives in New York. She worked as a cinematographer with Chantal Akerman, Yvonne Rainer, Michael Snow, Sally Potter, and Jean-Pierre Gorin, among others, and became known as a filmmaker through a trilogy of feature films exploring the use of the subjective camera. In the 1980s her films examined landscapes and colors; in the 1990s she focused on artists' processes. The digital revolution enabled her to combine photographs, films, and texts in installations exploring history and contemporaneity. In 1989 she joined the University of California, San Diego as a tenured professor. Recent films include Trisha Brown's choreography *Roof Piece on the High Line* (2011–12) and *Staging Lateral Pass* (1985/2013), *Steve Paxton at DIA* (2014), *I, Nous, I or Eye, Us* (2014), *Edward Krasiński's Studio* (Warsaw, 2011; Berlinale selection 2013), and her 2016 film on Anne Teresa de Keersmaeker's *Work/Travail/Arbeit* at WIELS Centre for Contemporary Art (April 2015). Mangolte's installations attempt to create architectural spaces exploring different modes of spectator interactivity. In *Looking and Touching* (John Hansard Gallery, Southampton, UK, 2007) she presented framed photographs of dance and performance on a wall that could only be seen at a distance next to print replicas on a table that the audience could manipulate and touch. In *TOUCHING III* (Inhotim in Belo Horizonte, MG Brazil, 2013) she used mostly theater images, followed by a script analysis, "Reading Yvonne Rainer's *this is the story of a woman who . . .*" (Whitney Museum of American Art, 2013). She reinstalled her first installation from 1976, *How To Look . . .*, at PS 1 in New York, renamed *How to Look . . . 2010*; it was acquired by the Tate Modern in 2011 and on display in 2018. Her solo show *Eye = I: Babette Mangolte* at the Vienna Kunsthalle (2016–17) focused on time, grouping several of her films with new installations and slide shows. The Sternberg Press is publishing Mangolte's selected writings (1998–2015). For further details, see www.babettemangolte.org.

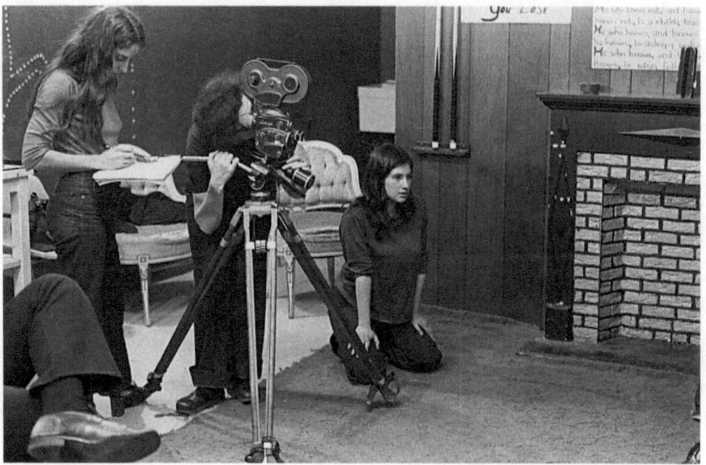

Figure 7. Shooting *Hanging Out Yonkers*, fall 1972. From left to right, Epp Kotkas taking script notes, Babette Mangolte with the Beaulieu camera, and Chantal Akerman. © 1972 Jane Stein (All Rights of Reproduction Reserved)

Hanging Out Yonkers: A Photographic Record

Jane Stein

Jane Stein, Myra Farhy (now Alfreds) and Chantal Akerman met in 1971 when the filmmaker knocked on the door of Stein's New York apartment, referred by a mutual friend. They remained friends for forty-five years. In 1972 Akerman worked on a documentary with youth participants in a citywide drug prevention and treatment program called RAP (Redirection and Prevention), where Farhy worked. Stein took these photos on a visit to the RAP lounge in Yonkers, where Akerman was shooting with cinematographer Babette Mangolte and Epp Kotkas. For an account of the project, see Janet Bergstrom's interview with Mangolte in this issue.
—Patricia White

Camera Obscura 100, Volume 34, Number 1
DOI 10.1215/02705346-7264104   © 2019 by *Camera Obscura*
Published by Duke University Press

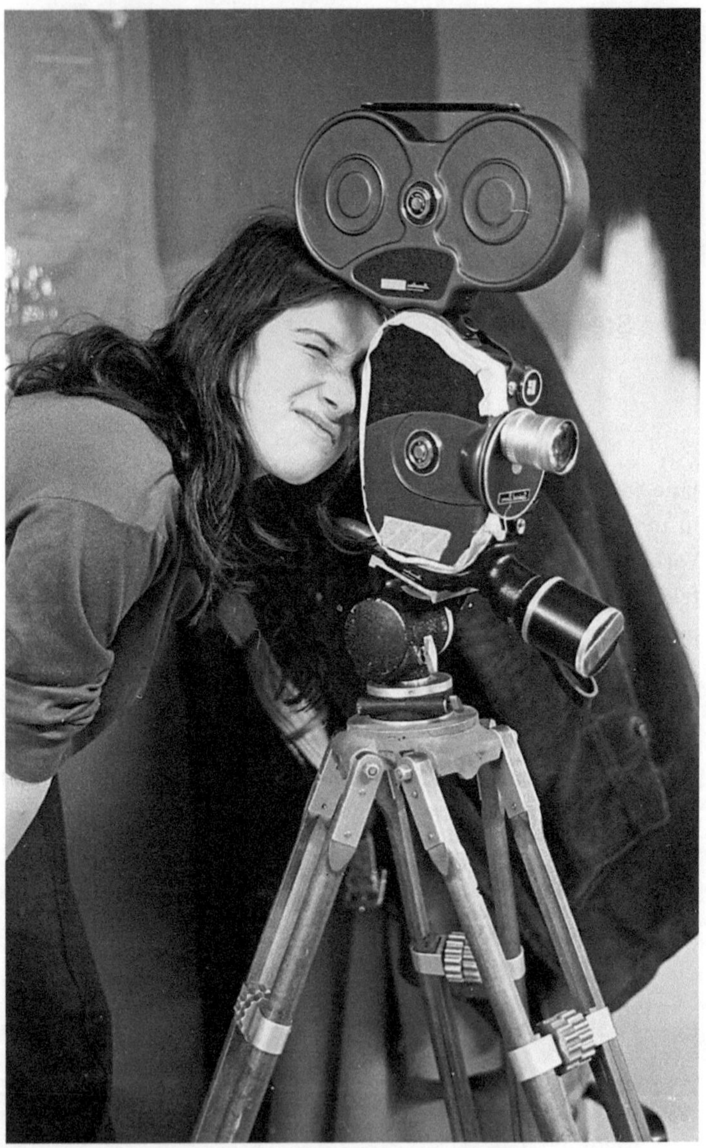

Figure 1. Chantal Akerman

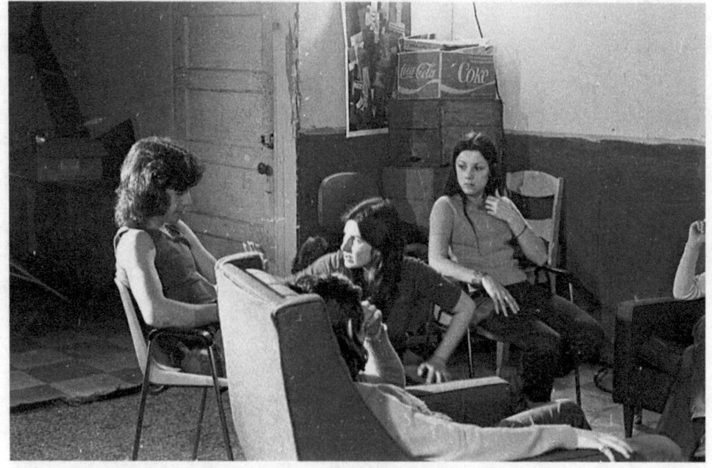

Figure 2. Chantal Akerman with program participants

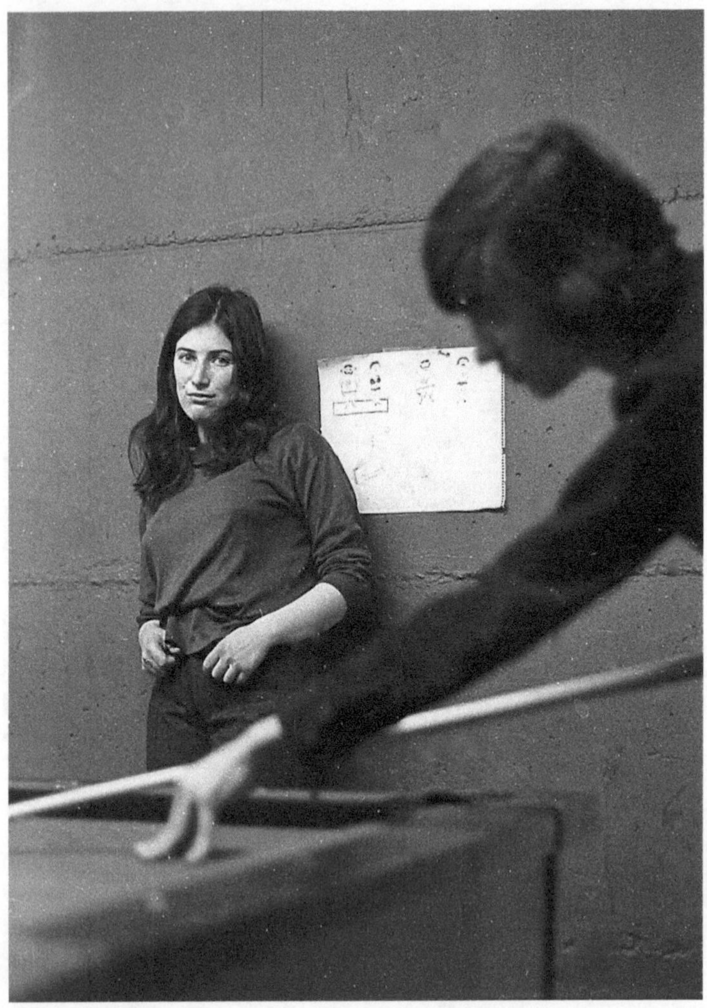

Figure 3. Chantal Akerman and program participant

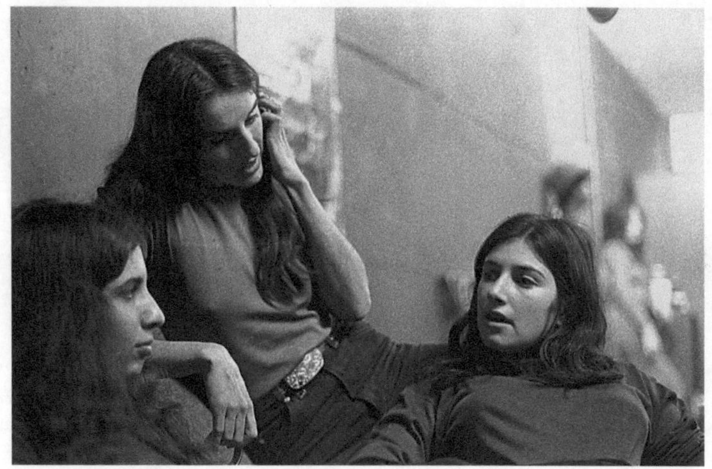

Figure 4. Left to right: Myra Farhy, Epp Kotkas,
Chantal Akerman

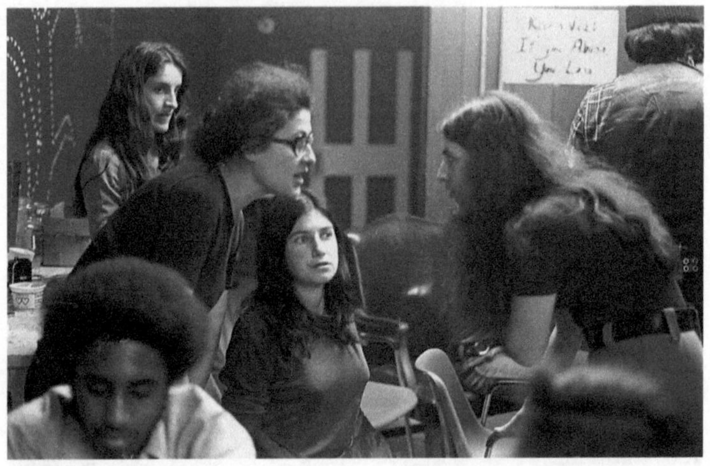

Figure 5. Program participant (bottom left foreground), Epp
Kotkas, Babette Mangolte, Chantal Akerman, Myra Farhy

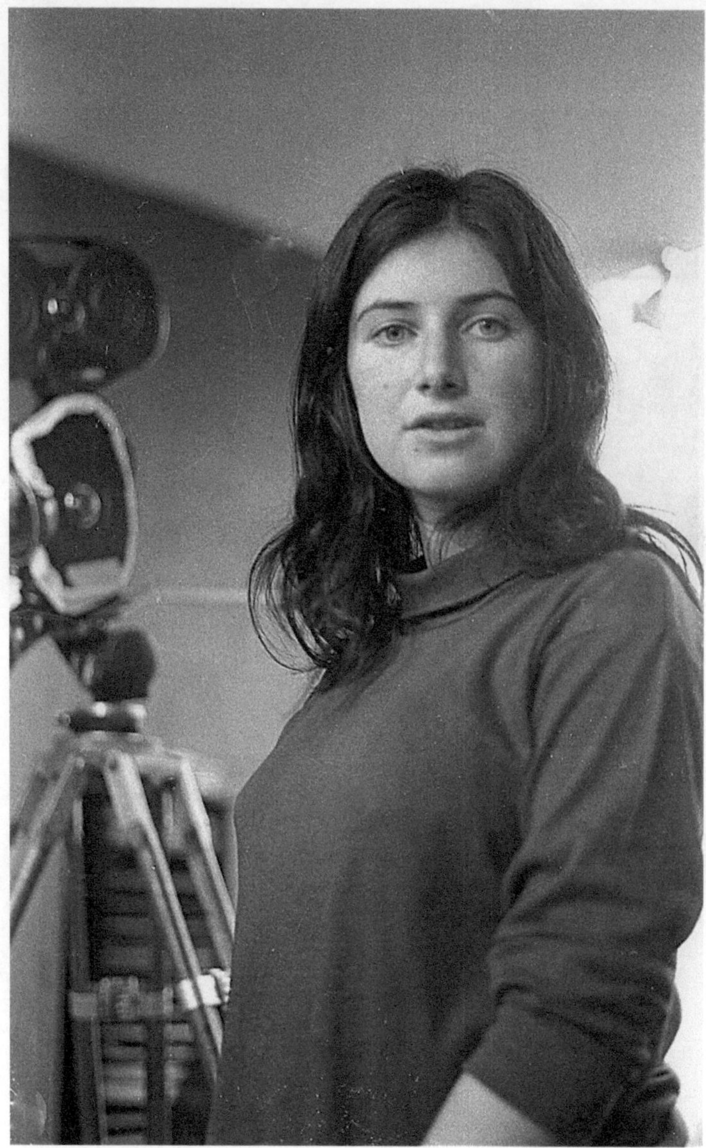

Figure 6. Chantal Akerman

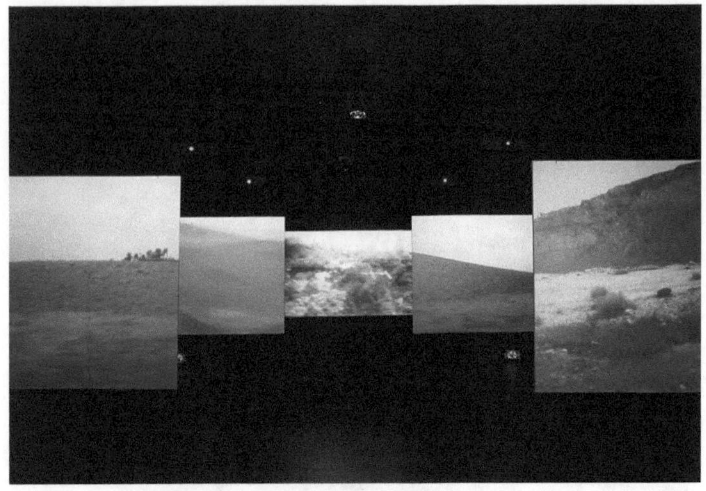

Figure 1. Chantal Akerman's *NOW*, at the Jewish Museum, New York, 2018. © 2018 Babette Mangolte (All Rights of Reproduction Reserved)

NOW, Chantal Akerman's Last Work

Babette Mangolte

NOW is a video installation made of multiple screens placed in three layers. When you see the installation for the first time, you feel that you are focusing only on the central layer (a single screen) and that the two outer layers—each composed of two screens, to the left and right of the central screen and progressively closer to you—reveal your eyes' peripheral vision that has been made visible for you by Chantal Akerman, the filmmaker who designed this installation between January and March 2015 and installed it in Venice for the April 2015 Biennale.[1]

I saw it there in July 2015 in the space where the installation premiered. But because the space was not enclosed, you could not isolate the Biennale crowd noises from the sound of *NOW.* You were aware of the obsessive sounds of motors that made you perceive that you were looking at the landscape from moving vehicles. You heard some gunshots, explosions, and loud noises that you could not identify. The clear association you got from what you heard was an allusion to guns, the sense of having to flee because of war, the need to be on the move. I knew that I was not really experienc-

Camera Obscura 100, Volume 34, Number 1
DOI 10.1215/02705346-7264094   © 2019 by Babette Mangolte
Published by Duke University Press

ing the immersion into the piece as it had been conceptualized by my friend Chantal, knowing how sound is a key component of her installations. They are works where actions and people are not always the driving parameters, so the context for what we see is conveyed by the offscreen sound that is of great importance in generating meaning.

The center screen is the farthest back. The four other screens are separated by the central one, but they are aligned in two layers at different distances from the center. The images on the five screens are tracking shots taken from moving cars. Everything was shot in the Negev desert—its bare vegetation, the dryness of the land, no water anywhere, and no clouds. At least that is what I assumed while in Venice.

I rediscovered the piece in February 2018 in a very contained room in the Jewish Museum in New York. Then I felt there could be exceptions to that one singular location, even one as vast as the Negev desert. The film could include elements shot in other places. But whatever you see is land that is barren of most vegetation, and the color is primarily that of sandy dirt, rocks, with white sky and some rare blue. At first you feel that the difference of the speed of each tracking shot is what distinguishes the five screens and the relation each screen has to the depth of the space. The layer closest to you (that I call layer 3, because for me, the center screen has to be layer 1, and therefore the intermediate layer has to be layer 2) always seems to have been shot from a faster car than layer 2, and it is the same for the center screen, where the tracking movement is not ever moving as fast as on layer 2 or 3. This is why the intention of exposing peripheral vision was so clear to me. The color palette of the center stage also distinctly shows more fertile land and more blue sky, some vegetation, not just rocks and gravel or sage. At a distance you perceive antenna-like satellite towers or electrical lines, so that we are in a man-made landscape after all. To the left of layer 3 you see parked cars briefly and an immobile truck that you pass by quickly. But the land behind the group of cars and the truck is the same as on the road before, with the same colored sand and dirt.

What you see is movement. I could notice only two exceptions, when there is a brief stop on an extreme close-up of a rocky wall, as if those rocks were blocking the road. Suddenly there is a jump cut, and we are back on the road. The two stops are actually the same image, but reversed, and you notice that there are multiple repetitions of tracking shots at every speed. You see the same footage used in a different order, so it is difficult to measure the duration of the various visual loops on the three layers of screens. Some tracking shots are too fast to be more than streaks of light indicating the sky and sandy terrain. Those are so distinctive that you know when they are repeated with their composition reversed. At first you think that each layer (that is, the left and right screens in layers 2 and 3) is contiguous in projecting the same movement from left to right or right to left. But that is not necessarily the case. The more you look, the more you discover that the movement jumps from layer 2 left to layer 3 right, continuing the movement initiated on layer 2 that is more distant than layer 3, which is the closest to the spectator. This shift of distance adds a complexity to the way the space is represented that is uncanny.

If you go behind the screens, you will find a small TV display with the little vignette in the back, with colored neon tubes that are pink on one side and blue on the other—both colors that are absent from the images projected on the screen. You do not feel that the installation encourages you to wander throughout the whole space, because it is too tight. So you stay put, transfixed in the center of the five screens, looking at the roads passing by, totally subjugated to the constant movement and aggressively loud sounds. The soundtrack is so packed with sound effects and an intense presence of people that the visuals of what appears to be a desert disappear behind the animation of the sounds, which evoke people talking and singing, church bells, a police siren passing by, a Muslim call to prayers, as well as musical fragments—even a solo played by a cellist in a concert that is almost buried under the soundtrack's cacophony of violence. The image is all about movement, but the predominance of the sounds of people transforms what you see and negates the empty landscape. Sounds from crowds of people in cities are mixed with the sounds of motor vehicles while the image shows a deserted landscape. The noises are from urban areas: police sirens, sounds of the subway, and crowds of people. When you hear people talking in Hebrew, English, Arabic, French, Hindi, or other languages, you feel that the movement you see is not part of what you hear. You become aware of two or three gunshots from a single revolver, and later rapid machine gun fire, and suddenly you—the viewer-listener—put together the sound you hear with what you see, and you decode a state of war in faraway places, as well as here in the cities we live in, and elsewhere, where the others live.

After a while, we feel that the five film projections become blurry, because we stop looking. Our attention becomes totally centered on listening to the enormous complexity of the sound and how evocative it is. It generates a rapid burst of associations that provoke zillions of impressions, evoking the extreme diversity of the places the sound is coming from. The sound is heavily mixed and distorted with echoes and decrepit public announcement speaker systems, which evoke the bad acoustics of the New York subway system and its train noises, and buses in Brussels or Paris or elsewhere. I remember that Chantal lived in both Paris and New York during the last three years of her life: all the sounds of her everyday life are there in *NOW*.

I contacted Claire Atherton, a close friend of Chantal's who edited many of her works starting in 1986. She sent me a description about making the film, in which she describes Chantal's intentions: she wanted to make the desert anonymous so that whoever sees the piece can imagine that what they see is what they know. Indeed, the landscape images could have been shot on different continents. But the point of departure for the installation piece was creating the multilayered sound mix around the idea of the five screens and the sound jumbled among all the screens. Claire writes: "*NOW* was born first of all with the sound. Chantal told me that she wanted the spectator to experience fear, war, flight, imminent catastrophe through the entanglement of soundtracks in a space inhabited by images of the desert. She wanted us to live the chaos, to feel the degree to which our world is haunted by violence."[2]

NOW is all about the present of its spectators, because the filmmaker has covered her creative traces and has made sure that the dense collage of sounds referring to multiple countries and cultures reveals nothing other than what is viewed and heard. There is no message, but there are sensations of being there, unable to see, unable to dominate the world that we are driven through. The past has disappeared. It is not there anymore, obliterated by violence. If the past affects the present through the act of unconscious memory as in Proust, there is no trace of it in *NOW*. We are moved through time by forces that are not in our power to control. Many of Akerman's works—*D'Est* (*From the East*, France/Belgium, 1993), *Sud* (*South*, France/Belgium, 1999), *De l'autre côté* (*From the Other Side*, Belgium, 2002), *Demain on déménage* (*Tomorrow We Move*, France/Belgium, 2004), *Là-bas* (*Down There*, Belgium/France, 2006), *La Folie Almayer* (*Almayer's Folly*, France/Belgium, 2011), and *NOW*—reflect on the idea that the present is what counts and nothing else, even if the present is haunted by the past, as in *Sud* and *La Folie Almayer* and her last film, *No Home Movie* (France/Belgium, 2015). For Chantal, living in the present was the most important thing to do. Many of her works, ever since her first film, testify to this philosophy.

NOW is Chantal Akerman's final work. When she was in Venice, unbeknownst to her, she had completed her creative trajectory. It began with *Saute ma ville* (*Blow Up My Town*, Belgium) in 1967 in the kitchen of a young girl, focusing on the individuality of one person, and it concluded in Venice in 2015 as a global statement about the world we live in, in which immersion in a crowd is part of every individual's trajectory.

Notes

1. *NOW* was commissioned as an installation for the 2015 Venice Biennale, and as of 2018 it is in the collection of the Jewish Museum in New York.

2. "*NOW* est née d'abord par le son. Chantal disait qu'elle voulait qu'on éprouve la peur, la guerre, la fuite, la catastrophe imminente par l'enchevêtrement de bandes sonores dans un espace habité par des images de désert. Elle voulait qu'on vive le chaos, qu'on ressente à quel point notre monde est détraqué par la violence." Claire Atherton, e-mail to the author, 28 February 2018.

Babette Mangolte (US, born in France) is an experimental filmmaker and photographer who is known internationally and lives in New York. Her installations create architectural spaces exploring different modes of interactivity for the spectators. Her writing on filmmaking practices and the impact that digital tools have had on filmmaking since the end of the twentieth century is soon to appear in a book edited by Luca lo Pinto. For further details, see www.babettemangolte.org.

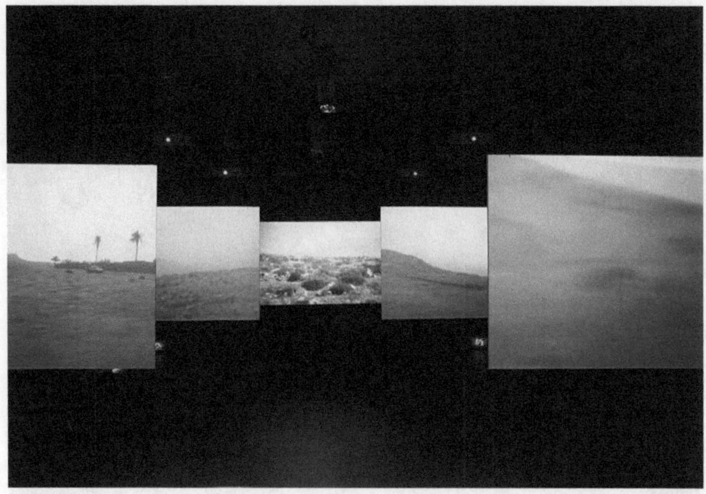

Figure 2. Chantal Akerman's *NOW*, at the Jewish Museum,
New York, 2018. © 2018 Babette Mangolte (All Rights of
Reproduction Reserved)

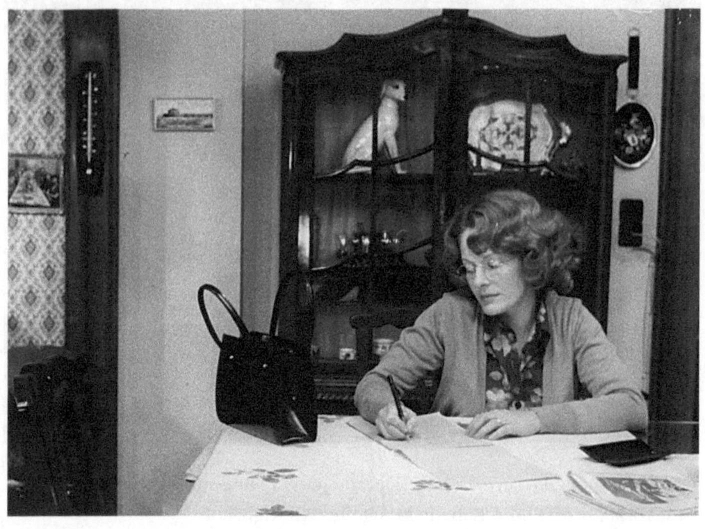

Figure 1. *Jeanne Dielman, 23 quai du Commerce, 1080 Bruxelles* (1975). Courtesy of Janus Films

Souvenirs de Chantal

Sandy Flitterman-Lewis

Chantal Akerman and Georges Perec share an aesthetic and a practice that probe the depths of identity, exile, memory, and displacement in an "invocation of and simultaneous distancing from autobiographical indices, [reflecting] on the porous boundaries between lived experience and fiction."[1] Perec had many affinities with Chantal, not the least of which was the generational memory of the Shoah. Perec, while eight years younger than Chantal's mother, Natalia (Nelly), belonged to the first generation; Chantal belonged to the second. They shared an interest in formal experimentation around an inexpressible traumatic past, the continuous evolution of form in whatever medium they were working, and a protean, almost joyous engagement with language—cinematic or written, or both. Perec has been described as a novelist, a filmmaker, a documentarian, and an essayist. Reverse the first two terms, add "installation artist," and you have a description of Chantal.

In the early seventies, Harry Mathews told Georges Perec about Joe Brainard's small book *I Remember* (1970), in which the American artist and writer developed an intriguing form of autobiography.[2] Perec began his own *Je me souviens* (1978) but made it

Camera Obscura 100, Volume 34, Number 1
DOI 10.1215/02705346-7264114   © 2019 by *Camera Obscura*
Published by Duke University Press

more characteristically observational, a chronicle of the quotidian as well as a self-portrait, and he dedicated it to Brainard.[3] After Perec died, Mathews began his own version of the familiar form, *The Orchard* (1988), "simply to avail [himself] of the written word in facing the dismay that at that moment was overwhelming so many of us."[4] My own contribution to this form is offered as a tribute to and appreciation of Chantal, a chronicle of our history, and an unusual glimpse into the highly productive career of one of our beloved pioneers. It is also a sort of memory work, which I hope through its scope will work on that porous border "between lived experience and fiction."

I REMEMBER my first meeting with Chantal in 1977, in her tiny Paris apartment, at the beginning of her career, after she had returned from Berkeley. *Camera Obscura* had published one of the first discussions of *Jeanne Dielman, 23 quai du Commerce, 1080 Bruxelles* (Belgium/France, 1975) in English, and Janet Bergstrom had organized an interview there. Connie Penley and I picked up the threads in Paris. This young, feisty, imaginative filmmaker gave me a poster for *Jeanne Dielman*, a realistic sketch of Jeanne and Sylvain waiting at the dinner table, and I had it framed. It became my muse for many years. It is worth a lot of money now.

I REMEMBER thinking, as a travel-weary Chantal opened a can of tuna and sat on the floor in 1977, how much, in retrospect, she reminded me of the weary Aurore Clément in *Les Rendez-vous d'Anna* (France/Belgium/Germany, 1978) and how human and endearing, even welcoming, was this young woman, almost a celebrity already.

I REMEMBER Berkeley professor Bertrand Augst plying us with French articles and interviews about this astounding young woman filmmaker while we were preparing the inaugural issue of *Camera Obscura*. Quite an origin story.

I REMEMBER Martin Walsh, a brilliant film scholar who could write about semiotics for *Jump Cut*, telling me about a film that baffled him when he saw it in Edinburgh. Really baffled him. It was *Jeanne Dielman*.

I REMEMBER loving Sami Frey's film *Autour de Jeanne Dielman*, now included in the Criterion DVD, shot simultaneously with the feature and later edited by Chantal in 2004, which gave such good insight into Chantal's process while working with Delphine Seyrig in conversations about space and time. Not character.

I REMEMBER being struck by the number of times that a typewriter, laptop, or the act of writing itself appears in Chantal's films. And then there are the letters.

I REMEMBER that when I started teaching "Women and Film," I planned to screen *Jeanne Dielman* near the end of the term. My colleagues all told me that I was crazy to show that film to uncomprehending undergraduates. Decades later, upon learning of Chantal's death, many students wrote to me, grateful that they had first seen her film in my course.

I REMEMBER Gwen Foster sending FedEx to my door to collect my chapter for her edited collection on Akerman just as I finished the last sentence. "What's Beneath Her Smile?" is about the cinematic and feminist relations between Germaine Dulac's film *The Smiling Madame Beudet* (France, 1923) and Chantal's film about an unsmiling housewife.[5]

I REMEMBER having dinner in London in the late spring of 2017 with filmmaker Ruth Novaczek and writer Cécile Chich at a restaurant that was Chantal's favorite. Therefore, her spirit also dined with us.

I REMEMBER this phrase of Harry Mathews: "I remember Georges Perec saying that buttered French bread [une tartine beurrée] was the most delectable food in the world. His usual breakfast consisted of a tartine and café au lait."[6] I thought of Jeanne and the thermos of coffee.

I REMEMBER with delight that my favorite photo (which I made into a postcard) was of a tartine and a café au lait.

I REMEMBER seeing the bookstore window in Paris when the Gallimard edition of Perec came out. We wanted the display poster, because of the cats, but it was not for sale.

I REMEMBER reading that in 1988, when the Avignon Festival honored Georges Perec with readings and an exhibition, Sami Frey performed *I Remember* on stage as a monologue with a minimal set and a stationary bicycle as his only prop.

I REMEMBER Sami Frey's set of incredible connections binding Chantal (a lifelong friend), the Shoah, memories of the maternal, *Cléo from 5 to 7* (dir. Agnès Varda, France/Italy, 1962), *Bande à part* (dir. Jean-Luc Godard, France, 1964), Samuel Beckett, Georges Perec, and Marguerite Duras in a sacred play of associations. Duras has said that she based one of her Aurélia Steiner texts on Sami's experience: during the war, his mother left him with a neighbor when he was five years old. She had promised him she'd be back soon, but she never returned, having perished in the camps.

I REMEMBER thinking how handsome Sami Frey was when I saw a screening of Chantal's *Le Déménagement* (*Moving In*, France, 1993).

I REMEMBER seeing *News from Home* (France/Belgium, 1976) for the first time when to me, as a Californian, the glaucous images of the New York subway seemed both scary and enchanting. Nelly's letters to her daughter, read in Chantal's soothing monotone, provided a kind of comfort.

I REMEMBER *News from Home* at the Jewish Museum, my adorable, diminutive in-laws attending my talk and saying that they liked "that meshuggenah film" even though they couldn't understand it.

I REMEMBER critic Jonathan Rosenbaum telling me that Chantal's face lit up when he said the word *mishpocheh*.

I REMEMBER discovering, for the first time, that Chantal's Jewish identity was central to her work when I saw the installation *From the East: Bordering on Fiction* (1995) at the Jewish Museum in New York City. Twenty-four television screens showed portions of the film *D'Est* (*From the East*, France/Belgium, 1993) in the middle room while the first room screened the film in its entirety. The

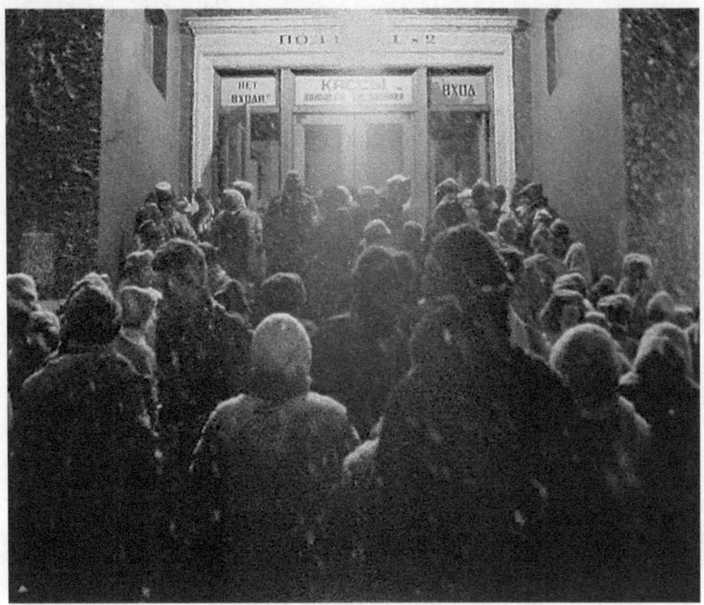

Figure 2. *D'Est* (1993). Courtesy of Fondation Claire Atherton
and Marian Goodman Gallery

third room held a twenty-fifth, black-and-white television monitor
on which Chantal pronounced the commandment against idolatry, first in Hebrew and then in English. But more important was
her voice-over:

Yesterday, today, and tomorrow, there were, there will be, there are at
this very moment, people whom history (which no longer even has a
capital "H"), whom history has struck down. People who are waiting
there, packed together, to be killed, beaten, or starved, or who walk
without knowing where they are going, in groups or alone. There is
nothing to do. It is obsessive, and I am obsessed. Despite the cello,
despite cinema. The film finished, I say to myself, *that's* what it was;
once again, *that.*

I REMEMBER asking my husband, Joel, what his conversation
with Chantal was about at the Jewish Museum's installation of
D'Est. "Being second generation," he answered. In 1996, I hadn't

really known how seriously the imprint of the Shoah had impacted Chantal's work.

I REMEMBER that I used the bit of money that I got for speaking at the Jewish Museum to buy Serge Klarsfeld's magisterial book *French Children of the Holocaust: A Memorial*, which gives a name, place and date of birth, last address, and convoy to Auschwitz of all 11,403 Jewish children deported from France.[7] There are pictures, too, for those that can be found. I was beginning to understand its crucial relation to Chantal's work, the book's explicitness working dialectically with Chantal's necessarily oblique and allusive reference to the Shoah in films and installations that bear its traces in less concrete terms.

I REMEMBER my high school friend Evy Kahan's French mother, a tiny woman with a haunted face and a number on her arm.

I REMEMBER that I wrote a poem for my father-in-law's funeral in which I reconfigured his Auschwitz number—141281—toward positive meanings in his life.

I REMEMBER being incredibly touched by the maternal kiss in Chantal's *Tomorrow We Move* (France/Belgium, 2004) and that I would later write that the film, in combination with her installation *Walking Next to One's Shoelaces in an Empty Fridge* (2004), represented for me the heart of many of Akerman's projects. The memory of the Shoah, never explicitly represented—yet transmitted through matrilineal silence, suffering, and strength—lies beneath and beyond everything that bears Chantal's signature.

I REMEMBER first learning of *Walking Next to One's Shoelaces in an Empty Fridge*, which was paired with an exhibition of Charlotte Salomon's work at the Jewish Museum in Berlin in 2007, from a talk given by Griselda Pollock at the Clark in Massachusetts. Both artists—Charlotte in painting and collage, Chantal in film, installation, and writing—"take confrontation with the past as a point of departure for their work," I jotted down. In fact, we do too.

I REMEMBER receiving Griselda Pollock's long-awaited book on Charlotte Salomon and finding that it opens with Israeli sculptor

Dani Karavan's contemplative memorial to Walter Benjamin at Portbou.[8]

I REMEMBER that Dani Karavan's environmental site sculpture contains my favorite Walter Benjamin quotation etched in glass: "It is more arduous to honor the memory of the nameless than that of the renowned. Historical reconstruction is devoted to the memory of the nameless."

I REMEMBER Chantal telling Nicole Brenez that the only thing that made her dying father feel better was her singing him songs in Yiddish. That reminded me of the time that my mother-in-law, Miriam, was in the hospital, and our rabbi brought his guitar to her bedside. The Yiddish songs made Miriam and Morty shine with delight.

I REMEMBER being stunned at Chantal's specificity about Nelly's Auschwitz experience, especially since *Tomorrow We Move* and *Walking Next to One's Shoelaces in an Empty Fridge* are notable for the lack of such detail in their reference to her mother and grandmother's Holocaust suffering. I know, for example, that Chantal has said that all of her films are in some way about her mother and that Nelly's silence was often her motivation. But her clarity regarding the memory about which her mother never spoke has haunted me. Nelly was fifteen at the time (like Marceline Loridan), manufacturing battle supplies for Krupp (like my father-in-law).[9] "My mother and her aunts were taken care of by an older woman who would save them a bit of bread so that they could stay alive. [During the death march] my mother didn't realize it, but her aunts supported her when she fainted, and they chewed her food for her so she could eat."[10]

I REMEMBER how impressed and moved I was by the phrase, "The Jewish tradition has no other history than its own memory," by Pierre Nora, quoted by Marion Schmid and by Janet Bergstrom in their analyses of *Histoires d'Amérique: Food, Family, and Philosophy* (France/Belgium, 1988).[11]

I REMEMBER shlepping out from Hoboken to BAM [Brooklyn Academy of Music] in Brooklyn to watch *Histoires d'Amérique,* a film that I'd often read about but never seen. It was worth the shlep—a more beautiful orchestration of immigrant voices with fanciful Mitteleuropean cultural touches, Yiddish phrases, and floating constellations of the Manhattan skyline I could not imagine. Chantal says of this film, "The Jews. (In exile, as usual.)"[12] In concrete terms, the film remains elusive.

I REMEMBER reading with a sense of happy recognition that, while working on *Histoires d'Amérique*, Claire Atherton and Chantal stayed at cinematographer Ellen Kuras's apartment near the Holland Tunnel, where the noise of the trucks always bothered them. Happy because the Holland Tunnel is what connects Manhattan to Hoboken, and it had its place in Chantal's narrative.

I REMEMBER Joel telling me that he and Chantal also spoke about their early Jewish education at Hebrew day school—and my bewilderment that I had known next to nothing about either. Chantal has said, "To go to yeshiva means learning the art of questioning and negation, and this after millennia, after the Hebrew Bible. The Talmud means learning how to discuss, to call things into question, to develop your thoughts."[13]

I REMEMBER thinking that the few breathtaking shots of the beach in Tel Aviv that Chantal disperses among the enclosure and voyeurism of *Là-bas* (*Down There*, Belgium/France, 2006) are some of the most beautiful images in the history of the cinema.

I REMEMBER the beautiful gold earrings, my favorites, that Miriam brought back from Israel. How did she know that they would look so good on me? I wonder why I never think of Chantal in earrings.

I REMEMBER my week in Israel, where I had been invited to be on a panel about *A Couch in New York* (France/Belgium/Germany, 1996). Jerusalem, Carmel Market, Beit Hatfutsot Museum—it changed my life. Being in places that have existed for thousands of years gave me a new perspective, something spiritual, and a sort of connection that I hadn't realized before.

I REMEMBER the cancellation of the panel on *A Couch in New York* in Tel Aviv after the previous night's typical Q and A debacle (owing to Chantal's characteristic hostility to audiences). Once it was reinstated, Chantal was still testy, but the atmosphere was calmed by the gracious and informed direction of Régine-Mihal Friedman of Tel Aviv University. Chantal had problems with the foray into commercialism that the film represented. People familiar with her films were disappointed by this straightforward narrative; conventional audiences avoided the film because Chantal's name evoked the avant-garde. Whether this fact or the location (Israel) led to her frustration is not clear, but the mercurial and unpredictable presence was pure Chantal.

I REMEMBER learning that Chantal was as horrified as I was to learn of the murder of James Byrd Jr., a black man, in Jasper, Texas, where he was dragged from the back of a truck down a country road by three white supremacists. Chantal made a film, *Sud* (*South*, France/Belgium, 1999); I made a collage, or, as I called it, a paper mosaic. Chantal extended her particular perception of human suffering beyond the specific trauma of her Jewish family to a wider understanding of social evil.

I REMEMBER thinking how exhausting and exuberant, how deadly serious and deadpan funny, the episodes in *Toute une nuit* (*All Night Long*, Belgium/France, 1982) were. A mad tango is funny; loneliness is not. And how beautiful was Natalia, who played a role in her daughter's episodic fiction film. Did she have a suitcase?

I REMEMBER telling my friend Marcelline that she hadn't missed much when she couldn't make it to *Maniac Shadows* (2012) at The Kitchen. How stupid of me. The more I learn about the installation, how Chantal used a Blackberry for some of it and how she read from *Ma mère rit* (*My Mother Laughs*, 2013), the more I understand how central it is to all of her work.[14] It's all there—the intimate personal stories, the documentarian's gaze on the everyday, the weight of the unsaid, the reciprocal respect between author and audience. But then, a lot of Chantal's oeuvre requires multiple screenings and readings.

I REMEMBER my happy recognition of the fact that Charles Denner, who played opposite Delphine Seyrig in *Golden Eighties* (France/Belgium/Switzerland, 1986), also played the Jewish father in Claude Berri's autobiographical film, *The Two of Us* (France, 1967), about his experiences as a hidden child in occupied France. Chantal has referred to Berri as "a small Jew who came from leather and fur, like my father."[15] Berri is the father of Thomas Langmann, another Chantal friend and actor (*Nuit et jour*, France/Belgium/Switzerland, 1991), who produced the commercially successful film *The Artist* (dir. Michel Hazanavicius, France/US/Belgium, 2011).

I REMEMBER noting with surprise that I actually knew all five of the writers for *Golden Eighties*: Chantal, of course; Jean Gruault, whom I had interviewed about Godard's *Les Carabiniers* (France/Italy, 1963); Henry Bean, from the Berkeley days, and his wife, Leora Barish, who wrote *Desperately Seeking Susan* (dir. Susan Seidelman, US, 1985); and Pascal Bonitzer, from the formative *Cahiers du cinéma* time. Such a lighthearted musical, so many high-powered voices.

I REMEMBER seeing Henry Bean at the Lincoln Center memorial and telling him how beautiful I thought his tribute to Chantal in the *Forward* was.[16] He told me that he hoped to get through reading it without crying. He didn't.

I REMEMBER a cute picture from the seventies: Agnès Varda and Chantal in profile, face to face. Perec remembers that Varda was a photographer for Jean Vilar's Théâtre Nationale Populaire. Varda remembers and reappropriates these photos in a recent installation at the Avignon Festival. Chantal tells Nicole Brenez that Varda's *Le Bonheur* (*Happiness*, France, 1965) "is the most anti-romantic film there is." While Agnès does not agree, Chantal thinks it is very daring for its time. Chantal's assessment of Varda: "Agnès has an intelligence that's attuned to the world."[17]

I REMEMBER dipping in to *Chantal Akerman: Autoportrait en cinéaste* numerous times, each random look a discovery.[18] Chantal's many haircuts, reflections on her films (read over and over again), the laughter, the seriousness, and the friends, people moving in and out of her (and my) life. Portrait, to be sure. But of whom?

I REMEMBER learning that Chantal loved Douglas Sirk's *Imitation of Life* (US, 1959): "The way he invites the viewer to feel what a black woman would feel."[19] It made me glad that I had written an article on that film in which I tried to say the same thing.

I REMEMBER wishing that every Chantal Akerman film would be put on DVD for endless thoughts, conversations, and inspirations. Perhaps the new archive, formed by Chantal's sister, Sylviane, and Marilyn Watelet (Fondation Chantal Akerman), will provide that.[20]

I REMEMBER finding a photo on Sylviane's Facebook page that made me smile. It was of the two sisters laughing unabashedly, an image close to my heart.

I REMEMBER thinking how the deserts of Arizona and Israel were so similar in Chantal's films (her concern with physical space and landscape eschewed the banality of identifying signs) and the apotheosis that was a sort of chaotic blurring in *NOW* (2015), her last installation, now in the permanent collection of the Jewish Museum, where five screens showing jumbled desert landscapes shot from a moving car are accompanied by a jarring, percussive soundtrack of brutal combat and other noises.

I REMEMBER noting that *I Don't Belong Anywhere: The Cinema of Chantal Akerman* (dir. Marianne Lambert, Belgium, 2015) contained—alongside clips from Chantal's films, discussions about editing between Chantal and Claire Atherton, commentaries by Gus Van Sant, Skype conversations with her mother, Natalia, images of abandoned artillery in the Negev dunes, and autobiographical musings—two iconic moments taken from two significant films: a small tree, sturdy in the fiercely blowing wind, from *No Home Movie* (Belgium/France, 2015), Chantal's last film and an homage to her dying mother; and a Chasidic tale about the sanctity of generational transmission of prayers, rituals, and stories from *Histoires d'Amérique*, which one could say is Chantal's film of Jewish identity about immigration, isolation, and Yiddish culture.

Both films provide a nexus of major Chantal thematics: mother, Shoah, memory, place, and identity.

I REMEMBER the last time I saw Chantal. It was after the screening of *Almayer's Folly* (France/Belgium, 2011) at the Museum of the Moving Image in Astoria, Queens, in 2012. I was still processing my thoughts. This was to be her last fiction film, one in which she extended her explorations of contemplative space and expanded time, begun, you could say, with *Jeanne Dielman*. Of course I mentioned how much I loved *Jeanne Dielman*, to which she replied, "That was forty films ago. Why do people act as if it's the only thing I've made?"

I REMEMBER a very short trip to Paris in April 2018 specifically to see the performance piece *CHANTAL?* in which Sonia Wieder-Atherton played her cello while *Saute ma ville* (*Blow Up My Town*, Belgium, 1968) was screened twice and Aurore Clément read from *A Family in Brussels*. This "dialogue between a movie, a cello, and a text," "structured around an absence," in Wieder-Atherton's words, evoked Akerman's oeuvre, and Chantal herself, with tenderness and love.

Notes

I dedicate this to my late mother-in-law, Miriam Lewis, a treasure of love and compassion. I wish to thank my twin sister, Sharon, for suggesting the original form of a memory chain, and Bertrand Augst for his continued inspiration. And of course my husband, Joel, whose contribution to this essay is evident throughout.

1. Marion Schmid, *Chantal Akerman* (Manchester: Manchester University Press, 2010), 77.

2. Joe Brainard, *I Remember* (New York: Angel Hair, 1970; New York: Granary, 2001).

3. Georges Perec, *I Remember*, trans. Philip Terry and David Bellos (Boston: Verba Mundi, 2014).

4. Harry Mathews, *The Orchard: A Remembrance of Georges Perec* (Flint, MI: Bamberger, 1988).

5. Sandy Flitterman-Lewis, "What's Beneath Her Smile? Subjectivity and Desire in Germaine Dulac's *The Smiling Madame Beudet* and Chantal Akerman's *Jeanne Dielman, 23 quai du Commerce, 1080 Bruxelles*," in *Identity and Memory: The Films of Chantal Akerman*, ed. Gwendolyn Audrey Foster (Carbondale: Southern Illinois University Press, 2003), 27–40.

6. Mathews, *Orchard*, 10.

7. Serge Klarsfeld, *French Children of the Holocaust* (New York: New York University Press, 1996).

8. Griselda Pollock, *Charlotte Salomon and the Theatre of Memory: Trauma, Representation, and Life Histories in Leben oder Theater, 1940–1942* (New Haven, CT: Yale University Press, 2018).

9. Marceline Loridan, as a young survivor, appeared in Edgar Morin and Jean Rouch's *Chronicle of a Summer* (France, 1961). As a seventy-five-year-old filmmaker, after a career in documentary with her husband, Joris Ivens, she made her first fiction film, *The Birch-Tree Meadow* (France/Germany/Poland, 2003).

10. Nicole Brenez, "Chantal Akerman: The Pajama Interview," trans. David Phelps, *Lola*, no. 2 (2012), www.lolajournal.com/2 /pajama.html. First published as *Chantal Akerman: The Pajama Interview* (Vienna: Viennale, 2011). Thanks to Adrian Martin for making this available to me.

11. Janet Bergstrom, "Invented Memories," in Foster, *Identity and Memory*, 111; Schmid, *Chantal Akerman*, 88.

12. Brenez, "Pajama Interview."

13. Brenez, "Pajama Interview."

14. Chantal Akerman, *Ma mère rit* (Paris: Mercure de France, 2013). An English translation by Corina Copp is forthcoming for the Song Cave. A British edition will be translated by Daniella Shrier for Silver Press.

15. Brenez, "Pajama Interview."

16. Henry Bean, "Our Lives with (and without) Chantal Akerman," *Forward*, 10 October 2015, forward.com/culture/322320/our -lives-with-and-without-chantal-akerman/. The Lincoln Center Memorial can be viewed online at vimeo.com/162304275.

17.   Brenez, "Pajama Interview."

18.   Chantal Akerman, *Chantal Akerman: Autoportrait en cinéaste* (Paris: Cahiers du cinéma, 2004).

19.   Brenez, "Pajama Interview."

20.   See the website-in-progress of Fondation Chantal Akerman, in collaboration with Cinematek, at www.chantalakerman .foundation/.

Sandy Flitterman-Lewis is the author of *To Desire Differently: Feminism and the French Cinema* (1990; expanded edition, 1996) and coauthor of *New Vocabularies in Film Semiotics* (1992). Her background in feminist film theory is largely due to her doctoral work in comparative literature at the University of California, Berkeley, where she earned her PhD in 1984. As one of the four founding coeditors of *Camera Obscura,* she helped formulate the aims and focus of this first journal of feminism and film theory. The journal's inaugural issue in 1976 was one of the first English-language publications to discuss Chantal Akerman's pioneering film *Jeanne Dielman.* Her work on the Shoah in France, *Essays on Childhood, the Family, and Anti-Semitism in Occupied France* (forthcoming) treats material culture and daily life before, during, and after World War II. She teaches courses in film through the English and comparative literature departments at Rutgers University in New Brunswick, New Jersey.

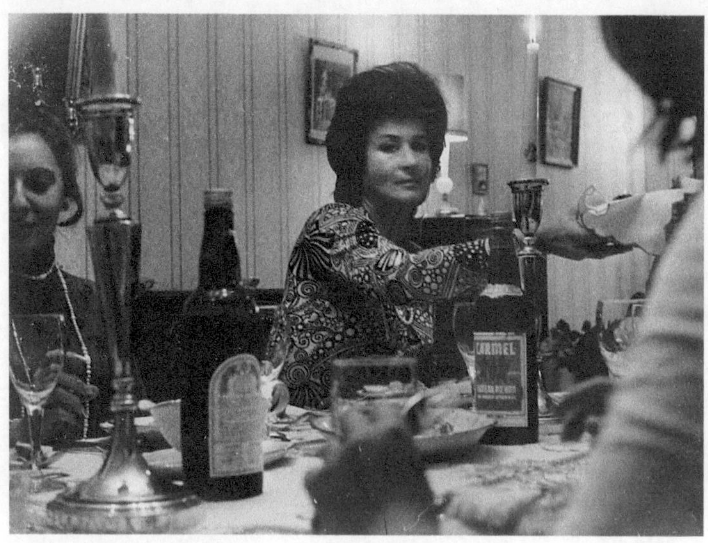

Figure 3. Natalia Akerman at home, mid-1970s.
Courtesy of Jane Stein

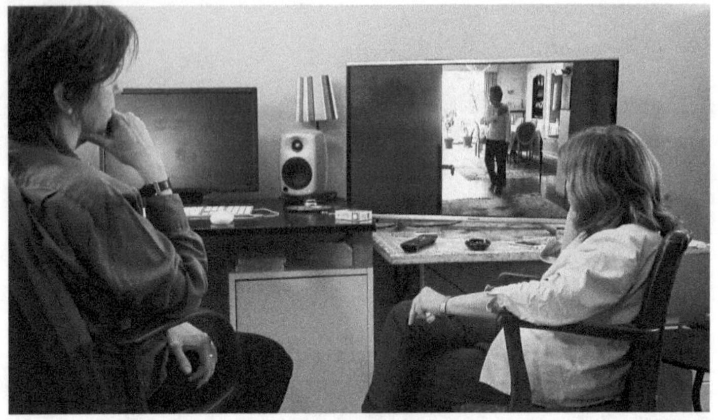

Figure 1. Claire Atherton and Chantal Akerman, 2014.
© Artémis Productions

Tribute to Chantal Akerman

Claire Atherton

Translated by Felicity Chaplin

A text written and read by Claire Atherton at the homage to Chantal Akerman at the Cinémathèque Française on 16 November 2015, before the premiere screening of *No Home Movie* (Belgium/France, 2015).

I often imagined the preview screening of *No Home Movie*. But never like this . . .

I want to speak to you about Chantal. To tell you everything she gave me, everything she taught me, everything we shared. To tell you how she was: luminous, intelligent, surprising, and funny too . . .

It is often said of Chantal that she had aesthetic principles. Well, I believe that principles protect us, and Chantal did not protect herself. She trusted what would happen. She knew how to welcome chance.

I am thinking of a story which shed light on her way of working. During the production of *La Folie Almayer* (*Almayer's Folly*,

Camera Obscura 100, Volume 34, Number 1

DOI 10.1215/02705346-7264124

France/Belgium, 2011), she needed a port. Her assistant asked her if she wanted a large port or a small port. She responded, "A large port." Then later she was asked if she was really sure that she wanted that, because perhaps a small port would be more convivial. I remember we were walking in the street, and Chantal was on the telephone. She stopped, stamped her feet, and said, "I want a large port. That's what I said. Don't ask me to explain why." She did not want to justify her gesture but welcome it, transform it, and, perhaps afterward, understand it.

Chantal was very free and intuitive, sometimes provocative. She had no prohibitions. She did not say, "We must film like this." "We must frame like that." "You can't do this." "You can't do that." Her choices came from within. She was guided by what she felt. She had more of a physical than cerebral rapport with the image, with colors, with sounds, with rhythm. When editing, I never heard her say, "I have an idea." She would say rather, "I heard that," or "I thought of that," or "I want that," or "I am obsessed with that." But it was never, "I have an idea."

When she was about to make a documentary, she did not want to explain what she would do. If she explained it, she no longer had the desire to make it. She wanted to go on location and be a sensitive plate, a sponge. She did not want to confine the film to a project but allow it to come to her and let herself be swept through by the material. If Chantal's images are so profound and strong—if they go beyond what they show—it is because they are not confined to intentions but are charged with all the concerns, the obsessions, which inhabited her.

This way of working, of "discovering while doing," was even stronger when making installations. Regarding one such installation project, Chantal wrote: "I had said a lot of things about the installation which followed *D'Est* [*From the East*, France/Belgium, 1993] before making it, and I understand that, more than a film, an installation for me cannot be described in advance, it is born little by little through the work itself. Here too, I will say nothing except for the necessity of fragmentation, because this demonstrates well that we cannot show everything of a world."[1]

During the editing of *D'Est*, we felt that the long tracking shots over the faces of the people waiting, the images of the people walking, referred back to other people waiting or walking, to other queues, to other stories within history, but we did not talk about it. It was only a year later, when we were setting up the installation *D'Est, au bord de la fiction* (*From the East: Bordering on Fiction*, 1995), that Chantal put the words over the echoes of these images. I will read to you these words from the last paragraph of the text of the twenty-fifth screen:

Yesterday, today, and tomorrow, there were, there will be, there are at this very moment, people whom history (which no longer even has a capital "H"), whom history has struck down. People who are waiting there, packed together, to be killed, beaten, or starved, or who walk without knowing where they are going, in groups or alone. There is nothing to do. It is obsessive, and I am obsessed. Despite the cello, despite cinema.

Once the film was finished, I said to myself, "So, that's what it was. That again."

Chantal liked frontal shots. It was not a formal decision but a taste, almost a need. The frontal axis does not describe, does not designate, but creates a space of perception and reflection. That space is also what we worked on during editing. It is a space left to the spectators so that they can experience, feel, and search. Chantal insisted that the spectators do their own work. She used to say that she wanted people to feel the passing of time in her films. When someone said, "Oh, I just saw a great film. I didn't notice the time passing," she did not think that was a compliment. She felt that the spectator's time had been stolen.

In editing, we never said, "Look, we need a long shot there." We chose the duration intuitively, and we understood why later. It is as if the shots themselves imposed their duration. Chantal liked to recount how we would hit the table at exactly the same moment to indicate that it was necessary to cut the shot. We saw the same things. I remember one time, after a work-in-progress screening of the film, one of us said that a certain tracking shot was too long and the other that it was too short. Chantal concluded: "We agree, this means that there is a problem!" From the moment the film started to exist, it rejected certain scenes, so we did not hesitate to subtract

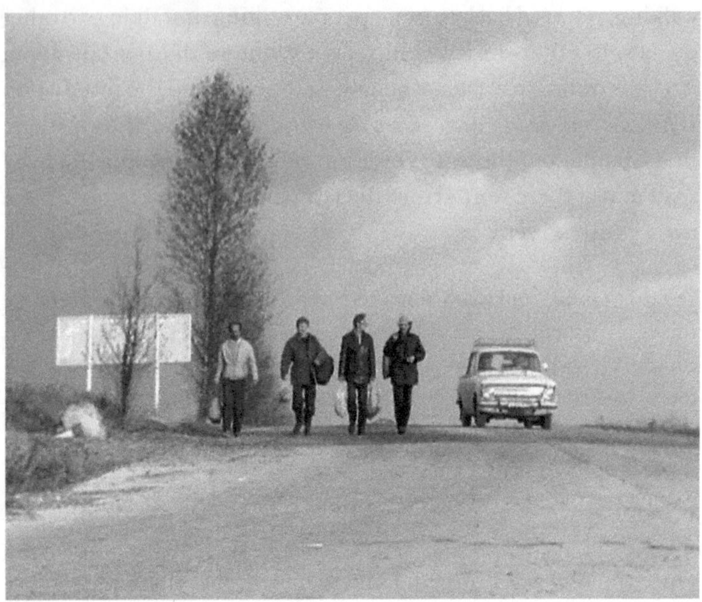

Figure 2. *D'Est* (1993). Courtesy of Fondation Claire Atherton
and Marian Goodman Gallery

or to shorten. If the film refused a shot—even a beautiful shot—
we did not insist. Often that gave a force to what followed, so the
film won. We used to say that in editing it is a game of "loser wins."

Each film, each installation, was like a first time. We had
no rules, fears, or barriers. Each time, we reentered a new sensory
and intellectual adventure. Our exchanges were very simple. We
said few words, as if too many words risked ruining something.
We often said, "It's beautiful" or "It's strong." We had words that
we liked. She said we must be drastic, without concessions. We also
said that we were to cut to the quick. I sometimes said to her, "We
have to complexify." She liked this word. She said to me: "Yes, that's
it: complexify a little." That was when we felt that there was something too overt, too linear. To complexify was not to complicate—it
was to add weights and counterweights, to shape the tension.

Chantal was not looking for verisimilitude or realism. She
was not afraid of anachronisms. She hated naturalism. She never
tried to copy reality or represent it; she transformed it. In her films

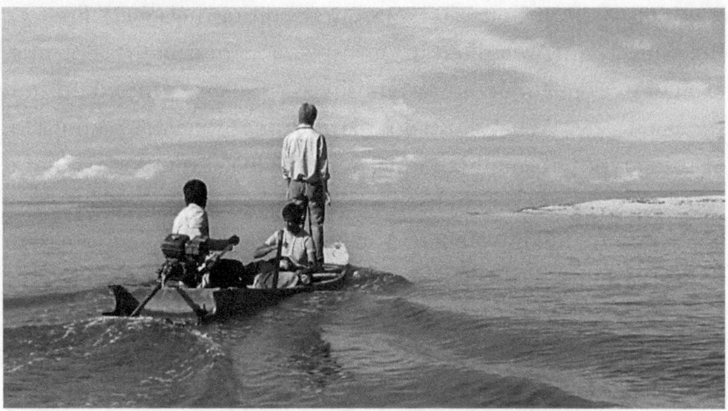

Figure 3. *La Folie Almayer* (2011). © Artémis Productions

and installations, the present, the visible are resonant with the invisible, the subterranean. She liked a quote by Edmond Jabès: "Every interrogation is linked to the gaze." She said that she did not know if it was true but that it spoke to her.

Chantal was allergic to psychologism. Psychologism is the psychological explanation of action and feelings. Chantal's cinema never explains. It questions us and confronts us with ourselves. This is why it is so powerful and alive.

For Chantal, everything was possible. She did not want to confine herself to a precise genre. She never wanted to make elitist or confidential cinema. When she made *Un divan à New York* (*A Couch in New York*, France/Belgium/Germany, 1996), she was hoping to make a commercial film that everyone would go and see. By the way, she always wanted everyone to go and see her films. When I started editing *Un divan*, Chantal was still filming. I was surprised that there were so many takes per shot. I was not accustomed to that with Chantal. Generally when she felt the take was good, she moved on to another scene. When she returned, she told me why. She said that there was such a financial stake in the film that she had been asked to do a lot of takes "for coverage." But she said to me, "This is no longer a cover—it's a pile of comforters!! And I am suffocating under these comforters!"

Yes, Chantal was funny. We forget it sometimes. Funny and

free. Out of the ordinary. When we were editing *Sud* (*South*, France/ Belgium, 1999), we edited in the afternoon, and in the morning, each of us went about our own business. One day I turned up, and she said to me, "What'd you do this morning?" She was asking a lot of these types of small-talk questions: "What'd you do?" "What'd you eat? . . ." And I said to her, "I made curtains." She replied, "You made curtains all by yourself? You know, that impresses more than if you'd won the Oscar for best editing!"

To speak to you about *No Home Movie,* I believe the most pertinent words are those written by Chantal herself, a few months after the editing was completed. It was in the autumn of 2014.

It's been years now that I have started to film all over the place, as soon as I sensed a shot. Without purpose really, but with the feeling that one day these images would make a film or an installation.

I was letting myself go, by desire and by instinct. Without a script, without a conscious project.

From these images were born three installations which were shown all over the place.

This spring, with Claire Atherton and Clémence Carré, I put together some twenty hours of images and sounds still without knowing where I was going.

And we started to sculpt the material.

These twenty hours became eight, then six, and then, after a certain amount of time, two. And there we saw, we saw a film, and I told myself: of course it is this film that I wanted to make.

Without admitting it to myself.

And, as one says, the red thread of this film is a character, a woman born in Poland, who arrives in Belgium in 1938 to flee the pogroms and the horror. This woman is my mother. Within and solely within her apartment in Brussels.[2]

Notes

This tribute originally appeared in *Senses of Cinema* and is available at sensesofcinema.com/2015/chantal-akerman/chantal-akerman-claire -atherton/.

1.   E-mail to author.

2.   E-mail to author.

Claire Atherton is a film editor born in San Francisco in 1963. She studied Chinese philosophy, language, and culture before turning toward cinema. In 1986 she started working with Chantal Akerman on *Letters Home* (France), which triggered a thirty-year collaboration until Akerman's last film, *No Home Movie* (Belgium/France, 2015), and last installation, *Now* (2015). She also works with a wide range of directors, artists, and young filmmakers.

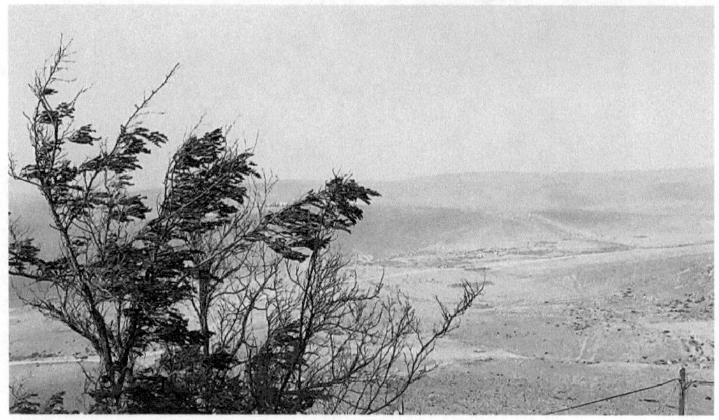

Figure 4. *No Home Movie* (2015). Photograph by Claire Atherton. © Paradise Films

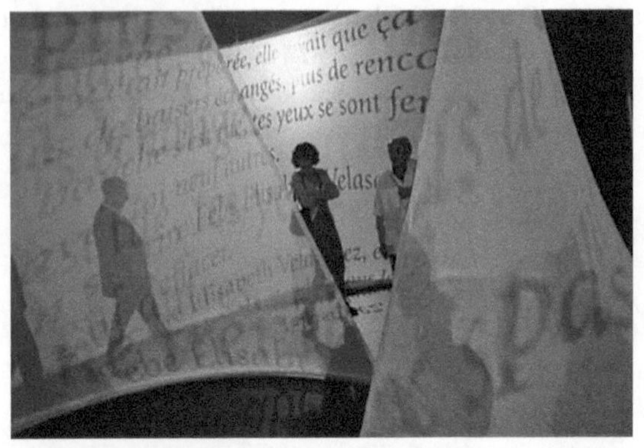

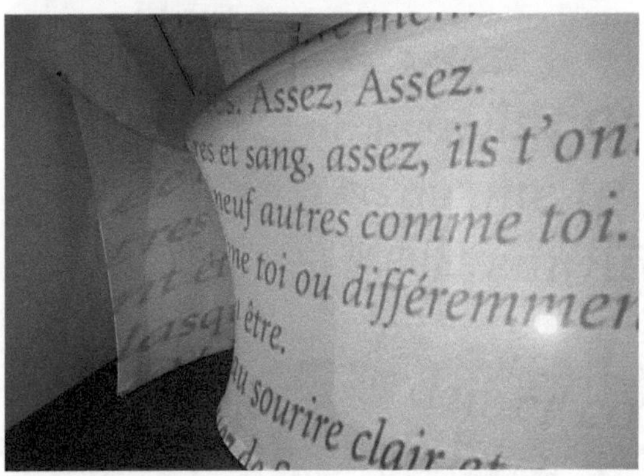

Figure 1. *Marcher à côté de ses lacets dans un frigidaire vide*
(*Walking Next to One's Shoelaces in an Empty Fridge*, 2004)

Next to Chantal Akerman: An Installation of Generations and the Shoah

Maureen Turim

Chantal Akerman's 2004 installation for the Marian Goodman Gallery, *Marcher à côté de ses lacets dans un frigidaire vide* (*Walking Next to One's Shoelaces in an Empty Fridge*), haunts. In one room is a large-scale sculpture composed of a gossamer spiral, an unfurled shroud of words that takes on a ghostly aspect, its diaristic free associations exposing a psyche (fig. 1). Projected on a gorgeous surround in a slow scrolling movement that effaces their reading as a whole, these words connect the filmmaker's work to her family. In another room we see a doubled projection: first, the pages of her grandmother's diary displayed on a scrim and, behind this, her mother and herself discussing this diary projected through the first image. Both of these rooms filled with the images of words are analyzed in detail below, but first let me attend to the installation's title.

The title suggests the absurdity and disorder of everyday life: *Walking Next to One's Shoelaces* is an image of untied laces straggling next to the walker, endangering each step, any forward

Camera Obscura 100, Volume 34, Number 1
DOI 10.1215/02705346-7264134   © 2019 by *Camera Obscura*
Published by Duke University Press

motion, and it has anecdotal reference to Akerman's tendency to leave her shoes untied. To walk next to one's shoelaces is also to be beside oneself and not entirely aware of one's circumstances or unwilling to take the simple measure of reestablishing a laced-up order. That this dishevelment is said to take place "in an empty fridge" creates a montage internal to this verbal construction that might recall the title of Hannah Höch's 1919 collage *Cut with the Dada Kitchen Knife through the Last Weimar Beer-Belly Cultural Epoch in Germany.* Yet Höch's montage suggests active rebellion; Akerman's title, in contrast, suggests a violence turned inward. In her first short film, *Saute ma ville* (*Blow Up My Town*, Belgium, 1968), Akerman exploded her living space. Here the fridge as enclosed space witnesses a slowly progressing incapacitation. Yet in creating under this title, Akerman does wish to move, to reach beyond. Through her installation, she uses the swirl of words, the imagistic investigation of her thoughts, as an ode to intergenerational inheritance. By remembering the Shoah in the most personal terms, by identifying with her grandmother and mother, by becoming an active artist who fulfills their promise, she strives to bring to light not just the weight of their legacy but its creative power.

Ironically, then, the title's imagery of incapacitation is contradicted by Akerman's desire to make art, to offer visual pleasures to others, even about the most dire of subjects. For one of her subjects here is *l'dor va dor* (to cite the Hebrew), the carrying of a legacy from generation to generation in a Jewish family marked by inheritances of the Shoah. Through this installation, Jewishness, Holocaust remembrance, and women's actualization of their beings and talents flow across generations, connecting the work, as I will show, to many of Akerman's other films.

In the first room of the exhibition, the scroll itself recalls the spatial delineations of Richard Serra's site-specific iron sculptures, as Scott Macaulay has noted.[1] But the difference is also worth taking into account. Serra's walls and curves confront the spectator with a barrier, emphasizing its power. In fact, while curves often figured in Serra's work, they would only take the form of spirals in work made after Akerman's piece. Yet Adrian Searle notes in his review of Akerman's installation that "one commentator has dismissed Akerman's installation as 'lightweight Richard Serra.'"[2] Let me suggest that Searle's second-hand snide dismissal misses Akerman's very gendered point, the connection she makes in both her words and her sculptural space of projection to *écriture feminine*, the French theory of female-voiced writing. She places her writing in light and movement, inviting the visitor into the text, its unfurling, its decipherment. Rather than a barrier, her installation is an immersive surround.

Thierry Kuntzel's 1974 sculpture *Le Tombeau de Saussure (Double Entrave)* [*The Tomb of Saussure (Double Hindrance)*], first shown at the Théâtre Campagne-Première and Galerie Ghislain Mollet-Viéville, is another important work for understanding Akerman's installation. Kuntzel engraves a citation from Saussure on a marble slab: "Que j'écrive les lettres en blanc ou noir, en creux ou en relief, avec une plume ou un ciseau, cela est sans importance pour leur signification." (Whether I write the letters in white or black, engraved or embossed, with a quill or a blade, is without any importance as to their signification.) Kuntzel uses tactility to transform, critiquing through his irony a view of language oblivious to the form of inscription as he shifts to one keenly attuned to the graphic arts, to writing as image that is at once spatial and visual. Akerman similarly uses spatial and visual dimensions of display to turn her writing into a form that signifies far beyond writing's ordered words as they might otherwise be reproduced. Her words drift, altered by the manner in which they are projected and displayed. They attain an aura in this presentation, all the more critical as the installation is not permanently displayed anywhere in the world.[3]

The material in the first room of the installation is heterogeneous, its diversity woven together artfully. I have excerpted some passages from the projected text corresponding to key concepts that build toward a metacritical commentary on Akerman's entire career, as well as her relationship to her family, to Jewishness, and to the intergenerational challenge of Shoah survival.

The first concept is to ruminate. Akerman remembers being chastised by her father for ruminating, for not letting go of old stories. Rumination has recently preoccupied French theorists, as several contemporary studies in literature and psychoanalysis attest.[4] In the scroll text of the artwork, Akerman connects her tendency toward rumination to repetitions she finds in her interviews: "Tout ou presque y était déjà." (It's all, or almost all, there already.) "Je relis aussi d'autres choses, des interviews données en français, en anglais, et je vois se dessiner une fois de plus quelqu'un qui ressasse." (I'm also rereading other things, interviews given in French, in English, and I see emerging once again the image of one who ruminates over things.) Akerman also acknowledges her tendency toward contradiction, encapsulated in a phrase that partakes of irony: "J'ai envie dans un ressassement toujours de dire le contraire mais pas toujours." (I always feel in any rehashing like saying the opposite, but not always.)

Tied to the notion of contradiction is another key concept, what she calls the tensions that pull her in different directions, the expression of which leads to her reference to the laces of the installation's title. In the scrolls, the laces are an evocation of her writing and of the relationship between filmmaking and writing in her works:

Laces

Et mon parcours est fait de toutes ces divisions, ces tensions, ça tiraille dans tous les sens. Et puis aussi que je sais marcher à côté de mes lacets. Ça c'est mon côté clown triste, comme dirait Sylvie. D'ailleurs je ne voulais pas faire du cinéma dans ma première adolescence. Je voulais écrire à côté de mes lacets.

(Laces

And my course is made of all those divisions, those tensions that pull in all directions. And also that I know how to walk without tripping over my laces. That's my sad clown side, as Sylvie would say. Besides I didn't want to make movies in my early years. I wanted to write outside my laces.)

She also addresses as a central concept being Jewish, and her mother's relationship to being Jewish, primarily as a reaction to films about Jewishness. Her mother reacts with disgust to *La vita è bella* (*Life Is Beautiful*, dir. Roberto Benigni, Italy, 1997), finding its comedic treatment of a fantasy that enables survival of a father-son pair in a concentration camp to be repulsive. Later in the scrolling text her mother also voices a negative reaction to an unnamed Israeli film about Orthodox Jews. Akerman, for her part, states that she rarely likes films about Jews even when made by Jews. One senses that Jewishness for her evinces tensions and contradictions yet remains something that should be guarded against false representations. Equally striking is her chastisement of those Jews whose Jewishness fades in their attempt to please a purely cosmopolitan or assimilationist goal, implicitly striving for an inconspicuousness meant to please others: "Parfois je me dis qu'il n'y a pas pire ennemi des juifs qu'eux-mêmes, surtout des juifs qui veulent plaire, plaire aux européens. Juifs ou non juifs." (Sometimes I tell myself that the Jews are their own worst enemies, especially the Jews who want to please Europeans. Jews or non-Jews.) The display on the scroll recalls the performative display of written pages in the first section of *Je tu il elle* (Belgium/France, 1974) as the character played by Chantal Akerman spreads out her writing on the floor in various configurations across disparate scenes, then rejects it.[5]

The scroll makes another Jewish reference by introducing Akerman's earlier *Histoires d'Amérique: Food, Family, and Philosophy* (France/Belgium, 1988) as a film about storytelling Jews, before reproducing dialogue from the film—a joke about insanity and fear. The joke has an incarcerated man finally able to leave an insane asylum, as he no longer thinks he is a grain of corn, only to tell us he now resides in a tree, because though "he knows he's not a grain of corn, . . . who knows what the chickens think!" This story resonates with Sigmund Freud's case history of Little Hans, whose paranoid fear of horses was analyzed as displacement. This story also serves Akerman by introducing a motif of a tree as shelter, only to have another tree emerge in the scroll's text in the form of the lyrics of Abel Meeropol's 1937 ballad "Strange Fruit," lamenting US lynching of African Americans, made famous by Billie Holiday's 1939 recording. Akerman ends this passage on *Histoires d'Amérique* with a very personal statement: "As a fifty-three-year-old woman, I'm better off in a tree because who knows what the chickens are thinking. It's not funny, and that's the funny part, that it's not funny." Akerman's *Histoires d'Amérique* borrows from Yiddish literature and theater its mixture of sad soliloquies and comic dialogue, staged to display the relationship between Jewish immigrants' sensibilities and Akerman's very personal pronouncements as filmmaker.

In the film's stunning opening offshore footage, we track a present-day nighttime New York skyline bathed in deep blue tones as Akerman voices a version of Baal Shem Tov's parable of intergenerational loss, though transmission of a prayer survives. This parable has been cited frequently, notably by Elie Wiesel in the preface to *Gates in the Forest* (1966). Akerman uses it not so much as a religious allegory of recognition of Jews no matter how or where they pray, as others have, but rather as a striving for Jewish identity through diasporic transformations and losses from generation to generation. She ends this introductory sequence with a lament, "And I don't even have children." Childlessness will echo through her later films; however, the chain of intergenerational inheritance is not broken. The works themselves embody her role in the transmission.

The spiraling text also anticipates the second room of the installation as it speaks of filming her mother: "C'était la première fois qu'elle et moi étions ensemble devant une caméra, même si ce n'était qu'une petite caméra digitale." (It was the first time that she and I were together in front of a camera, even if it was just a little digital camera.) In this other room, the recovered diary of fifteen-year-old Sidonia Erenberg, written in Polish in the 1920s, takes both physical and metaphorical center stage, as its pages are projected on a scrim through which we watch another film in which it is translated and discussed. Sidonia Erenberg was Akerman's maternal grandmother, a religious Polish Jew who would perish at Auschwitz. The second film, seen through the diary scrim, is projected as a diptych of two different views of a filmed conversation of the filmmaker and her mother about the recovered diary. The materiality of the translucent diary projection binds this section of the exhibit to the first room's luminous transparency of spiraling, diaristic verbal display (fig. 2).

Chantal relies on her mother's translation to recover the

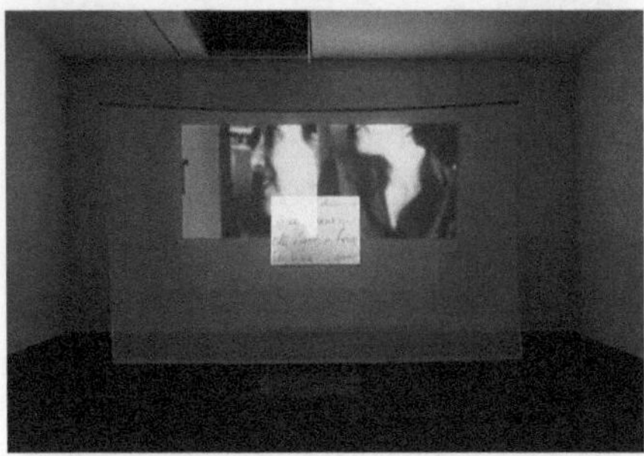

Figure 2. *Marcher à côté de ses lacets dans un frigidaire vide* (*Walking Next to One's Shoelaces in an Empty Fridge*, 2004)

desires confided in this *Tagebuch*. Her mother hesitates, apologizes for her difficulty in remembering Polish, and the conversation proceeds as if the diary's secrets are being translated for the first time, though we have every reason to believe there were earlier such conversations, earlier sharing of this diary. Those who have read Akerman's books *Une famille à Bruxelles* (*A Family in Brussels*, 1998) and *Ma mère rit* (*My Mother Laughs*, 2013) recognize in this coy staging of the translation the self-consciousness with which her writing treats the familial repetition of stories; stories told many times serve as a structural motif.

A backstory may help explain why Akerman stages the discussion with her mother this way: the diary translation film was reportedly first made to serve the cast of a fiction film Akerman was shooting, *Demain on déménage* (*Tomorrow We Move*, France/Belgium, 2004). That film treats in tragicomedic fashion a similar mother-daughter relationship, as well as, through a secondary character, the topic of Holocaust survival. The recording's casualness can be attributed to its initial utilitarian purpose; only later would Akerman mine it for the revelatory beauty that becomes key to this artwork. Overall, an air of spontaneity distinguishes this work from a polished documentary style in which preplanning would define the footage to be shot. In such a work, professional translation would eliminate the struggle with the diary's decipherment. Here it is a performative ritual that eases the mother and daughter into an open dialogue about their faith in each other.

The play with repetition is echoed in the diptych format, in which one side consists of a refilmed version of the image seen in the other, creating a continual play of magnification and emphasis of one image beside the other. This formal play amplifies the intimacy of the interaction between the filmmaker daughter and her mother. This visual intimacy is in sharp contrast to the distance used in Akerman's *Les Rendez-vous d'Anna* (Belgium/France/Germany, 1978) to portray the meeting between a fictional filmmaker and her mother after three years of separation. The film's studied distance will culminate in a tight embrace, one that follows a relation drawn between the daughter's lesbian romance and her desire for her mother's encompassing love. Distance reemerges as they part company on a train platform the next day.

It is my contention that the intimacy with her mother and her extended family displayed in Akerman's later works has everything to do with her gradual working through the contradictions and tensions of her Jewishness. Here, she looks to the diary to understand her grandmother's becoming-woman in the context of a Jewish Orthodoxy that would restrict her voice.[6] The beginning of the diary clarifies the intimate relationship with the diary, as she writes her desires as a woman in this patriarchal context: "Je suis une femme, donc je ne peux pas . . ." (I am a woman, therefore I cannot . . .) Addressing the diary, the grandmother, as fifteen-year-old girl, writes: "Je peux écrire sur ses feuilles et ce sera ma seule confidente." (I can write on your pages, and this will be my only confidant.) Akerman's mother speculates on the mystery of the diary's survival, wondering why she can't remember how they came to possess it. The survival of this precious writing induces renewed mourning for the loss of its writer. Akerman's mother touchingly yearns for her mother's eyes and regrets the loss of her talents. This exchange leads the mother to make a connection between Chantal's creativity and the grandmother's; the daughter embodies a regaining for the mother. The loss of the previous generation is eased by her daughter's presence. Then the filmmaker transitions into questioning her mother about the latter's regrets in life: "Est-ce qu'il y a des choses que toi, tu regrettes?" (Are there things that you regret?) "Ne pas avoir finir mes études." (Not having finished my studies.)

In *News from Home* (Belgium/France, 1976), a very young Akerman created a film that tried to mark her distance from her mother's letters, consigning their obsession with the metonymic hold of everyday life and their indirect demand for closeness to a soundtrack that haunted her structurally articulated images of Manhattan streets. Yet those letters read by the daughter simultaneously traced the strength of the mother-daughter bond, even for a daughter seeking to explore a world and her creativity. *News from Home* marks the hold of the mother's voice over the filmmaker, a hold that resonates ever more strongly as the film is replayed in more recent decades.

In the interim between that early film and the installation, Akerman interviewed other grandmothers. In her film *Dis-moi* (1982), originally made for broadcast on French television, she interviews three women, never named, each a survivor of the Shoah. Each meeting is framed with shots of Akerman emerging from the metro at Place de la République, on the street outside, on a staircase, knocking on the door, or being anticipated from a window. Two of the women prepare food for Akerman and urge her to eat as if she were their daughter. Engagingly, she lets them tell their stories, with whatever asides and meanderings they wish, for that is her own style of prose—the significant interwoven with the mundane, the everyday interrupting the revelation. It is the second woman, seated alone on a chair—not like the others at the table (amid interior decorations that speak to the comfort of their successful integration in France)—who most speaks in echo of Akerman's grandmother's diary, as well as of the words that we will hear her mother speak in *No Home Movie* (Belgium/France, 2015).

This woman begins, "I don't have much to tell you," echoing the self-deprecation of Akerman's grandmother, who feels as a woman only able to speak to her diary. This disclaimer is pre-

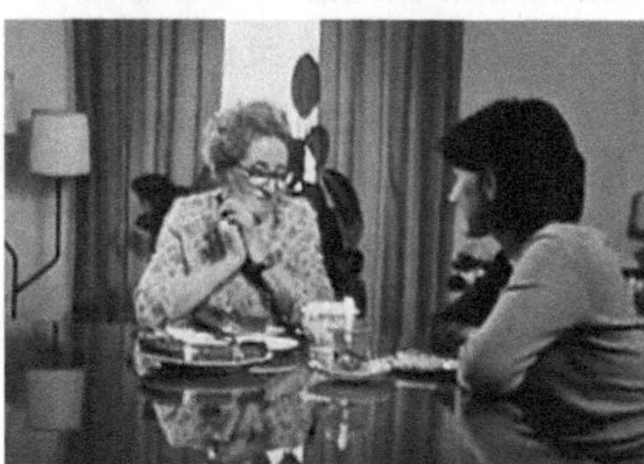

Figure 3. *Dis-moi* (1980)

lude to a most significant story of her family's political engagement with the resistance and the French role in deporting Jews, punctuated with a powerful line to speak on French television: "After that, there was no question of feeling French." In *No Home Movie*, Akerman's mother will say something similar when talking of the family's deportation from Belgium and of how her husband's knowledge of the Belgian anti-Semitism he had witnessed filled him with fear.

Think about the distance traveled to make the world so much smaller that a new intimacy is displayed in the Skype and kitchen-table conversations with her already ill mother in Akerman's last film, *No Home Movie*. Distance has been bridged. In this now-cherished intimacy, her mother can give her the gift of recalling some aspects of the family's Holocaust history, as well as its abandonment of some Jewish rituals following the death of Akerman's paternal grandfather. In addition to the loosening of Kashrut observance, his passing also meant the end of Chantal's Jewish education. Yet despite their less rigorous observance, her mother says, the rituals still lived in her heart.

I am suggesting that, laced through many of her films, Akerman had been seeking the Jewish heart of the socialist relatives she brings up in conversation with her mother in this last film. This secular, creative woman still feels her ties to the Jews who perished in the Shoah and also to those who survived to celebrate brisses and weddings. Their lives remained shadowed by a horror and by the knowledge of the betrayal of which their neighbors were capable. So simply does her mother tell of returning to Belgium after her family was deported. Chantal quietly but insistently reminds her mother of how active the king was in those very deportations. Belgium is home, but it was no home, and the movie made in her mother's comfortable apartment in the last months of her life is the most complete excursion into the world of the Jewish Akermans. A brief conversation between Akerman and her mother's caregiver, perhaps an immigrant herself, shows this other woman's empathy with the family's suffering and its generational transmission. As Akerman makes a home movie for international distribution, it is, in ironic contradiction, no home movie, just as she writes diaries, then turns these pages into art, confiding to the world.

I have placed Akerman's installation in the context of other works: the fraught relationship with her mother at the moment in her twenties when her desire to make art takes her an ocean away; the film she makes documenting women in Paris who have survived the Shoah; the film she makes of sad stories and trenchant jokes of an American immigrant generation. *Walking Next to My Shoelaces in an Empty Fridge* may also be seen in relationship to her imagistic documentary essays. Precisely because as she looks at troubled areas of the world, sites of conflict, she takes on the vocation so often assumed by Jews, both secular and practicing, of attempting to repair the world through devotion to social causes. Thus we see the reclamation of Holocaust survival as investment in social justice in *Sud* (*South*, France/Belgium, 1999), which investigates how the African American man James Byrd Jr. was dragged to his death for three miles behind a pickup truck by three white supremacists, ending with a haunting tracking shot that retraces the route of this ignominious murder, and *De l'autre côté* (*From the Other Side*, Belgium, 2002), which examines the bleak landscape of border crossings between Mexico and Arizona, in which many emigrants have lost their lives. The metaphoric, sad slowness of *D'Est* (*From the East*, France/Belgium, 1993), both as film and as installation, draws a contemplative comparison between the Jews who are no longer in Eastern Europe and the population that remains awaiting changes that will accompany the collapse of communist governments. She will examine the enclosed room of Jewish identity in *Là-bas* (*Down There*, Belgium/France, 2006), as a visitor to Tel Aviv who visually questions her place, just as she questioned her place in an apartment in Brussels in the first segment of *Je tu il elle* in 1974.

Akerman's minimalist aesthetic, her understatement, her formal constraints, her refraining from the melodramatic build slowly, patiently, page by page, shot by shot, into an exposure that remains discrete. I have tried to respect that discretion. For Akerman, rumination and contradiction, this turning over and over, is the process of thought itself, inscribed with the willingness not to resolve into certainty. Finally, this is how she sees herself as a Jewish woman, fascinated by her ties to the generations who preceded her and offering her works to generations to come. *L'dor va dor*: Chantal Akerman has fulfilled the mitzvah of generational legacy.

Notes

1. Scott Macaulay, "*To Walk Next to One's Shoelaces in an Empty Fridge*," *Filmmaker*, 8 July 2005, filmmakermagazine.com/1981-to-walk -next-to-ones-shoelaces-in-an-empty-fridge/.

2. Adrian Searle, "Smoke and Mirror-Images," *Guardian*, 15 July 2008, www.theguardian.com/artanddesign/2008/jul/15/art .film.

3. The work is neither on permanent display nor well documented. The catalog of its German exhibition attests to how it would be served by more documentation: *Chantal Akerman: Neben seinen Schnürsenkeln in einem leeren Kühlschrank laufen*, ed. Cilly Kugelmann (Berlin: Jewish Museum Berlin and Laconic Press, 2007).

4. François Roustang, *La Fin de la plainte* (*The End of the Complaint*) (Paris: Odile Jacob, 2000); *Ecritures du ressassement*, ed. Eric Benoit (Bordeaux: Presses Universitaires de Bordeaux, 2001); Domitille Dupoux, "Dynamique du ressassement: Les récits concentrationnaires de Jorge Semprun" ("Dynamics of Rumination: The Concentration Camp Stories of Jorge Semprun"), (PhD diss., Université Lyon 2, 2008).

5. Maureen Turim, "Personal Pronouncements in Two Akerman Films: *I . . . You . . . He . . . She* and *Portrait of a Young Girl at the End of the 1960s in Brussels*," in *Identity and Memory: The Films of Chantal Akerman*, ed. Gwendolyn Foster (Wiltshire, UK: Flicks, 1999), 9–26.

6. See Camilla Griggers, *Becoming-Woman* (Minneapolis: University of Minnesota Press, 1996). The term "becoming-woman" derives from Gilles Deleuze.

Maureen Turim is professor of film and media studies in the Department of English at the University of Florida. She is author of *The Films of Oshima Nagisa: Images of a Japanese Iconoclast* (1998), *Flashbacks in Film: Memory and History* (1989), *Abstraction in Avant-Garde Films* (1985), and *Desire and Its Renewal in the Cinema* (forthcoming). She has published over one hundred essays in journals and books, including on Akerman.

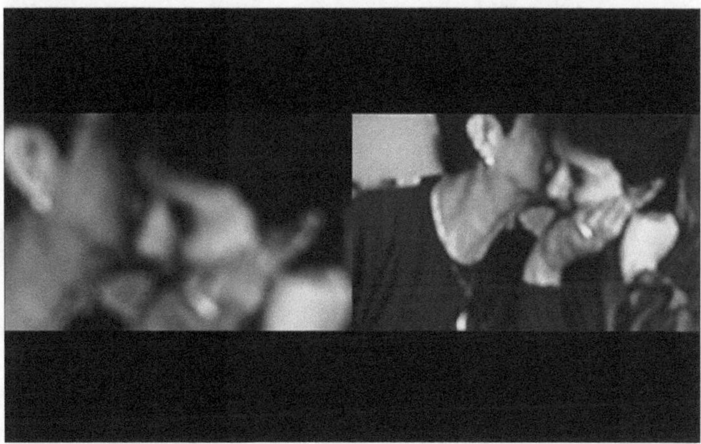

Figure 4. *Marcher à côté de ses lacets dans un frigidaire vide* (*Walking Next to One's Shoelaces in an Empty Fridge*, 2004)

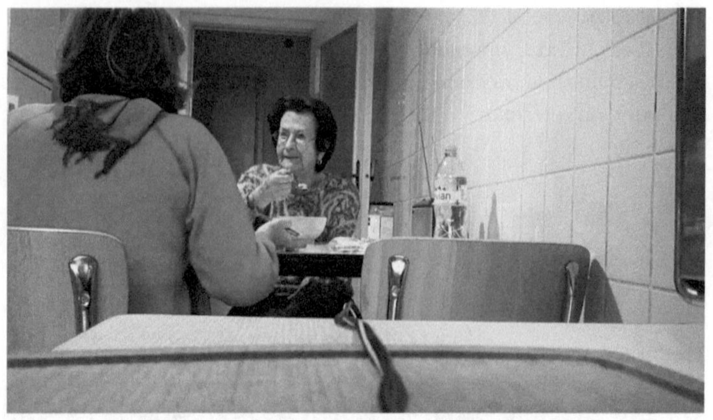

Figure 1. The humane gaze of the daughter.
No Home Movie (2015)

The Matrixial Borderspace: The Complex Inscription of Trauma in Chantal Akerman's *No Home Movie*

Brenda Longfellow

When I want to speak about things that are too close to me, I take a detour. The detour is shattering . . . but it is still not the direct path.

—Chantal Akerman

"Chantal Akerman's cinema is within me."[1] These words from Élisabeth Lebovici's homage in *Senses of Cinema* capture, more than most, the particular affective bond that feminist film scholars and critics, particularly those who came of age in the 1970s and 1980s, have with Akerman's work. This affective hold is clearly witnessed in the plethora of elegies and special issues, the outpouring of writing following Akerman's untimely suicide (but what suicide is ever timely?) in October 2015. But for me, no film of Akerman's generates the feeling of intimate address more than *No Home Movie* (Belgium/France, 2015), her last film, which observes

Camera Obscura 100, Volume 34, Number 1

DOI 10.1215/02705346-7264144   © 2019 by *Camera Obscura*

Published by Duke University Press

113

her frail eighty-year-old mother Natalia (Nelly) as, day by day, sequence by sequence, she moves closer to death. For anyone who has gone through the excruciating process of tending to a mother who is dying, who has felt the shocking depth of bereavement— how it unhinges, whether one is confronted with becoming an orphan at thirty-five, as I was, or at sixty-four, as Akerman was— *No Home Movie* provides an immediately recognizable view of the devastation and bittersweet aspects of the experience.[2]

Shot by Akerman on a small digital camera, the film records Natalia's last days as she putters around the family apartment in Brussels. There are other images in the film—a startling four-minute opening shot of a thin tree battered by a desert wind, for instance, or various shots where our attention is diverted outside the apartment through an impassive glance out the window at an overturned chair or women waiting for a bus. Later, halfway through the film, we are catapulted into a strange desert landscape (more on that later), but for the most part we remain cloistered inside as Akerman records the mundane details of daily life and her mother's increasing fragility.

No Home Movie has had a mixed response, to put it mildly. The audience at the Toronto International Film Festival in 2015 (where I first saw the film shortly before the filmmaker's death) was mainly puzzled; there were many walkouts and only a small blurt of tepid applause when the final credits started to roll. Programmer André Picard proclaimed it a masterpiece, and Kent Jones, director of the New York Film Festival, called it "one of her greatest films."[3] But I want to explore what happens when we think of *No Home Movie* as an anomalous film, even as a "failed" film. The cinematography is crude: the image is muddy and frequently badly lit. Digital resolution is very low, and there appears to be little color or exposure correction. Akerman has always played with duration via an attentiveness to the gestures and details of the everyday, but here each shot shades into a kind of unremitting banality. A five-minute sequence of the mother moving aimlessly in and out of frame as her daughter films her from the other side of an open door serves as a synecdoche of a film that seems to evolve in the absence of purpose or cinematic propriety. Is this why certain members of the press allegedly booed the film at a preview screening during the Locarno Film Festival, where it had its world premiere?[4]

In *The Queer Art of Failure*, Jack Halberstam rescues failure from its negative connotations to reframe it as an act of aesthetic and political resistance. Failure, he writes, is bound up with "the refusal of legibility, and an art of unbecoming," a queer mode of resisting heteronormativity, the belief that we live in the best of all possible worlds or that individual happiness represents the pinnacle of accomplishment.[5] If *No Home Movie* fails, it fails as an act of deep subversion. Failure, of course, is inscribed in the emphatic *no* of the film's title that immediately distinguishes Akerman's film from the conventions of home movies with their nostalgic fictions of home as a place void of trauma. But the *no* also negates home: *no home* is a suspended declaration that alerts us to the work of the film, which makes of *home* something strange, even unbecoming. It is built around two formidable acts of resistance: one on the part of the mother, Natalia, who refuses to recount her experiences of the Holocaust, and the other on the part of the daughter/filmmaker, who refuses to fill in, to speak, for the other.

In this essay I explore the complex way in which trauma is inscribed in *No Home Movie* as a transitive and transsubjective encounter mediated through a relation to the maternal that stands, in many ways, as an alternative paradigm of subjectivity coded in the feminine. Though I've suggested *No Home Movie* is, in certain aspects, anomalous, I'd like to nuance my framing of the film as an outlier by suggesting that there are certain aesthetic and ethical strategies in the film, both formal and affective, that form a continuity with her other work and that may be read in relation to recent scholarship on Akerman that foregrounds the central role of trauma to her multiple artistic practices.[6]

In her remarkable book *After-Affects, After-Images: Trauma and Aesthetic Transformation in the Virtual Feminist Museum*, the feminist art historian Griselda Pollock recounts her intense psychic reaction to seeing Chantal Akerman's installation *Marcher à côté de ses lacets dans un frigidaire vide* (*Walking Next to One's Shoelaces in an Empty Fridge*, 2004) at the Jewish Museum in Berlin in 2007. Pollock writes, "I was emotionally undone by this kiss in Akerman's installation." Pollock is referring to the final double-screen projection where an improvised conversation between Akerman and her mother on her mother's experience during the Holocaust and her reintegration into Belgium at the end of the war concludes with the mother reaching for the daughter's face and kissing her cheek. That corporeal, affective reaction leads Pollack to the epiphany that all of Akerman's work "could be re-read, retrospectively, as a long journey home, namely as a journey towards the trauma that is finally claimed and transformed in this work—transformed by a process of filmmaking that hovers undecidably between fiction and memory."[7] What Pollock's epiphany reveals, in other words, is that if the mother is central to Akerman's oeuvre—as every feminist film scholar who has ever written on Akerman avows—it is because of the particularity and intensity of this relationship, forged through a transgenerational transcription of trauma: the murder of Natalia's mother and father in Auschwitz and Natalia's own experiences of being interned in the death camp as a teenager.

The centrality of the Holocaust and inherited trauma to Akerman's work is, obviously, not buried. In multiple interviews, Akerman is explicit about the psychic primacy to her of her mother's devastating experience. It is crucial to attend to this insistence as a complex articulation of the inherited and imagined traumatic memories that fueled and informed her life and work. As Akerman remarks in an interview about *No Home Movie* published by *Mubi* in 2015: "I was always aware. Even though my mother never said anything. Okay, so she had that number on her arm, but when I was a child of three years old I had *dreams* about the camps, every night. Very precise dreams about Hitler being in a big chair in a concentration camp. It was like a Pina Bausch scene. Jews were playing violins with strange smiles."[8]

Over the years, scholars have referenced these issues as central to Akerman's creative process, perhaps none other with the theoretical ambition of Janet Bergstrom and Alisa Lebow.[9] Both writers probe the way in which autobiographical material is embedded in Akerman's films through highly mediated processes of displacement and distancing. Bergstrom suggests that these processes are unconscious symptoms linked directly to the psychic defense mechanism of splitting provoked, in Akerman's case, by a reaction to maternal trauma.[10] Lebow reads Akerman's *D'Est* (*From the East*, France/Belgium, 1993) in a more Benjaminian frame as a "transitive autobiography," where Akerman's journey through the landscapes and villages of Eastern Europe is formally translated into an encounter with multiple temporalities—the present where the charged absence of the Jewish community is palpable and the spectral past's images of wartime evacuations and forced marches.

While both of these approaches are richly suggestive, I want to explore the particular representation of trauma in *No Home Movie* through an alternative, though related, framework posed by artist, psychoanalyst, and writer Bracha Ettinger's work on matrixial borderspace. Ettinger is also the primary theoretical source for Pollock, who appropriates Ettinger's concept of the matrixial to read a range of feminist work, including Akerman's, where the aftereffects and afterimages of trauma are paramount to the aesthetic process and to the transferential relation between artwork and spectator. According to Pollock, "Ettinger's contribution to the field of trauma studies in general and that of trauma and aesthetics in particular is her emphasis on the very early emergence of psycho-aesthetic and trans-subjective processes to facilitate transmission and transformation of residues and traces of traumatic events personal and historical." These processes, furthermore, are "premised on a specific human capacity that is primordially (in the Real) linked to a non-phallic feminine difference"—the matrixial.[11]

For Pollock, the matrixial provides a rich conceptual frame to think the transmissibility of historic trauma as modeled on and reiterating the atavistic relation to the maternal other, a relation that is prior to gender and is conceived "in jointness" as fundamentally intersubjective and transitive. The matrixial is foreclosed in patriarchal culture, but it subsists, nonetheless, *in potentia*, as a psychic dimension adjacent to and outside the phallic symbolic and as a residue open to retrieval through art-making practices. For Pollock, the advantage of the matrixial is that it "expands the range of founding traumas of subjectivity identified by psychoanalysis by identifying a primordial sense of becoming a humanized being . . . in co-emergence with a co-other" (xxiv). The matrixial is a supplement, an alternative nonphallic and female-centric subjectivizing process that is open to all subjects, male or female. In a preemptive move against criticism that might read the matrixial as an overly idealized (if not essentialist) concept, Pollock assures us that the matrixial is distinct from other feminist accounts of the preoedipal and "has nothing to do with symbiosis or fusion" (xxiv). Ettinger clarifies that "by Matrix I do not intend the organ but a complex psychic apparatus modeled upon this site of feminine/prenatal encounter—not fusion—that puts in rapport any human becoming-subject-to-be, male and female, with female bodily specificity and her encounters, trauma, jouissance, phantasm and desire."[12]

Since the early 1990s, Ettinger's essays have appeared in publications ranging from psychoanalytic periodicals and limited-edition artist's books to multidisciplinary cultural theory anthologies and art journals.[13] While Pollock's work has ensured an ongoing uptake of Ettinger's theories in feminist art circles, Ettinger has been less remarked upon in feminist film and media theory, although her usefulness seems compelling.[14] Ettinger explicitly positions her work as a working through the inability of Sigmund Freud, Jacques Lacan, and Emmanuel Levinas to think outside a phallic symbolic posed as "neutral" and "universal."[15] More to the point, Ettinger's theories of the matrixial and of the specific role of art making as a transitive process mapped onto the archaic relation to the m/other seem uncannily appropriate for a reading of Chantal Akerman's work.

In "Art as the Transport-Station of Trauma" Ettinger, who like Akerman is a child of Holocaust survivors, argues that secondary or historic trauma is processed through the archaic relation to the maternal as a compassionate and hospitable "differentiating-in-jointness." That is, unlike the phallic scenario of absolute separation, matrixial becoming is predicated not on the cut or the production of defensive ego boundaries but on a process of coeval becoming, "joining-in-separating." The space between "I" and "not

I" is not a boundary but a threshold where exchanges of psychic matter may take place, including unsymbolized traumatic residues, affective intensities, and silences. For Ettinger, art represents a privileged space where the transmission of trauma may be reencountered as a "transport-station," which allows "for certain occasions of occurrence and of encounter . . . [a] *borderlinking and borderspacing in a matrixial trans-subjective space.*"[16]

The core impulse of *No Home Movie* situates it as a "transport-station"—a film that stages an encounter between the mother and daughter observed through their on-camera interactions and through the ongoing and humane gaze of the daughter at the mother (fig. 1). Both are mediated by the urgent desire on the part of the daughter to record and acknowledge the unspoken traumas that bind them: the trauma of the mother's imminent death and the trauma of that other death, the death that could have happened sixty years prior in the nightmare of Auschwitz. Reading the film as a transitive and transsubjective encounter allows us to highlight what is as pertinent to Akerman's cinema as it is to Ettinger's theorization of the matrixial: the elaboration of an alternative paradigm of meaning, subjectivity, and aesthetic and ethical practice mediated through a coeval and compassionate relation to an other coded in the feminine.

According to Ettinger, the matrixial foregrounds the relationship to the other as a primary coeval "hospitality" where the "I" and "not I" are conjoined in a complex mutuality she names *metramorphosis.* Metramorphosis involves a qualitatively different passageway to others who are not "frozen into objects" but who emerge as partners in a complex transsubjective relation.[17] From a very broad perspective, Ettinger's theoretical move is aimed at the dismantling of the subject-object paradigm that has structured Western thought and been so perilous for others throughout history (women, colonial and racialized subjects, immigrants, Jews, gender nonconforming people, indigenous peoples).

For the most part, feminist scholars have tended to gloss over the distinction between Akerman's fiction and documentary work, arguing that the similarity of formal strategies, the use of extended duration in particular, undermines the significance of any separation. But as documentary theorists remind us, documentary is of a different signifying order than fiction, representing as it does actual others in a world that is materially contiguous with our own. Moreover, the manner in which the representation of others is articulated has immediate ethical consequences for subjects, directors, and spectators who are reflexively remanded, as Vivian Sobchack argues, "to ourselves as embodied, culturally knowledgeable and socially invested viewers."[18] All of Akerman's documentaries acknowledge the heightened ethical stakes in documentary and, in so doing, capture something of the quality of metramorphosis as an ethical and erotic passage to the other. For Akerman, as much as for Ettinger, the central question is not the one of traditional ethics—what is good or just?—but the more grounded and possibly more urgent question of how to respond to the other.

This question seems to me to be at the heart of Akerman's documentary practice, a practice engaged less with politics than with a moving and profound meditation on ethical response to the other. Of course, this is also the question asked by Levinas,[19] with whom, incredibly, Akerman studied as a young woman in Paris (at the École Normale Israelite Orientale), an experience that clearly made a significant impression on her.[20] The definition of responsibility as the first order of moral being is also a well-acknowledged Jewish proclivity rooted in teachings in the Hebrew Bible.[21] This may be what Akerman refers to when she acknowledges that Levinas is "part of my culture."[22] The call of the other obviously takes many different iterations in her documentaries: African Americans in *Sud* (*South*, France/Belgium, 1999), Mexican migrants in *De l'autre côté* (*From the Other Side*, Belgium, 2002), Polish working-class men and women in *D'Est*, and finally her mother in *No Home Movie*. But as Akerman herself has avowed—and as critics like Bergstrom, Lebow, and Pollock have underlined—her response to the other is continuously, even obsessively, mapped onto the primal scene of Jewish trauma, the Holocaust. In an interview with Élisabeth Lebovici, Akerman spoke of the way the border wall between Mexico and the US, which features so prominently in *De l'autre côté*, functions in a dual sense as a material embodiment of historical racism and xenophobia and as an allegorical referencing of previous historical traumas of othering:

My obsession with borders comes from the camps. When you touch on that limit—and I touched it very closely through my mother, who was in the camps but was never able to talk through her anxiety—this border becomes the source of anxiety, it becomes an "anxious Abject." In *From the Other Side*, for instance, I show the wall to my mother and ask her what it brings to mind, and she says: "You know what." When it is internalized, experience is given without speaking, transmitted as a spectral presence; you cannot separate yourself from it.[23]

In *No Home Movie*, the spectral presence of trauma haunts every moment and imbues Akerman's compassionate observation of her mother with poignant affect. Here Akerman is not simply bearing witness. Rather, she orchestrates the silences, the movement of bodies, the sudden eruptions of intimacy as performative gestures that bear traces of the nonlinear, fragmented, and partial transmission of trauma as the sign of loss and as the primal link (a borderlinking, Ettinger would say) that binds her to her mother.

As a distillation of the notion of the transitive aesthetic encounter, Ettinger coins the term *aesthetic wit(h)nessing*, a formulation that carries the ethical and truth-telling connotations of witness while replacing any notion of an objective or detached observer through the supplement of the *h*. *Wit(h)nessing* implicates the production of meaning and affect as a process that is coeval and shared. Aesthetic wit(h)nessing seems a provocative frame to consider how trauma is woven into the texture of *No Home Movie* through a deeply affective and relational mode of film practice.

In one of the last interviews Akerman gave, she commented on the ethical paradox of making a film about her mother: "I had the feeling for a long time—my mother went into the camps and never said a word about it—that I had to talk for her, which is crazy because you cannot talk for someone else. . . . So I thought that I was the one who had to make, because she would not say anything, that I was the one who was going to testimony [*sic*] instead of her."[24] If Akerman was ever inspired by the desire "to testimony" for her mother, it is clear that she quickly recognized that the impulse had, of necessity, to take a different form than "speaking for." In *No Home Movie*, Akerman doesn't set out to elicit testimony. She lets silence speak, and not in any literal way but through a complex orchestration of form and affect that is more performative than constative, more corporeal than verbal, and more subject to a logic of association than a logic of revelation.

As Pollock points out, the emphasis on gesture, performance, allusiveness, and complex temporalities and spatialities distinguishes Ettinger's concept of the rendition of trauma in art making from the more constative emphasis that has dominated trauma studies, such as the work of Cathy Caruth and Shoshana Felman, where spoken or recorded testimony is given as the primary modality.[25] In *No Home Movie*, trauma is rather mediated through what Kent Jones has identified as "savage silences." It is a film less about final verbal reckonings than, as he puts it, "intensities of feeling and the spaces in which they occur."[26]

This is not to say there aren't crucial scenes of verbal articulation in the film. Halfway through the film there is a crucial shift away from the meditative and durational rhythms where silence predominates. At about the forty-minute mark, a dinner conversation between Akerman and her mother begins to approach the core thematic of the film. Natalia begins by recollecting how little Chantal ate as a child, and their exchange flows through reminiscences about family—the father who pulled Chantal out of Jewish school the minute his Orthodox father died. The conversation drifts to the war. Natalia is more rueful than anguished, even speaks about how the Germans were nice at first, buying things in shops. Akerman asks how Ethy and Gusta (an aunt and cousin) escaped from Germany, and her mother replies that it was her grandfather who paid a smuggler to get them out. "It was 1939," she remarks. "He understood what was happening." The conversation ends with Natalia's rueful comment: "We thought we were safe here in Belgium. We were naïve, weren't we? . . . If only we had only known."

The other scene also takes place in the kitchen, but in this instance, Akerman remains out of frame, filming her mother's Mexican caregiver Clara. Clara seems uncomfortable, and to make conversation she asks Akerman about the nationality of her mother. Akerman responds by giving a blunt and condensed version of her mother's Holocaust experience. "She ran away because the Poles were very harsh. So they fled here, but afterwards the SS captured them and sent them back to Poland to the concentration camps. That's why my mother is like that." "I see," Clara responds. "To Auschwitz," Akerman clarifies. It is not clear whether Clara understands the implications of Akerman's account as she immediately turns the conversation toward more normative topics. "You're not married? You have no children?"

These conversations circle or mark trauma but without elaboration. Ghosts are conjured only to be repressed, and the dialogue evokes fragments of history only to expose the gross inadequacy of language as a medium for the processing of trauma. If language is abjured as a medium where trauma might be narrativized or resolved in *No Home Movie*, so too is the photographic archive. This marks another of Akerman's unique contributions to trauma studies. The archive is crucial, of course, to what Marianne Hirsch has called *postmemory*, referring to the complex legacy of the Holocaust for children of survivors who incorporate the burden of their parents' memories "so deeply as to seem to constitute memories in their own right."[27] Hirsch cautions, however, that these so-called memories are distinguished from those of the first generation by the fact that they are produced "not by recall but by imaginative investment, projection, and creation," processes mediated by the vast public repertoire of photographic and film imagery released and produced around the Holocaust.[28]

I believe this is what Akerman is talking about when she insists in a 1979 interview with Jean-Luc Godard that her own filmmaking is a process of inscription. "I say that, yes, there are images already inscribed, and it is exactly *under* those that I work: over the inscribed image and the one I want to inscribe."[29] For Akerman, inscription is a manner of resisting both spectacle and brute literalism. It inflects her filmmaking with complex temporalities, where past and present are conjoined through an associative logic, but it is also, in the case of *No Home Movie*, related to her ethical refusal to speak for the other, for her mother.[30] Even if we had no extratextual information about Natalia's past, if Akerman had never spoken of the impact of the Holocaust on her mother (though she does this repeatedly in interviews), as spectators we would be left to imaginatively fill in for Natalia's silence and to draw from the repertoire of preexisting images our own visceral sense of horror as we attempt to reconcile the image of this frail individual with what we already know of the history of the Holocaust. Akerman's refusal to fill in or to speak for the other is markedly different from the claim that the reality of the Holocaust can never be adequated through representation, because for Akerman history is written not with a capital *H* but through the personal bond with her mother, in the words and narrative that cannot be spoken but that imbue the present with a weight of ghosts and spectral imaginings.

"All you have is time," Akerman once told an interviewer. "In my films you are aware of every second passing by. Through your body. You are facing yourself." Is this why the sequences of Akerman's mother living and dying in the apartment are so moving? Each plays with extended duration, testing our tolerance for the absence of action, narration, or purpose, but in so doing they allow us to feel the phenomenological press of time, the irresistible movement toward an end of time from which there is no escape. They capture the poignancy of a moment in time, a moment that is already past and that, like the image of the young man condemned to death that had so struck Roland Barthes, is moving toward death. "He is dead, and he is going to die," wrote Barthes.[31] This doubled temporality, of the present-past and viewing future, mediated through our extratextual knowledge, also applies to the filmmaker herself, whose omnipresence in the film, onscreen and off, now reminds us that "She is dead, and she is going to die," a fact that charges every viewing with a bittersweet and retroactive sense of loss.

At the most obvious level, time passes in *No Home Movie*, although we are never clear whether the film takes place over days or months or even years. Natalia is frail at the beginning of the film, but she seems whimsical, lighthearted, and affectionate with her daughter and caregiver. She engages in conversation and is present to those around her. As the film progresses, her deterioration becomes palpable. She has difficulty eating and swallowing; dinner becomes a painful process interrupted by coughing and distress. By the end of the film, she lapses into sleeping for long stretches in her chaise lounge in the living room, even when prodded aggressively by her daughters to "tell them a story," as if beckoning her back in time. In one of the last sequences in the film, Natalia lies immobile in the chaise, an indecipherable figure obscured in the penumbra of the living room that is suddenly cast into darkness. Bodies are silhouetted as if they are on the very edge of representability. Visibly distressed and anxious, Akerman paces, talks on the phone, and smokes on the balcony, finally entering the living room to plant a kiss on her mother's head as we hear her mother's plaintive cry, "But I want you here every day." This is the last trace of her mother in the film: a cry in the dark.

While the sequences in the apartment each unfold through extensive duration, they are elaborated into the whole through radical ellipsis and by a subtle undoing of linear time via repetition and redundancy—as in those sequences where a passage of time is inferred, but Akerman or her mother appear dressed in the same clothes we had seen earlier in the film. However, these slow and passively observed sequences are critically framed by the opening four-minute shot of a wan tree battered by the desert wind (fig. 2) and by a series of static traveling shots through a parched desert, including a seven-minute traveling shot that tears us out of the cloister of the apartment an hour into the film. What are these sequences doing? For Jeremy Gerrard, these are "passages of raw unfolding time."[32] They are that to be sure, but they also need to be read relationally as an absolute rupture and resistance to the stasis and repression of the domestic and to the final immobility of death. While shot in the Negev desert in Israel, these images could, as Akerman herself avowed, represent "any kind of desert."[33] They do not index singularity, geography, or history; they are pure velocity and perpetual movement, marking a dramatic separation from the maternal space and narrative to embody a kind of virtuality, a suspension of time and a dissolution of identity of space and person. They mark a space of psychic "unbecoming."

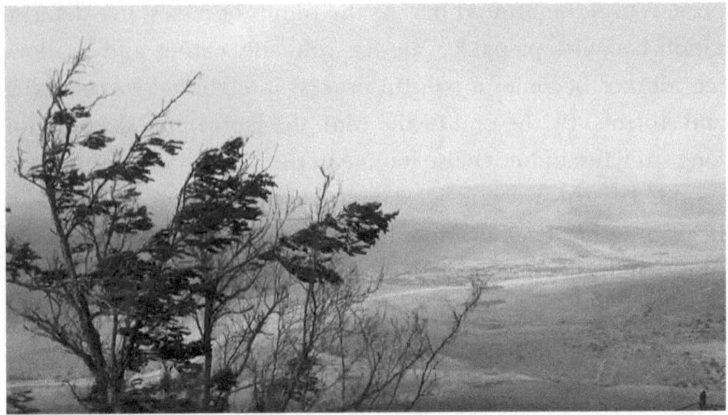

Figure 2. The Negev desert—a space of psychic unbecoming.
No Home Movie (2015)

This is a radically distinct space from that which occupies most of the screen time in *No Home Movie*: the space of the domestic and the everyday, where intimate gestures, daily routines, and small dramas unfold in repetitive patterns. We have been in this space before, at least imaginatively so, in *Jeanne Dielman, 23 quai du Commerce, 1080 Bruxelles* (Belgium/France, 1975): the same pastel colors, the same bourgeois propriety of carpets, polished surfaces, and tasteful decoration, the curtains drawn against the outside world. But while the fictional rendition of space in *Jeanne Dielman* is mediated through a highly formal hyperrealism, as Ivone Margulies has so brilliantly argued—one that amplifies the referential aspect of representation while defamiliarizing it through "an excess of detail" and "theatricality"[34]—the domestic space of *No Home Movie* arrives only through an obdurate minimalism that is void of any trace of hyperbole. As Kent Jones has put it, *No Home Movie* is "as elemental" a film as exists in the history of cinema.[35] But as "elemental" and purposely dedramatized as *No Home Movie* is, the film, through its complex pacing and montage, its attentiveness to the meaning of silence, and its quiet observations, represents a highly aesthetic mediation of the experiences recorded with Akerman's camera. The simplicity of the surface details belies the complexity and profundity of the charges of desire, memory, and traumatic exchange that animate *No Home Movie* and render the film a performative staging of psychic dramas of repression, regression, and traumatic transaction.

I have argued that *No Home Movie* can be productively read through Ettinger's concept of aesthetic wit(h)nessing as a complex, transsubjective processing of trauma modeled on the archaic mutuality of the matrixial. To be clear, the m/other that Ettinger speaks of is not, and never could be, fully represented by an actual mother. The matrixial references an archaic psychic substratum, not a literal relation, even as that relation might very well carry residues and traces of archaic psychic elements.[36] This distinction, of course, seems key to *No Home Movie*, where the director's mother—an ailing, elderly Jewish woman, sweet and needy in equal measure—is the primary subject of the daughter's gaze. I have also argued here that the daughter's gaze is compassionate and humane, a model of matrixial relation in its ability to meet the other, not as a "frozen" object but as coeval subject in becoming. This does not mean, however, that the relation is exempt from ambivalence or contradiction. In an astonishingly candid interview Akerman gave to Nicole Brenez in 2011, she spoke to this aspect of her relationship to her mother:

[My mother's] got a lively spirit, completely the opposite of me. Because, for 15 years, before being taken to the camps, she could believe in the world. While for me, I was born into trauma. . . . I was born with anxieties. My mother never let me negotiate a real separation from her—or maybe I'm the one who couldn't do it, as I have trouble even existing. My mother still calls me "mon amour" all the time, I can't stand it. In Judaism, you're not required to love your parents, only respect them. Sometimes I don't feel either love or respect and, sometimes, the very next day, there's too much of it.[37]

Akerman's insight here reveals much about how her relation to her mother is represented in *No Home Movie*, where the desire for passionate attachment alternates with an equally powerful demand for distance and detachment. In particular, the sequences in which the itinerant Akerman Skypes with her mother from hotel rooms in New York and Oklahoma feel like exemplars of "too much" as they play out as an exaggerated, almost embarrassingly regressive, exchange. "Why are you filming me?" her mother asks at one point. "I film everyone," Akerman responds, "but of course, you especially more than the others," as she zooms her camera into the mother's face, now a haptic moiré of pixels as if visually evincing a desire for an impossible fusion and intimacy (fig. 3). While their verbal exchanges are mainly banal—talk of family members, future visits, and the like—their goodbyes slip into a heightened emotional intensity. Sixty-year-old Akerman calls her mother "Mama," "Mamika," "Mami," without a shred of self-consciousness and, as if purposefully goading her mother, repeatedly stalls the end of their conversation, extending the goodbyes as the two exchange the kind of endearments that Akerman avows "she can't stand": "Grand bisous," "Je t'embrasse, mon amour." At one point, Natalia even confesses to Chantal that "when I see you like that, I want to squeeze you in my arms." And later, as if she is speaking to a lover: "I'd like to say even more, but when I think that someone else will hear it, I don't want to. I don't want everyone to hear what I want to say to you." The heightened emotional intensity of these sequences is, however, enabled by geographic distance and by the technological mediations of laptop and Skype. If Akerman and her mother exchange these avowals of love in person or face to face in the mother's apartment, they are not included in the film, which purposefully frames these scenes of exaggerated pathos with sly humor and reflexivity, as they are viewed only through the framing of screens within screens and faces within Skype windows.[38]

Reflexivity is elsewhere inscribed through formal strategies that deploy what Giuliana Bruno calls "an elaborate geography of thresholds" via Akerman's signature frontal long takes and compositions that rely on frames within frames.[39] Shooting down hallways, through half-open doors, and across rooms, the camera gives us a view of the space of Natalia's apartment that is always partial, located, and mediated through the gaze of the daughter. Akerman recorded much of *No Home Movie* by placing her small digital camera on pieces of furniture or by leaving the camera on tripods at fixed locations around the apartment. At one point, we even see the filmmaker enter the living room with a small palm-sized camera to crouch on the floor before her mother, a doubling of the gaze as the camera films her filming. As with all of Akerman's cinema, we are acutely aware of the presence of the camera even as this presence remains completely unacknowledged by the denizens of the apartment: Natalia; Akerman's sister, Sylviane; and Clara, the caretaker, who all seem oblivious or have learned to indulge Chantal's caprices. The camera's gaze and the filmmaker's gaze are, of course, entwined, but there is also a measure of autonomy in the camera's gaze, a disembodied look that is particularly evident in scenes where Akerman appears onscreen. She enters and exits frames, paces and smokes in the background, and sits with her back to the camera while engaging in the dinner conversation with her mother, shifting her chair to the left to ensure spectators a better view of her mother's face. Akerman is obviously the orchestrator of the gaze, but she is also frequently its subject, performing a role and occupying a place within the onscreen domestic world as the daughter of Natalia who comes and goes, who travels and works elsewhere, who Skypes from hotel rooms around the world, and who performs her filial duties while at the same time observing herself and her mother. Within this complex imbrication of observation and performance, on- and offscreen space are rendered irreducibly separate but adjacent spaces, crossed by the filmmaker's gaze, body, and voice.

In her essay "Splitting," Janet Bergstrom argues that one of the dominant characteristics of Akerman's cinema is precisely "the rigorous separation she maintains between two distinct visual fields: the field occupied by the camera which Akerman has often equated with her own view, and the field observed by the camera."[40] The deliberate referencing of offscreen space, Bergstrom argues, foregrounds the process of enunciation and, as such, may be associated with the formal reflexiveness of avant-garde cinema. But for Bergstrom, Akerman's doubling of visual fields evolves from something more than a formal affectation. It has an "unconscious motive" and functions as a manifestation of the psychic process of splitting as a defense mechanism against maternal trauma. While we might be wary of Bergstrom's appropriation of the Freudian notion of splitting given its link to fetishism, castration anxiety, and other oedipal or phallic dramas, I find something enormously generative about her insight that maternal trauma in Akerman can be, and is only ever to be, represented "at a distance."

In *No Home Movie*, our gaze as spectators is mapped onto Akerman's gaze. We look with her as she observes her mother. The quality of this observation is never probing or aggressive; *No Home Movie* is as far from vérité voyeurism or confessional documentary as one could imagine. We look with Akerman, and the quality of this look is patient, empathetic, weirdly attentive, and, for the most part, emotionally detached—although this is absolutely not to say that the film, in its complex textual address, is void of emotion. Giuliana Bruno beautifully described this quality of Akerman's cinema as one of "distant intimacy," and her felicitous phrase captures something of the affective atmosphere of *No Home Movie*, where the familiar is defamiliarized, and "home" is made into something strange through the formal rigor of duration and framing.[41] The long shot predominates through the rhythms of Akerman's montage and, most of all, through the repeated shots of the empty foyer, the large living room, the empty rumpled bed where, to quote Margulies, "nothing happens." Gestures and bodies periodically fill these spaces—pills are consumed, dinner is eaten, pleasantries exchanged—but these spaces are also weighted with the spectral presence of an eerie emptiness and by the burden of a history that has marked both mother and daughter.

As much as we may read Akerman's work, as Pollock suggests, "as a journey towards the trauma that is finally claimed and transformed,"[42] we might hesitate a moment on the nature of that transformation, for what the obdurate silences and the compassionate waiting and observing witness in *No Home Movie* is the fact that trauma, particularly the trauma of the second generation, may never be easily resolved or processed. *No Home Movie* flows from that irresolution as unspoken trauma inflects the daughter's relation to her mother with a profound ambivalence, where regressive declarations of love coexist with an affective mode of "distant intimacy" as if distance was as necessary as love to the daughter's psychic survival. Again, for me, this is why Ettinger's theorizations seem so uncannily appropriate to a reading of *No Home Movie*. For Ettinger, the matrixial transsubjective space is above all a space marked by ambivalence where identities, part-objects, and traumatic residues are held in a paradoxical relation through a process that is never fixed into static attitudes or binary identities. In this, Ettinger's work is indebted to Melanie Klein's object relations theory, for which ambivalence marks an important passage from "black and white thinking" to a mature ability to hold irreconcilable feelings at the same time without destroying the subject or freezing the other into an object.[43] As I have been arguing, there are many ways in which ambivalence is formally articulated in *No Home Movie*—through the complex "border-linking" of on- and offscreen space, through the paradoxical affective tone of "distant intimacy," and through the rhythm of montage that alternates moments of contemplative observation with explosive eruptions of affective intensity.

It is to the latter that I would like to turn in considering two sets of sequences in *No Home Movie* that embody a markedly different affective and formal quality. The first set of these sequences takes place in the mother's apartment, but here the static, observational camera yields to camerawork that is unmoored, hand-held, uneasy in space, that moves rapidly through rooms and halls, searching without a destination or motivation. There is no narrative or rational provocation for these shots. They are random, abrupt, and infrequent—a subjective embodiment of the filmmaker's anxiety in the face of her mother's inevitable demise.

The second set of shots includes the prolonged four-minute static shot of a lone tree wracked by a desert wind that opens the film and the series of traveling and static shots of a rocky desert landscape inserted into the later part of the film, which catapults us into another time-space continuum entirely. What would this film be like without these strange images that tear us out of the domestic space into a larger world, an exterior, an unmarked landscape that figures far more as wasteland than oasis? Margulies introduced her book on Akerman with the insight that "Akerman's films seem to alternate between containment, order, and symmetry, on the one hand, and on the other a dry intensity that registers as the reverse of restraint: lack of control, obsession, explosion."[44] The traveling sequences register the antinomy of the restraint embodied in the observational sequences in her mother's apartment. Shot on a Blackberry held out a car window, these images are tethered less to an embodied persona (as are the scenes shot in the apartment) than to the impersonal, externalized technologies of car and recording device. They are abstract, perplexing, and, of course, open to multiple interpretations. I would like to venture that they at least partially represent a desire for another space, freed of the enormous weight and responsibility of trauma and maternal relation.

In *No Home Movie*, the rhythms of montage alternate domestic intimacy with the defamiliarizing observation of a maternal space where emptiness and silence register a trauma that resists representation. What is shaped in silence—what shadows the death we observe happening—is that other death, the death that could have happened in Auschwitz. There is another specter haunting the film, of course, and that is the death of Akerman herself. For spectators who have carried Akerman's films and installations with them over the course of her forty-year career, her last offering provides a final and poignant reflection on the themes of trauma and mother-daughter relation that have animated all of her work and that leave such a unique and powerful legacy.

Notes

1. Elisabeth Lebovici, "Her Cinema, Even," *Senses of Cinema* 77 (December 2015), sensesofcinema.com/2015/chantal-akerman/her-cinema/.

2. Of course, this might also speak to the importance of attending to the context of viewing. For me, watching *No Home Movie* on my home computer was entirely different than viewing the film in a

large theater during a press and industry screening at a frenetic film festival. At "home," the film's personal, affective address seemed far more heightened and immediate, and I often cried as the film sparked a range of memories. See Francesco Casetti, "Filmic Experience," *Screen* 50, no. 1 (2009): 56–66.

3. Kent Jones, DVD notes, *No Home Movie* (2015; New York: Icarus Films, 2016).

4. Peter Debruge, "*No Home Movie*," *Variety*, 10 August 2015, variety .com/2015/film/reviews/no-home-movie-film-review -1201566469/.

5. Jack Halberstam, *The Queer Art of Failure* (Durham, NC: Duke University Press, 2011), 88.

6. An important corrective to reading all of Akerman's work via the framing of trauma and its aftereffects is provided by B. Ruby Rich in her editorial comments for the recent *Film Quarterly* special dossier on Chantal Akerman. Rich argues that Akerman's suicide should not shape all scholarship on the director, given how Akerman's work included so many different genres, including joyous comedies and musicals. See B. Ruby Rich, "What Is at Stake: Gender, Race, Media, or How to Brexit Hollywood," *Film Quarterly* 70, no. 1 (Fall 2016): 8–9.

7. Griselda Pollock, *After-Affects, After-Images: Trauma and Aesthetic Transformation in the Virtual Feminist Museum* (Manchester: Manchester University Press, 2013), 324.

8. Daniel Kasman, "Chantal Akerman Discusses *No Home Movie*," *Mubi*, 17 August 2015, mubi.com/notebook/posts/chantal -akerman-discusses-no-home-movie.

9. Janet Bergstrom, "Chantal Akerman: Splitting," in *Endless Night: Cinema and Psychoanalysis, Parallel Histories*, ed. Janet Bergstrom (Berkeley: University of California Press, 1999), 273–90; Alisa Lebow, "Memory Once Removed: Indirect Memory and Transitive Autobiography in Chantal Akerman's *D'Est*," *Camera Obscura*, no. 52 (2003): 35–83.

10. Bergstrom also appropriates André Green's clinical definition of the "dead mother" as a phenomenon particularly related to subjects whose mothers suffer chronic depression and emotional withdrawal. Bergstrom sees this as particularly evident in

Akerman's characterization of Jeanne Dielman as an "affectless" mother. Bergstrom, "Splitting," 283–84.

11. Pollock, *After-Affects*, 12.

12. Bracha Lichtenberg Ettinger, "Wit(h)nessing Trauma and the Matrixial Gaze: From Phantasm to Trauma, from Phallic Structure to Matrixial Sphere," *Parallax* 7, no. 4 (2001): 89–114.

13. See "Works by Bracha L. Ettinger," a selected bibliography, in Bracha L. Ettinger, *The Matrixial Borderspace*, ed. Brian Massumi (Minneapolis: University of Minnesota Press, 2006), 227–38.

14. Pollock has been singularly responsible for introducing Ettinger's thought into English-speaking feminist art theory and history, beginning with a special issue of the feminist journal *differences* in 1992 and culminating in the curation of an exhibition of Ettinger's art in the Freud Museum in London in 2009, as well as the publication of numerous essays, most notably "Femininity: Aporia or Sexual Difference," in Ettinger, *Matrixial Borderspace*, 1–41.

15. Ettinger, "Wit(h)nessing Trauma and the Matrixial Gaze," 101.

16. Bracha Lichtenberg Ettinger, "Art as the Transport-Station of Trauma," in *Bracha Lichtenberg Ettinger: Artworking, 1985–1999* (Brussels: Palais des Beaux-Arts, 2000), 91.

17. Bracha L. Ettinger, "Matrixial Trans-subjectivity," *Theory, Culture, and Society* 23, no. 2–3 (2006): 218.

18. Vivian Sobchack, *Carnal Thoughts: Embodiment and Moving Image Culture* (Berkeley: University of California Press, 2004), 284.

19. Levinas says: "I speak of responsibility as the essential, primary and fundamental structure of subjectivity. For I describe subjectivity in ethical terms. Ethics, here, does not supplement a preceding existential base; the very node of the subjective is knotted in ethics understood as responsibility." Emmanuel Levinas, *Ethics and Infinity: Conversations with Philippe Nemo*, trans. Richard A. Cohen (Pittsburgh, PA: Duquesne University Press, 1985), 95.

20. Élisabeth Lebovici, "No Idolatry and Losing Everything That Made You a Slave: Chantal Akerman," *Mousse*, no. 31 (December 2011–January 2012), moussemagazine.it/chantal-akerman -elisabeth-lebovici-2011.

21. See Carol A. Newsom, "Models of the Moral Self: Hebrew Bible and Second Temple Judaism," *Journal of Biblical Literature* 131 (2012): 10.

22. Lebovici, "No Idolatry."

23. Lebovici, "No Idolatry."

24. Kasman, "Chantal Akerman Discusses *No Home Movie*."

25. Pollock, *After-Affects*, 15.

26. Jones, DVD Notes, *No Home Movie*.

27. Marianne Hirsch, "The Generation of Postmemory," *Poetics Today* 29, no. 1 (2008): 103.

28. Marianne Hirsch, *The Generation of Postmemory: Writing and Visual Culture after the Holocaust* (New York: Columbia University Press, 2012), 39. The problem with the archive, as Hirsch points out, is that it frequently naturalizes persistent gender stereotypes, as "preformed images" and "pre-established forms" undergird a "fundamentally oedipal and heteronormative, reproductive form of social organization" (107).

29. Jean-Luc Godard, "Entretien sur un project: Chantal Akerman," *Ça Cinéma* 19 (1980): 11.

30. For the installation version of *D'Est*, Akerman included a long meditative monologue where she avows that the landscapes and faces she filmed stood for her as "a primal scene": "It is far behind or always in front of all images barely covered by other, more luminous or even radiant ones. All images of evacuation, of walking in the snow with packages toward an unknown place, of faces and bodies one placed next to the other, of faces flickering with robust life and the possibility of a death which would strike them down without their having asked for anything." Quoted in Lebow, "Memory Once Removed," 42.

31. Roland Barthes, *Camera Lucida: Reflections on Photography*, trans. Richard Howard (New York: Hill and Wang, 1981), 95.

32. Jeremy Gerrard, "Chantal Akerman Will Be Remembered at 'No Home Movie' Screening—New York Film Festival," *Deadline Hollywood*, 7 October 2015, deadline.com/2015/10/chantal -akerman-remembered-new-york-film-festival-1201568816/.

33. Kasman, "Chantal Akerman Discusses *No Home Movie*."

34. Ivone Margulies, *Nothing Happens: Chantal Akerman's Hyperrealist Everyday* (Durham, NC: Duke University Press, 1996), 42–46.

35. Kent Jones, "On Chantal Akerman," *FilmLinc Daily*, 7 October 2015, www.filmlinc.org/nyff2015/daily/on-chantal-akerman/.

36. The matrixial rather references an alternative psychic potentiality where the m/other is multiple, constituted in what Ettinger names *severality*. "If the Matrix points to that which is not reducible to the one and does not yearn for one," Ettinger writes, "it is because it never was One." Bracha L. Ettinger, "Metramorphic Borderlinks and Matrixial Borderspace," in *Rethinking Borders*, ed. John Welchman (Minneapolis: University of Minnesota Press, 1996), 125.

37. Nicole Brenez, "Chantal Akerman: The Pajama Interview," trans. David Phelps, *Lola*, no. 2 (2012), www.lolajournal.com/2 /pajama.html. First published as *Chantal Akerman: The Pajama Interview* (Vienna: Viennale, 2011).

38. A scene in Marianne Lambert's documentary *I Don't Belong Anywhere: The Cinema of Chantal Akerman* (Belgium, 2015) features Akerman, naked from the waist up, Skyping with her mother, a scene not included in *No Home Movie* perhaps for the way in which it makes all too literal a fantasy of regression.

39. Giuliana Bruno, "Projection: On Chantal Akerman's Screens, from Cinema to the Art Gallery," *Senses of Cinema* 77 (December 2015), sensesofcinema.com/2015/chantal -akerman/projection/.

40. Bergstrom, "Splitting," 279.

41. Bruno, "Projection."

42. Pollock, *After-Affects*, 324.

43. Meira Likierman identifies Melanie Klein's essay "A Contribution to the Psychogenesis of Manic-Depressive States" (1935) as a "watershed" intervention in the development of Klein's theory of ambivalence. See Likierman, *Melanie Klein: Her Work in Context* (London: Continuum, 2001), 100–112.

44. Margulies, *Nothing Happens*, 1.

Brenda Longfellow is associate professor in the Department of Cinema and Media Arts, York University, Toronto. She has written extensively on feminist, Canadian, and documentary cinema and is the coeditor of *Gendering the Nation: Canadian Women's Cinema* (1999) and *The Perils of Pedagogy: The Work of John Greyson* (2013). Her documentaries have been screened and broadcast internationally. Her most recent project, *Offshore*, an interactive documentary on offshore oil disasters, is available at offshore-interactive.com.

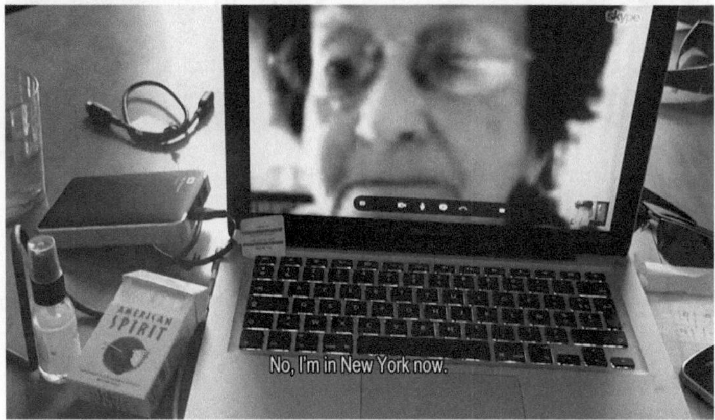

Figure 3. Skyping with Natalia—an intimate distance. *No Home Movie* (2015)

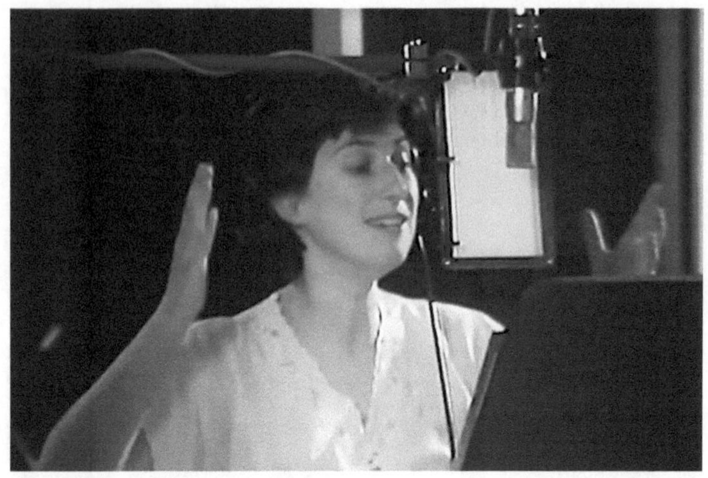

Figure 1. Chantal Akerman in *Les Années 80* (1983)

Lyrical Akerman

Kelley Conway

J'ai tant aimé faire [*Demain on déménage* (France/Belgium, 2004)]. Nous n'avons fait que chanter. J'aime chanter. C'est ce que j'aime le plus. . . . On chantait puis on tournait. Quelle joie. Quoi qu'il arrive, il ne faut pas que j'oublie ça. Ce bonheur-là. C'est pas si souvent. Loin de là.

(I so loved making [*Demain on déménage* (*Tomorrow We Move*)]. All we did was sing. I love to sing. It's what I love the most. . . . We would sing, and then we would shoot. What a joy. Whatever happens, I must not forget that. That happiness. It doesn't happen so often. Far from it.)
—Chantal Akerman, *Autoportrait en cinéaste*

At the conclusion of the memorial held in 2016 for Chantal Akerman in New York, a clip from *Les Années 80* (*The Eighties*, France/Belgium, 1983) was screened. Midway through the experimental film, which Akerman created in preparation for her musical *Golden Eighties* (France/Belgium/Switzerland, 1986), the director stands in a recording studio. She is conducting actress Magali Noël, who sings a song Akerman cowrote with Marc Hérouet. Akerman directs Noël with extraordinary energy and enthusiasm,

Camera Obscura 100, Volume 34, Number 1
DOI 10.1215/02705346-7264154   © 2019 by *Camera Obscura*
Published by Duke University Press

moving her arms with such force that she appears to be dancing. In another surprising development, Akerman sings (fig. 1). Wearing headphones and communicating with an offscreen pianist, she sings inexpertly but with great passion and obvious sincerity. The choice of the clip was inspired, no doubt, by a desire to leave mourners with an image of Akerman at work, joyous and inventive. This moment in *Les Années 80* provides comfort in the wake of Akerman's death, but it also raises questions. Given the love of song Akerman demonstrates here, we might ask: What did songs and the act of singing mean to her? What are the songs' relationships to the narratives in which they are embedded? An examination of Akerman's use of song shifts our conception of her work, allowing for an expanded understanding of her aesthetic exploration and commitments and, specifically, her foregrounding of the female voice.

Film critics and historians typically characterize Akerman's films as minimalist and melancholy. Her signature long takes and understated acting performances, combined with her predilection for ellipsis, repetition, and duration, are rightly perceived to result in "antipsychological, sparse, and dedramatized narratives."[1] Yet Akerman's films also express extraordinary lyricism and euphoria. Amid the highly patterned narratives and the exquisitely precise repetition and variation of stylistic strategies, songs periodically imbue Akerman's films with a range of meanings and experiences we rarely associate with her work: a jolt of joy, an impression of intense human connection, a reference to popular culture. Ivone Margulies asserts, "When a song's lyrics are heard in an Akerman film, it is always a corny love song, or else a classical musical cliché, like the 'Für Elise' heard over the radio in *Jeanne Dielman*. Even the films' cheerful original songs, with lyrics by Akerman, appeal to what Theodor Adorno disparagingly called the 'emotional listener.' Akerman's songs are the lighter side of a darker, more powerful drive."[2] Akerman's films do indeed contain love songs and classical music clichés, but the significance of song in her films deserves a closer look. Akerman employs songs in a range of ways, weaving them into her avant-garde and more traditional works alike while tapping into traditions of popular song, opera, and less classifiable vocal performance. From unpredictable humming to an opera duet exactingly shot and performed, and from a modest a cappella solo performance to full-fledged production numbers, Akerman's work is infused with the sound of the female singing voice.

In her very first work, the short film *Saute ma ville* (*Blow Up My Town*, Belgium, 1968), Akerman plays the role of a young woman who enters an apartment, scrubs and sullies it, prepares and consumes a meal, and then turns on the stove's gas, causing a huge explosion. The soundtrack is unusual from the beginning. We hear the protagonist before we see her. Fast-paced, asynchronous humming serves as the introduction to a character who will engage in increasingly maniacal activities before causing a total destruction of the domestic environment.[3] The character's humming and la-la-la-ing are utterly unpredictable. The speed, volume, and timbre of the vocal performance vary considerably during the thirteen-minute film. Occasionally the humming ceases for a time and then resumes without warning or clear motivation. There is no attempt to suggest synchronization between the movement of Akerman's lips and the sounds we hear, although sound and image are synchronized from time to time elsewhere in *Saute ma ville*, such as when the protagonist drops a key onto the floor or puts tape around her door frame.

The gulf between voice and image in *Saute ma ville* persists when, after the explosion occurs and the screen goes dark, the humming returns. Has the character somehow managed to survive the explosion? This seems unlikely, but it nevertheless raises the question of whether the voice—which is Akerman's voice, in fact—emanates from the character at all. Is the vocal performance an aural corollary to the frantic, unpredictable, and often humorous actions of the character? Or is the soundtrack a relatively autonomous channel of aesthetic material, detached from what we see, operating according to its own logic? Paul Hegarty suggests the multiple functions of sound in *Saute ma ville*, describing Akerman's voice as "both outside of the film's visual space and somehow inside her head and/or apartment" and as "an extra-diegetic sound with the capacity to comment on, mirror or pre-empt events and actions in the apartment."[4] Not only does Akerman's soundtrack roam across the divide between the diegetic and the nondiegetic, but the choice to employ intermittent humming (instead of dialogue or lyrics) and the film's unusually loud ambient noise also challenge conventional sound/image relationships and the norms of aural expressivity more generally. Even the credit sequence extends Akerman's playful treatment of the soundtrack: she voices the credits, a gesture that further lifts us out of the story world and serves as an emphatic assertion of authorship on the part of an insouciant, audacious, first-time auteur.

As a whole, the film foregrounds contradiction: domestic labor leads to the annihilation of the home and lighthearted humming precedes suicide. Image and sound seem connected at times but ultimately remain autonomous entities. Barbara McBane astutely observes of Akerman's soundtracks in general, "Akerman brings such attention to bear on the soundtrack—carefully selected, choreographed, and precisely mixed sounds modulated to certain ends—that her technique has the effect of lifting the soundtrack away from the images and inserting a space between them. An awareness of the condition of sound and image tracks as separate constructions is generated and sustained."[5] The "constructed" quality of the vocal performance constitutes a rejection of the impression of fidelity typically created in cinema's sound-image relations. The experimental nature of the film is enhanced by vocal utterances that are unintelligible, unpatterned, and unpredictable, a distinct departure from the lyrics and verse/chorus structure characterizing traditional songs. Finally, the voice is female. As I discuss here, female vocal performance is a central component of Akerman's stylistic and narrative experimentation.

In *Je tu il elle* (*I, You, He, She*, Belgium/France, 1974), Akerman's first feature, she again uses vocal performance in a surprising fashion, very different from her first film. Here, too, Akerman plays the main character and lends her singing voice to the soundtrack. In the first section of the film, the protagonist ruminates alone in her apartment for several weeks in the aftermath of a breakup. In the second portion of the film, she hitches a ride from a male truck driver, whom she manually pleasures. In the third and final section of the film, she spends the night at the apartment of her exlover, a woman. In a lengthy scene, the two women make love. The following morning, Akerman's character gets up, leaves her lover asleep in bed, and exits the frame. The camera stays on her sleeping lover for several seconds in silence, and then we hear birds chirping and children singing. Credits on a black screen follow, and a woman's voice joins those of the children, singing "Nous n'irons plus au bois" (We'll to the Woods No More), a well-known eighteenth-century French folk song that is often sung in rounds. In a call-and-response style, the woman (perhaps a teacher) and the children (perhaps her students) sing,

Nous n'irons plus au bois.
Les lauriers sont coupés.
La belle que voilà.
Ira les ramasser.
Entrez dans la danse.
Voyez, comme on danse.
Sautez, dansez, embrassez qui vous voudrez.

(We'll to the woods no more.
The laurels are all gone.
The pretty lass has gathered them all.
See the people dance.
Come join in the dance.
Leap and dance and kiss whom you please.)[6]

Eventually, the children drop out of the song. Attentive listeners will note that Akerman herself begins to sing with the woman, replacing the students. An alternation between Akerman and the other woman is first established and continues for a few lines, but eventually their voices merge.

The merging of these two female voices aurally suggests what we have just seen in the love scene: the fusion of two bodies. But just as the film refrains from implying that Akerman's character will form a long-lasting couple with her ex-lover, the soundtrack suggests the maintenance of autonomy. Akerman's charming but untrained singing voice remains distinguishable from her partner's more confident performance. This technique of joining together two female voices, while retaining their vocal differences, will be used by the filmmaker again decades later in another lesbian love story, *La Captive* (*The Captive*, France/Belgium, 2000), a film I return to below.

Akerman extends the use of the a cappella female singing voice in *Les Rendez-vous d'Anna* (*The Meetings of Anna*, Belgium/France/Germany, 1978), a film chronicling several days in the life of an enigmatic filmmaker (Aurore Clément) as she travels through Europe promoting her film. The protagonist engages in repetitive actions, says little, and remains enigmatic throughout the film. As she travels from Essen to Cologne, on to Brussels, and then to Paris, she has extended interactions with a number of characters. She embarks upon, but then aborts, a sexual encounter with a man she meets in Germany, listens patiently to the life story of a man she meets on a train, cuddles up with her mother in bed for a long chat in a hotel room in Brussels, and spends part of an evening with her current lover in a Paris hotel room. In most scenes she says little, frequently gazing out of the windows of hotel rooms and trains. She often appears to act as a kind of receiver for the stories of others.

Song becomes important in the Paris hotel room scene with her companion, Daniel (Jean-Pierre Cassel). Daniel appears depressed and mentions that he is tired of his job and the constant effort to get ahead. He muses that if he were a woman he would have a baby, breastfeed his baby every two hours, live close to nature, and forget about everything else. Daniel then extends his expression of gendered fantasies, asking, "What is lovelier than music, than a woman's voice?" and "Where does a woman's voice come from?" He then asks Anna to sing for him. While he reclines in bed, she stands before him and sings "Les amants d'un jour" (Lovers for a Day), a ballad created for Edith Piaf in 1956. The song tells the story of two devoted young lovers who rent a room in a shabby hotel and are found dead in each other's arms the following day, having committed suicide. The narrator of the song is a cynical waitress worn down by her work in the café:

Moi j'essuie les verres au fond du café
J'ai bien trop à faire pour pouvoir rêver
Mais dans ce décor banal à pleurer
Il me semble encore les voir arriver.

(I'm the one who washes the glasses in the back of the café
I've much too much to do to have time to dream
But in this lamentably banal décor
I still seem to see them arrive.)[7]

Anna sings to Daniel, without pretense or polish, in a static, frontal long take lasting more than three minutes (fig. 2). This is the only song performance in *Les Rendez-vous d'Anna*, and therefore the scene is not at all typical of the film as a whole. Nor is the song typical of musical performance in other, more conventional films. There is no music: the song is sung a cappella. Anna's singing voice is that of an amateur, and yet it is not flamboyantly imperfect or idiosyncratic. Adding to the sparse quality of the performance, there is no dancing or distinctive movement. A woman stands still in a hotel room, wearing a white terry cloth bathrobe, and sings a mournful song to her companion. Anna's song performance has been interpreted as a "perverse twist on the maternal-feminine lullaby-function" and as "resistance to conventional romance and

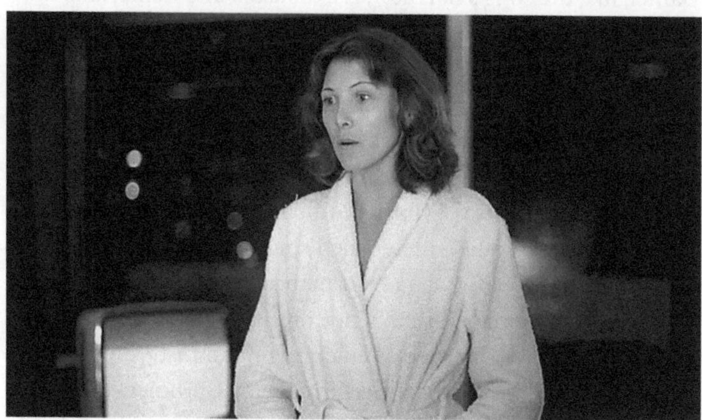

Figure 2. Aurore Clément in *Les Rendez-vous d'Anna* (1978)

its attendant inequalities," but this moment evokes more than a rejection of the conventional maternal or romantic female role.[8]

That Akerman chose a song associated with Edith Piaf for this scene is significant. Piaf was an internationally successful singer active from the mid-1930s to her death in 1963. Her repertoire comprised largely the *chanson réaliste*, a song genre that emerged in fin-de-siècle France and typically consisted of a first-person narrative performed by a woman. Realist songs tend to be set in the working-class or criminal milieu and chronicle sexual desire, failed love affairs, poverty, or depression. The figure of the *chanteuse réaliste* (a topic I address in greater depth elsewhere)[9] has a rich history in French cinema: Fréhel evokes depression and nostalgia in *Pépé le Moko* (dir. Julien Duvivier, France, 1937); Florelle sings of poverty and prostitution in *Le Crime de M. Lange* (dir. Jean Renoir, France, 1935); and Piaf herself appeared in several films from the late 1930s to the 1950s to similar effect. *Les Rendez-vous d'Anna* implicitly attributes value to the work and the persona of Piaf, an iconic popular singer who incarnated female pain and fragility, but also resilience. Anna serves, in part, as a stand-in for the realist singer, telling both the melodramatic tale of a young couple's suicide and the narrator's own, more workaday story of a worn-out woman washing dishes in a cafe. The song echoes the film's larger narrative in that its lyrics parallel the state of the male character: Daniel, like the song's narrator, is exhausted and demoralized.

Akerman's choice of Piaf's song also creates an interesting mismatch. Piaf is indelibly associated with the working-class and criminal margins of French society, while Daniel is a middle-class businessman and Anna is a working artist. More pertinent for my analysis is that Piaf's extraordinary capacity to project her voice and her distinctive use of vibrato could not be more different from Aurore Clément's quiet, unadorned singing voice. Claudia Gorbman calls this type of vocal performance "artless singing": a kind of singing performance that is not presented as a musical number but, rather, is construed as emerging naturalistically from the diegetic world.[10] Such vocal performances, Gorbman notes, are often without the "magical" backing of an orchestra and are shot in sync sound with indices of spatial realism. Clément's startlingly simple singing performance generates pleasure for the internal audience (the lover) and for viewers of the film, but Akerman undercuts the utopian function often performed by film songs. The flickering television screen in the background becomes distracting and irritating, suggesting that even this tender performance cannot heal the man's malaise. And yet despite the song's dark theme, its performance suggests an emotional generosity in Anna hinted at earlier in a tender scene with her mother. A moment of connection occurs through the performance of the song, even if that sense of connection quickly dissipates. Following the singing performance, Anna takes off her bathrobe and arranges her nude body on top of Daniel's clothed form. But he has a fever and feels too ill for intimacy. The scene concludes with Anna leaving the hotel in search of medicine for him, tears rolling down her face.

The scene thus asks the viewer to reconcile several apparent opposites: a supine, ailing man and a healthy, mobile woman, certainly, but above all, the evocation of Edith Piaf's powerful voice with Aurore Clément's modest singing voice used in this scene. The scene foregrounds misalignment and then hints at dysfunction in her relationship with Daniel. The fragility of their relationship is underscored further when, upon arriving at her apartment, Anna listens to messages on her answering machine left by her female lover. The film's conclusion, admittedly ambiguous, leaves open the possibility and promise of a lesbian relationship.

The performance and the staging of song in *Les Rendez-vous d'Anna* are quite different from those in both *Saute ma ville* and *Je tu il elle*. Unlike Akerman's humming in *Saute ma ville*, the vocal performance in *Les Rendez-vous d'Anna* possesses intelligible lyrics and is clearly generated by the film's female protagonist thanks to its use of synchronized sound. Moreover, unlike the offscreen children's song in *Je tu il elle*, the song lyrics in *Les Rendez-vous d'Anna* tell a story with obvious connections to the film's narrative. The song emerges upon the request of a character and is thus narratively justified. Its lyrics express the lassitude and despair of the male character who requested it. The a cappella, artless singing and static staging result in a dedramatized, melancholy use of song. Yet the singing performance constitutes a gift on the part of a woman to her lover and crystallizes a moment of intense, if temporary, connection between two characters.

Akerman's use of song intensified in the 1980s, finding its most elaborate and, in many ways, most traditional expression in *Golden Eighties*, a musical about shopkeepers and hairdressers who seek, find, and lose love at a shopping mall in Brussels. The film's production history is unusually circuitous. By the end of the 1970s, after making the monumental *Jeanne Dielman, 23 quai du Commerce, 1080 Bruxelles* (Belgium/France, 1975) and a number of experimental short films influenced by the New York avant-garde, Akerman decided to move in a new direction.

Akerman initially planned to direct a film based on an adaptation of two novels by Isaac Bashevis Singer, *The Manor* and *The Estate*, but struggled to raise production funds for the project. Advised to make a modest comedy before tackling the Singer adaptation, Akerman embarked on a project that eventually evolved into the *Golden Eighties*. But before making *Golden Eighties*, she created the feature-length *Les Années 80*, which has been called "a kind of demo tape, or proof of concept" for the subsequent film.[11] Ultimately an unclassifiable work, *Les Années 80* features a series of auditions and rehearsals, operating more as an avant-garde film than a pilot or a "making of" documentary. The film does not have the traditional self-celebratory tone of a making-of film. It does not, for example, culminate in the successful completion of the casting process or the steady march from awkward rehearsal to finalized perfection. The film conveys only a few slivers of the future film's plot; there are no interviews with Akerman, the cast, or the crew. Instead, *Les Années 80* offers a mesmerizing series of scenes emphasizing repetition and process. Amid the line readings and song rehearsals, the timbre, volume, and rhythm of the female voice are foregrounded.

The film opens on a black screen, and for nearly three minutes we hear, but never see, Akerman working with an actress on the delivery of one line. Over and over, the actress utters, "A ton âge, le chagrin est vite passé" (At your age, grief soon wears off). Akerman murmurs, sometimes barely audible, indicating the changes she desires in the reading of the line. In other sections of the film, actors rehearse songs or vamp and prance through warehouse-like interiors. Most of the performers in *Les Années 80*, some of whom were students at the film school where Akerman taught at the time, do not appear in *Golden Eighties*. For example, Magali Noël and Aurore Clément, perhaps the best-known actors in *Les Années 80*, had other commitments by the time Akerman pulled together the funding for *Golden Eighties* and had to drop out of the production.

Perhaps the most intriguing performer in *Les Années 80* is Akerman herself, who conducts and sings. She becomes a character, as it were, singing passionately while accompanied by someone named Marc offscreen, who is perhaps Marc Hérouet, the composer for *Les Années 80* and *Golden Eighties*. (Akerman wrote the lyrics to the songs.) *Les Années 80* and *Golden Eighties* have been interpreted as a postmodern critique or a parody of the musical.[12] However, Margulies rightly emphasizes instead Akerman's genuine investment in the emotional power of song, observing that "French modern films check the dryness of their antinaturalism with a nostalgia for the emotional affect of singing."[13] The scenes of Akerman conducting and singing in *Les Années 80* do not necessarily imply that she intended to play a role in *Golden Eighties* but, rather, wanted to convey her love of song and the physicality of singing.

While *Les Années 80* revels in the repetition, fragmentation, and imperfection inherent in the rehearsal process, *Golden Eighties* offers the result of that process. By turns sincere and cheeky, the film is in many ways a conventional film musical, with its alternation between narrative and numbers and its mix of ordinary and rhythmic movement. Robert (Nicolas Tronc) works at his parents' clothing store and sings of his love for the opportunistic Lili (Fanny Cottençon), the hair salon manager who works next door, while two hair stylists—one of whom is played by the Belgo-Portuguese pop singer Lio—pine for Robert. Sylvie (Myriam Boyer) tends the mall's snack bar and sings excerpts from letters written by her lover, who has moved to Canada to find his fortune. Delphine Seyrig incarnates another "Jeanne" for Akerman, Jeanne Schwartz, a married shopkeeper and the mother of Robert. She sings movingly of her love for an American man, Eli (played by the previously black-listed American director John Berry), who sheltered Jeanne after she survived the concentration camps during the war and has now wandered into the mall.

The soundtrack is a distinctive mix of sound effects, music, and dialogue. Adrian Martin describes it well:

The constant clackety-clack footsteps; the signifying of boutique muzak by a drum machine loop that gets busier each time it reappears; the deft conversion of an air-conditioner's "whoosh" or a pesky dress zipper's noise into synthesized, rhythmic elements of the music; and the ever changing acoustics of voice and speech—spoken, sung, whispered, solo, en masse, with and without echo. One has the sense of hearing a sound "mix," complete with stops, starts, modulations, tryouts . . . laboratory experiments of all kinds.[14]

There are three basic types of singing performance in *Golden Eighties*. Most commonly, individual characters sing, often directly to the camera and accompanied by nondiegetic music, songs about love or financial troubles that contain the conventional alternation between verse and chorus. Monsieur Schwartz (Charles Denner), Jeanne's practical husband, sings of the recession and his desire to expand his clothing store, but most of the songs evoke emotions of desire and disappointment around romantic love. In "Cette Nuit," Jeanne sings of her passion for Eli in the dimly lit underground mall as shopkeepers arrive to open their stores: "Enferme-moi dans tes bras, ne me quitte pas, ne t'en vas pas" (Lock me up in your arms, don't leave me, don't go away) (fig. 3). Seyrig's breathy and fragile voice, apparently the only singing voice that is not dubbed in the film,[15] is moving in its imperfection, like that of Aurore Clément in *Les Rendez-vous d'Anna*, but the song as a whole is more conventional, with its nondiegetic piano and string accompaniment. The songs are squarely in the mode of the popular (as opposed to classical) as defined by Rick Altman: they rely on language and are rhythmically predictable, "singable," and memorable.[16]

In addition to the film's ballads, there are witty and playful

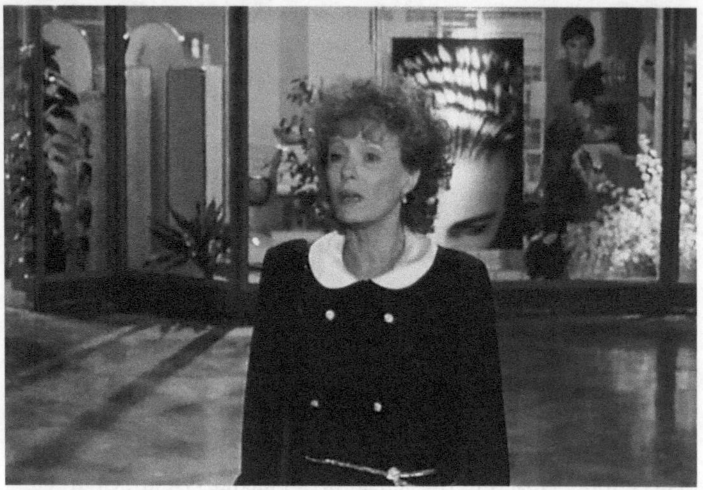

Figure 3. Delphine Seyrig in *Golden Eighties* (1986)

group numbers. The female employees of the hair salon vigorously shampoo and spray customers' hair while relaying gossip through song about the film's main love triangle (the scheming Lili, the lovesick Robert, and Jean, Lili's married lover and source of financial support). There are also numerous brief a cappella passages sung by a chorus of young men who gently mock the principle characters. The chorus often taunts the young and foolish Robert, singing repeatedly the nonsensical rhyme "Robert, camembert, tout vert . . ." Marion Schmid observes of such scenes, "The chorus deflates the romantic clichés that are lived and repeated by the central characters, its malicious comments distancing the spectator from the spectacle on display."[17] But the chorus and the salon scenes function less as criticism of cliché than as humorous and affectionate nods to the conventions of the musical, whether Hollywood or European. Akerman had often experimented with a sparse soundtrack, precise and repetitive human movement, and confining interior spaces.[18] Like *Les Années 80, Golden Eighties* offered Akerman a new arena for experimentation. In an interview with Nicole Brenez, Akerman expresses her desire to embark on something new in the making of *Les Années 80* and *Golden Eighties*:

NB: I remember just how out of place and explosive it seemed in the landscape of the time; nobody was expecting such a joyous, colourful musical. That kind of exhilaration ran completely against the dominant taste in auteur films of the '80s.

CA: They kept wanting me to remake *Jeanne Dielman*, but I wanted to *spurn* everything—spurn my father's name, not repeat myself. I did a number of trial runs for it, and *Les Années 80* (*The 80s*) and the others are possibly more joyous than the final film, which suffered from a lack of resources, among other reasons. In any case, I was very happy to write the songs. [She sings.][19]

Golden Eighties alternates between narrative and number, like the classical Hollywood musical, but the film's bittersweet quality connects it more closely to the sensibility of Jacques Demy. Characters do not get the lovers they prefer. Seyrig's character refuses Eli's proposal and remains in the shop with her husband. On the eve of their wedding, Mado loses Robert to the vampy salon manager. Sylvie is still waiting for her lover to return at the end of the film. Other references to the work of Jacques Demy abound, supporting Schmid's assertion that Akerman's film draws explicitly upon Demy's melodrama and sentimentality.[20] *Golden Eighties* cites the famous opening credits of *Les Parapluies de Cherbourg* (*The Umbrellas of Cherbourg*, France, 1964) with overhead images of women's feet in ballet flats or high heels moving briskly across the floor of the shopping mall. Akerman also cites Demy in her use of a network narrative: like *Les Demoiselles de Rochefort* (*The Young Girls of Rochefort*, France, 1967), *Golden Eighties* rejects the strict dual-focus structure of the classical musical, constructing instead a plot in which several possible couples are proposed. In another nod to Demy, Jeanne and Sylvie are trapped in their shops and preoccupied with absent lovers, just like *Rochefort*'s café proprietor, Yvonne Garnier (Danielle Darrieux), while Eli's entrance into the film—he bends down to pick up a paper dropped by another character—evokes the entrance of Andy Miller (Gene Kelly). *Golden Eighties* cites *Rochefort* once again in the numerous missed connections among its characters. Jeanne identifies Eli from behind, gasps, and then decides she was mistaken. In the salon, where Eli is getting a shave, he starts when he hears Jeanne's voice but fails to confirm her identity because she moves quickly out of view. Finally, Sylvie, like Demy's Lola, is a single mother waiting patiently for her boyfriend to return from a years-long effort to find his fortune in North America.

Golden Eighties proposes two kinds of love: the fiery and brief love of the young and the stable, sensible relationships of the old. Akerman savors, and upends, romantic clichés but ends on a note of practicality. Embracing the young woman her son has abandoned, Jeanne murmurs that they will all be okay "as long as there's enough to eat." In the wake of the Holocaust, the film suggests at several points that romance is a luxury one cannot afford. Jeanne's husband, for his part, compares the choice of a romantic partner to the choice of a new dress. "You'll meet someone else. . . . It's like with a dress. You love a dress, but it's too expensive or doesn't look good on you . . . and you have to choose another." The film ends as they stroll along on a sunny street, temporarily released from the stuffy underground mall but still confined by their fears and economic condition.

If the women in *Golden Eighties* are ultimately trapped in conventional heterosexual and economic relationships, Akerman suggests a different female existence in *J'ai faim, j'ai froid* (*I'm Hungry, I'm Cold*, France, 1984). In this exuberant short film made for the omnibus work *Paris vu par, 20 ans après* (*Paris Seen By, Twenty Years Later*), Akerman again foregrounds female singing performance. Here, however, female singing is neither a gift to an ailing male lover (as in *Les Rendez-vous d'Anna*) nor a lament for impossible love (as in *Golden Eighties*). This fast-paced, twelve-minute narrative offers a droll chronicle of a day in the life of two eighteen-year-old women who have fled Brussels for Paris. The women roam the city, intermittently uttering the phrases "I'm hungry" and "I'm cold." Throughout most of the film, the characters' similarities are emphasized through their robotic delivery of dialogue and their way of striding briskly, side by side. But their differences are emphasized once they run out of cash and decide to sing. One character (Pascale Salkin) says, "I sing off key. I yell when I sing."

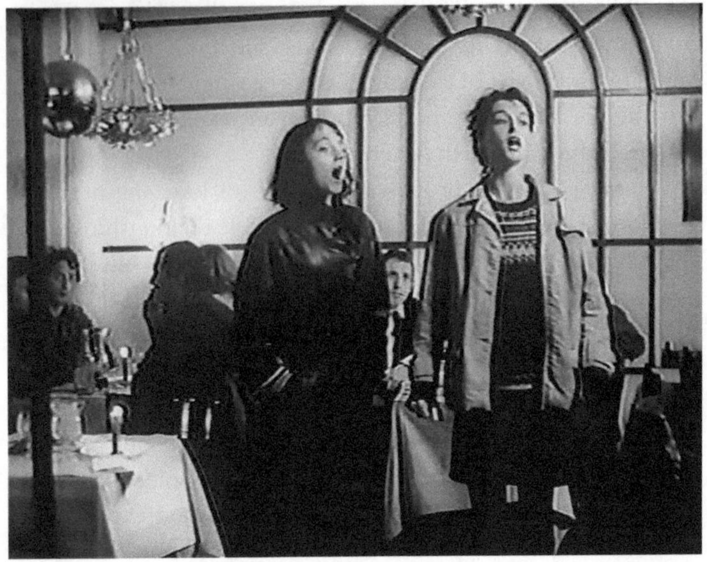

Figure 4. Maria de Medeiros and Pascale Salkin in *J'ai faim, j'ai froid* (1984)

The other (Maria de Medeiros) says, "I like to yell, and I sing in key." The young women pause in front of several restaurants to assess their appropriateness as a performance space. They go back and forth several times in their negotiation: "Chantons ici?" (Shall we sing here?). "Non, ailleurs!" (No, elsewhere!). They finally choose a restaurant and, immediately upon entering, boldly sing a snippet of Verdi (fig. 4). Their performance is another "artless" performance, somewhat akin to Akerman's humming in *Saute ma ville*. They sing "la la la" instead of lyrics, veer off-tune, and trail off into awkward pauses. And yet their performance is successful. Their audacity is riveting, and when they are asked to leave by the management, a patron invites them to dine. Later that night, one of the women loses her virginity to the dining companion. But rather than creating a suffocating atmosphere of heterosexual obligation and constraint, *J'ai faim, j'ai froid* ultimately suggests the pleasures of female friendship. Their singing voices—similar, yet different—symbolize both their solidarity and their individuality.

The two young women in *J'ai faim, j'ai froid* share a few

kisses, suggesting the possibility of a lesbian love affair, and *La Captive* employs song to express lesbian desire overtly. In this loose adaptation of *La Prisonnière*, the fifth volume of Marcel Proust's *À la recherche du temps perdu* (*In Search of Lost Time*), Akerman's use of song both references her earlier work and ventures into new territory. The film tells the story of Simon (Stanislas Merhar), a wealthy man in his twenties who is obsessed with his enigmatic lover Ariane (Sylvie Testud). She reassures him that all is well but frequently disappears from his apartment. Simon follows Ariane obsessively through the streets of Paris and the rooms of the Musée Rodin, evoking Scottie's trailing of Madeleine through the streets of San Francisco and the Palace of the Legion of Honor in *Vertigo* (dir. Alfred Hitchcock, US, 1958). Ariane's transgressions, perceived or real, crystallize around female singers. She takes singing lessons from a woman and attends the concert of a beautiful soprano (Aurore Clément).

The film's most sustained use of diegetic song occurs when Ariane steps out onto her balcony one evening to cool off from the summer heat and sings, apparently spontaneously, with a woman perched on her own balcony across the courtyard (fig. 5). They sing a duet from Mozart's *Così fan tutte*, "Ed intanto che diletto, Che spassetto io proverò!" (And meanwhile, what sport, what pleasure I shall have), in which sisters Dorabella and Fiordiligi sing conspiratorially to one another about the love affairs they are plotting and the pleasure they anticipate. Ariane responds, seemingly spontaneously, to a woman perched above on the perpendicular facade of the courtyard. The woman is behind a grated window that confines her and serves as the material expression of Ariane's captivity. McBane observes that the scene provides a link to Akerman's earlier use of the children's song in *Je tu il elle*. Mozart's lyrics "And in May as the proverb goes / Do what comes your way" recalls the children's invitation to "kiss whom you please," the lyrics employed after the explicit lesbian love scene in *Je tu il elle*.[21] But lyrics are not the only realm in which a transgressive fusion of two women is suggested and celebrated. The scene produces a contrast in female singing voices analogous to the mixture of voices in *Je tu il elle*. A trained soprano (Sophie Assante) begins singing, a cappella, and is answered by the untutored voice of Sylvie Testud. The call-and-response structure gives way to the melding of the two women's voices and offers the film's most persuasive evidence of Ariane's preference for women. Simon, ever vigilant, witnesses the women singing together from the courtyard below and seems to understand that this performance is not for him. The camera lingers while he listens in an intimate close-up that seizes on the cold, almost feminine fineness of his cheekbones, in contrast to the wider shot of Ariane that emphasizes her languid sensuality in the heat of the night. He is buttoned up, stiff and arrogant, in his trench coat, while she is exposed in a willowy nightdress. We see him looking, but his look is not returned. The gazes of the women are trained on each other, connected through their performance *for* each other as they seem momentarily to escape their respective prisons. In the context of a film full of ambiguity about characters' intentions and desires, the scene confirms Ariane's inscrutability and inaccessibility. Her erotic energy will never flow exclusively toward Simon.

Akerman once again stages a frontal a cappella female singing performance in *La Folie Almayer* (*Almayer's Folly*, France/ Belgium, 2011), her last fiction feature. The film is a loose adaptation of Joseph Conrad's 1895 novel about a Dutch trader in the jungles of Borneo. Akerman sets her story in 1950s Malaysia and explores the isolation and physical degradation of a French colonist. Early in the film, Almayer (Stanislas Merhar) forces his mixed-race daughter Nina (Aurora Marion) to leave her home to attend a European-style boarding school so that she can get a "white girl's education." The film's opening hints at the alienation that results from this action.

A powerful and perplexing performance of two songs, diametrically opposed to each other in performance style and genre, takes place on the stage of an open-air nightclub. A man lip-synchs to "Sway" (music Luis Demetrio, 1953; English lyrics Norman Gimbel) while female dancers wearing denim miniskirts stand in a line behind him, swaying inexpertly and robotically to the beat. The kitschy performance is interrupted when another man—an anticolonial insurgent, we later learn—emerges from the crowd and stabs the singer to death. The stage empties, but one woman remains, still swaying rhythmically, as if in a trance. She moves to the front of the stage and sings, in close-up and a cappella, Mozart's "Ave verum corpus." As we will soon learn, this is Nina, Almayer's daughter, who has returned home embittered and numb from her forced exile.

But before we know this, the performance of the songs alone hints at the trauma of colonialist, imposed identities. "Sway," initially a mambo instrumental called "¿Quién será?," was written in 1953 by Mexican composer Luis Demetrio. The song became a hit for Dean Martin in 1954 and has since been recorded dozens of times by singers ranging from Rosemary Clooney to Michael Bublé. In Akerman's film, the use of "Sway" evokes a hybrid, international pop culture: Mexican-Cuban dance music grafted onto American big band music infused with Dean Martin's Rat Pack finesse is transposed to a Southeast Asian outdoor bar. The strangeness of that mélange is enhanced by Akerman's use of Mozart's religious hymn, which introduces yet another musical tradition into an atmosphere where it does not seem to belong. Explaining her choice of the song, Akerman said, "I hesitated before taking Mozart's 'Ave Verum' in Latin, a Christian song in a greasy nightclub— but it's more amusing and totally out of place. It's one of the few songs I learned in school."[22] The hymn, no doubt something Nina learned at the religious boarding school she loathed, is delivered with apparent sincerity but is painfully ironic. The character of Nina is now "totally out of place" and full of quiet rage; there will be no spiritual grace for her or for her depressed, broken father. Nina's a cappella performance of Mozart in *La Folie Almayer* echoes Aurore Clément's chanson réaliste in *Les Rendez-vous d'Anna*, but here the female singer is boxed in by colonial greed and patriarchal imperatives.

Akerman's use of song is distinctive in its generic heterogeneity, its varied connections to her narratives, and its specific connection to unconventional female representation. For a director known for her minimalist visual design and sparse soundtracks, Akerman privileges the singing voice to a surprising degree, whether working in an avant-garde, art cinema, or more classical narrative register. As Akerman's career developed, her employment of song shifted. She left behind the gleeful rejection of synchronization and aural fidelity in *Saute ma ville* for the diegetic, synchronized songs of *Les Rendez-vous d'Anna*, *Golden Eighties*, and *La Captive*, employing song to represent strong emotion and to suggest human connection in films whose characters' lives are marked by solitude.

Akerman's most distinctive contribution to the mise-enscène of song is her commitment to the amateur, nonstandard female singing voice, whether that of her own or others. The untutored and "artless" female singing voice is a source of unexpected pleasure and a disruption of convention on its own, especially in Akerman's own imperfect, but exuberant, singing performance in *Les Années 80*. When Akerman combines the amateur singing voice with a trained one (in *Je tu il elle* and *La Captive*), the female singing voice suggests the capacity to connect while remaining autonomous. The female singing duo is linked specifically to lesbian love (or at least its possibility) in no fewer than three of Akerman's films: *Je tu il elle*, *J'ai faim, j'ai froid*, and *La Captive*. Akerman also links female singing performance with destruction or dysfunction, whether through the humming that accompanies domestic devastation in *Saute ma ville*, the parting gift of a chanson réaliste by a woman to her lover in an ailing heterosexual relationship in *Les Rendez-vous d'Anna*, the production numbers that express longing and disappointment in *Golden Eighties*, or the song as postcolonial critique in *La Folie Almayer*. Akerman's minimalist modernism makes room for the emotion of song, reminding us of her films' extraordinary stylistic range, her constant thirst for experimentation, and her commitment to the female singing voice as a portal to joy, longing, and rebellion.

Notes

1. Ivone Margulies, *Nothing Happens: Chantal Akerman's Hyperrealist Everyday* (Durham, NC: Duke University Press, 1996), 4.

2.   Margulies, *Nothing Happens*, 211.

3.   Akerman's vocal performance in *Saute ma ville* figures centrally in Sonia Wieder-Atherton's performance *CHANTAL?*, described in Sandra Percival's contribution to this issue.

4.   Paul Hegarty, "Grid Intensities: Hearing Structures in Chantal Akerman's Films of the 1970s," in *The Music and Sound of Experimental Film*, ed. Holly Rogers and Jeremy Barham (New York: Oxford University Press, 2017), 156–57.

5.   Barbara McBane, "Walking, Talking, Singing, Exploding . . . and Silence: Chantal Akerman's Soundtracks," *Film Quarterly* 70, no. 1 (2016): 39.

6.   Jean-Claude Klein, *Florilège de la chanson française* (Paris: Bordas, 1989), 29.

7.   Author's translation.

8.   Ivone Margulies, "Echo and Voice in *Meetings with Anna*," in *Identity and Memory: The Films of Chantal Akerman*, ed. Gwendolyn Audrey Foster (Wiltshire, UK: Flicks, 1999), 73.

9.   Kelley Conway, *Chanteuse in the City: The Realist Singer in French Film* (Berkeley: University of California Press, 2004).

10.   Claudia Gorbman, "Artless Singing," *Music, Sound, and the Moving Image* 5, no. 2 (2011): 157.

11.   Steven Shaviro, "Clichés of Identity: Chantal Akerman's Musicals," *Quarterly Review of Film and Video* 24, no. 1 (2007): 11.

12.   Shaviro, "Clichés of Identity," 14.

13.   Margulies, *Nothing Happens*, 189.

14.   Adrian Martin, "Golden Eighties," *Film Critic*, accessed 1 April 2018, www.filmcritic.com.au/reviews/g/golden_eighties.html.

15.   Shaviro, "Clichés of Identity," 16.

16.   Rick Altman, "Cinema and Popular Song: The Lost Tradition," in *Soundtrack Available: Essays on Film and Popular Music*, ed. Pamela Robertson Wojcik and Arthur Knight (Durham, NC: Duke University Press, 2001), 24–25.

17.   Marion Schmid, *Chantal Akerman* (Manchester: Manchester University Press, 2010), 81.

18. Babette Mangolte, "The Loudness of the World: Listening to What Is Out There: Sound Strategies in Akerman's Fiction and Documentary Films," *Senses of Cinema*, no. 77 (2018), sensesof cinema.com/2015/chantal-akerman/sound-strategies/.

19. Nicole Brenez, "Chantal Akerman: The Pajama Interview," trans. David Phelps, *Lola*, no. 2 (2012), www.lolajournal.com/2 /pajama.html.

20. Schmid, *Chantal Akerman*, 80.

21. McBane, "Walking, Talking, Singing, Exploding," 42.

22. Brenez, "Pajama Interview."

Kelley Conway is professor in the Department of Communication Arts at the University of Wisconsin–Madison. She is the author of *Chanteuse in the City* (2004) and *Agnès Varda* (2015). She has also published articles on popular song in Jean Renoir's films, songs in recent French cinema, the ciné-club, the installations of Jean-Luc Godard and Agnès Varda, genre and gender in sexually explicit French films, and Varda's documentaries.

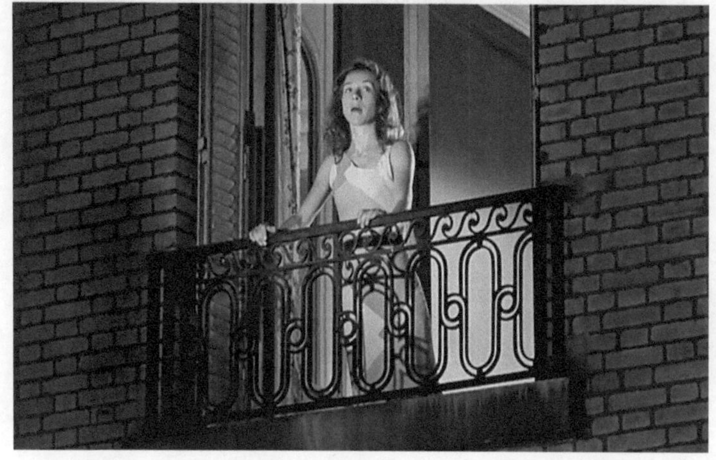

Figure 5. Sylvie Testud in *La Captive* (2000)

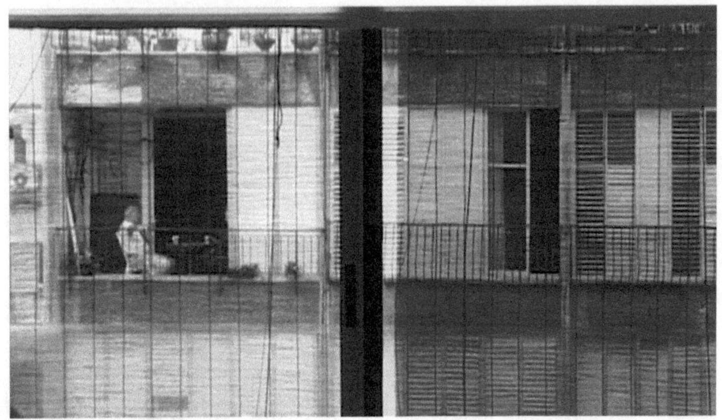

Figure 1. *Là-bas* (2006)

On the Difficulty of Forgetting: Recollections of the Basel Symposium on Chantal Akerman

Edited by Eva Kuhn and Ute Holl

In October 2016, we organized a symposium in Basel, Switzerland, in commemoration of Chantal Akerman. Through screenings of her films, as well as talks, presentations, and accounts from friends and collaborators, the event focused on issues of remembering and forgetting. In Akerman's films, history insists, returns, refuses to disappear—memories are haunting and haunt those who were and are persecuted. The conference examined Akerman's cinematic strategies of taking time to forget, transforming the traces of history into resistant forms. In working with cinematic forms of alienation, repetition, and permutation; in inventing shots that point to the lacking and the missing; in transmitting unexpected voices and sounds; and in creating hybrid forms of unadaptable identities, Akerman unflinchingly produces forms of persistent memories.

Akerman masterfully deploys comedy, drama, the musical, documentary, essay, and adaptation to depict history as a bold confrontation of catastrophe and comedy, duration and explosion. In

Camera Obscura 100, Volume 34, Number 1

DOI 10.1215/02705346-7264184   © 2019 by *Camera Obscura*

Published by Duke University Press

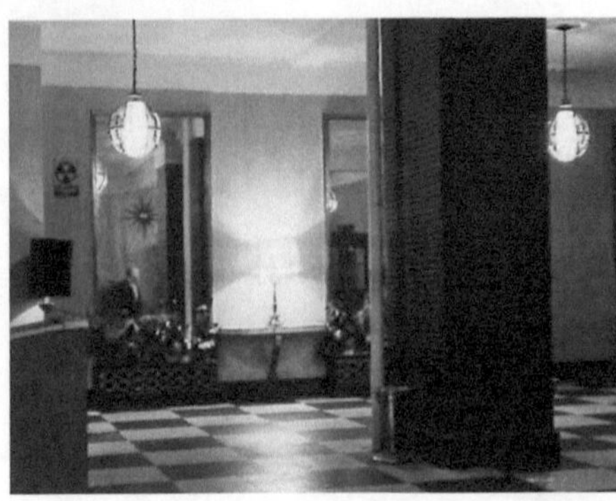

Figure 2.
Hotel Monterey (1972)

her films, outbursts of rage are dealt with silently. The everyday takes place with force. Normality breaks through unexpectedly. Everything moves calmly against the grain. In her early film *Hotel Monterey* (Belgium, 1972), shot by Akerman together with camerawoman Babette Mangolte, the camera suddenly moves after forty minutes. An exit sign appears in the corridor, but there is no way out in sight (fig. 2).

The following short texts by the participants in the symposium condense their contributions, their thoughts, and the sometimes contradictory positions that surfaced after the viewing of Akerman's films. Films served as spaces of resistance, reconsidering the boundaries of history and presence, of fiction and document, and of biography and historiography. The authors are scholars, curators, and collaborators; some were her friends; many share several of these attributes. As organizers of the symposium, we asked them to shed light on their papers by returning to the theme of the difficulty of forgetting. "My story is full of holes, full of blanks," Akerman wrote.[1] The only thing she forgets, Akerman said, are her dreams. That's not entirely true. In her films we can see her transgressing the borders of memory and projection, dreams and reality.

The Wish for Unknowing: Exhausted Finales
Ivone Margulies

Chantal Akerman's ruminative aesthetics balance the active wish for unknowing with the difficulty of forgetting. The object of forgetting changes, but the exhaustiveness of the rumination and the flight from certainty are perceptible under the surface of her characters' faces as fatigue.

Emmanuel Levinas, a philosopher with whom Akerman felt a special affinity, invested fatigue with a moral dimension, seeing it as a horizon of subjective self-consciousness, a product of effort, and a confrontation with indeterminacy.[2] This indeterminacy courted by Akerman (and manifest in her shots' irresolution and her pronouns' and deictics' ambivalence) structures the memorial dynamic she installs through her sitting "portraits."

Starting with *Jeanne Dielman, 23 quai du Commerce, 1080 Bruxelles* (Belgium/France, 1975), what is at stake for all of Akerman's tragic characters is the desire to endlessly retrace and erase what one knows. One could, of course, place pressure on the author's own thematic obsessions and ask what Simon (Stanislas Merhar) in *La Captive* (France/Belgium, 2000), Almayer (Stanislas Merhar) in *Almayer's Folly* (France/Belgium, 2011), and Jeanne Dielman (Delphine Seyrig) have in common. The last shot of each film provides some answers: these shots are protracted, and in each, the insistent focus on the protagonist produces at once a sharp image and a corresponding *horror vacui*. In these tour-de-force scenes in which barely anything happens, we watch, in a distilled form, the constitutive and destabilizing potency of Akerman's durational and cumulative strategies. The only conclusion for the films is to return their protagonists to a state of suspended, inconclusive uncertainty (fig. 3).

Working as a coda to the films, what I call Akerman's "portraits" unremittingly display characters who lose and belatedly

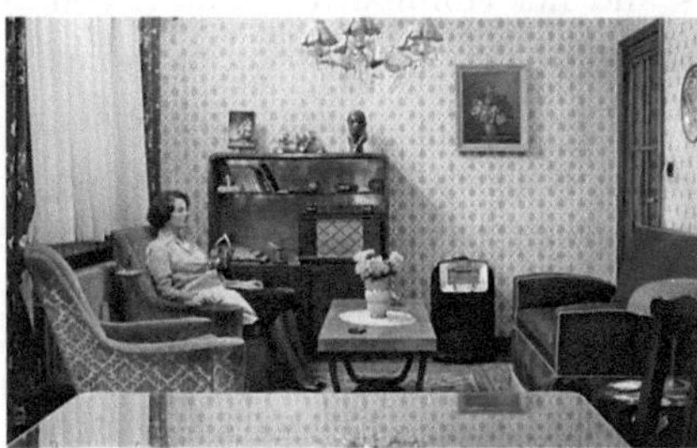

Figure 3. *Jeanne Dielman, 23 quai du Commerce, 1080 Bruxelles* (1975)

attempt to reestablish their equilibrium. It is therefore not by chance that one recognizes in the weariness of Almayer some of the gestural components of Jeanne Dielman and her breakdown.

Abandoned by his beloved daughter Nina, Almayer vows to forget her, to erase her from his mind. In Joseph Conrad's novel, he reinscribes his loss as memorial mounds of sand, covering over the footprints that Nina has left on the beach. In the film, the ambivalence between forgetting and remembering appears through the un/certainty that flickers through Almayer's maddened face. We watch him as he understands something and denies it, exposing a disjointed consciousness coming, in spurts, into being. This extended close-up has a relentless continuity, growing closer under a cold light that spells out the inescapability of the present. We can make out the mesh of tears and sunlight, the inward smile, but this visual definition comes at a cost. We fully register the character's horrific will for, and the actor's terrific performance of, unknowing.

The matrix for this oscillatory unknowing dynamic is the mother, a character in Akerman's novel *A Family in Brussels*: "Thanks to her daughter from Ménilmontant she knows what's going on . . . and with what's going on there she'd rather not think about it anyway. If she thinks about it, she starts thinking about everything that she doesn't let herself think about. She's very good at not letting herself think about what she doesn't want to think about, at least she is trying to be good at it. She's trying and it's so tiring."[3]

In rethinking Akerman in the context of the Basel conference's "difficulty of forgetting" theme, the exhausting push-pull between fusion and autonomy (with her mother) that so thoroughly structures Akerman's work and her ruminative dynamic comes to the fore. *Exhausting* refers to the tiring succession of thoughts following one another in flight so as to avoid any flash of actual knowledge—in this case, of her mother's experience at a concentration camp. But I also have in mind Gilles Deleuze's distinction, regarding Samuel Beckett, between tiredness and exhaustion: "The tired has only exhausted realization, while the exhausted exhausts all of the possible. The tired can no longer realize, but the exhausted can no longer possibilitate. . . . He exhausts himself in exhausting the possible, and vice versa."4

Akerman operates in between the psychic and the artistic notions of *exhaustive*. In true minimalist fashion, the artist exhausts the possible through alogical series, quirky dialogues, and a textured accumulation of time. Duration and seriality, formal strategies in Akerman's work, are the mechanisms of exhaustiveness, a Beckettian exercise around particularly haunting voids.

The Partition of Absence
Cécile Tourneur

In 1972, the young Chantal Akerman left Brussels for New York. Four years later, she made *News from Home* (Belgium/France, 1976), a film about her experience of exile, superimposing different spaces and time frames through sound/image disjuncture, as well as two experiences of absence (fig. 4). Akerman reads aloud the many letters she has received from her mother since arriving in New York. Her voice attempts to extend the "home" of the title from Brussels to New York (and vice versa), across geographical and temporal distance, by creating a third space, the space of the correspondence itself. The vocal interpretation of her mother's written words is an echo of her initial, presumably silent, reading of them. These painful words, rehashing the absence of the daughter, resonate as a score among the other sounds of the city: the roaring of the subway, cars passing by, a boat leaving the harbor. Those recorded sounds are the symbols of movement and travel and are, in a certain way, addressed to her mother as a replay. If Akerman's life experience at this time was impossible to describe with words, she could share it with images and sounds, as if she were trying to find her cinematographic alphabet. These repetitive noises can be connected directly to the eternal return of the voice-over, singing the same melody over and over again, with slight variations, sometimes swallowed by the *rumeur* of the city. The frenetic rhythm of the writing style and the way Akerman chooses to read the letters seem to fill up any space that

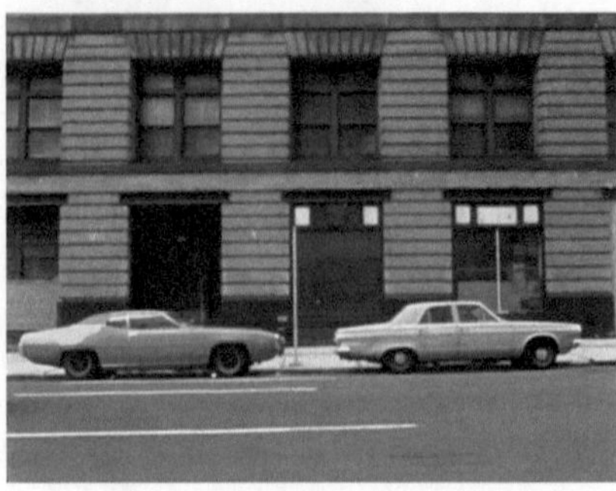

Figure 4. *News from Home* (1976)

might have been available to tell another story, one relevant to Akerman's mother's life. The words are missing. The soundtrack could have been played more slowly, but its pace fits perfectly with the emergency contained within the letters. It is halfway between the hurried discourse of her mother and Akerman's own tone and rhythm, instantly recognizable to those familiar with her work. The fragile tie between the mother and daughter exists through a common breath. Each of them is the absent one, playing simultaneously the part of the one who is longing for the other and the one who is trying to compose with her memories but never forgets.

On the Necessity of Forgetting
Alisa Lebow

Although our task was to write about "the difficulty of forgetting in Akerman's work," I feel compelled to write about its necessity. Memory and its correlate of forgetting have ample resonance in the themes and scenes of Akerman's films and installations; the invocation to remember drives much of her documentary work and her fiction films as well. Whether through the loving reenactment of her mother's gestures in *Jeanne Dielman, 23 quai du Commerce, 1080 Bruxelles* or the agonizing retracing of the length of rough Texas road on which James Byrd Jr. was dragged in *Sud* (*South*, France/Belgium, 1999), Akerman revisits sites and movements that clearly haunt her memory and in turn come to haunt ours. And yet, by her own admission, forgetting is an integral aspect of her filmmaking. Two confessional moments attest to this: first as parable, second as method.

In the beginning of *Histoires d'Amérique: Food, Family, and Philosophy* (France/Belgium, 1988), as the Staten Island Ferry approaches Manhattan, Akerman recounts the story of a rabbi: "He passed through a village to get to the forest, and there, at the foot of a tree (and it was always the same tree), he began to pray, and God heard him." Generations pass, and his progeny increasingly forget the details: first the location of the tree, then the locations of the forest and village, and eventually the words of the prayer. The great-grandson only remembers the vaguest details of the story, yet at the mere telling of it, "God heard him." Akerman admits at the end of this parable that not only does she not know the place or the prayer, but she doesn't even have children to whom to recount the story. Not knowing as a form of cultural forgetting begets its own inquiry.

The second confessional moment that institutes forgetting as a structural necessity in and for Akerman's work, and even a guide by which others might also learn to make films, is when she tells us, in the last chamber of the installation *From the East: Bordering on Fiction* (1995), that "One must write when you want to make a film, although you know nothing about the film you want to make. And yet you already know everything about it. But you don't realize this. Fortunately, I would say. Only when it is confronted with the act of making it will it reveal itself. . . . And slowly we all realize that it is always the same thing that is revealed." The filmmaker must forget what she knows in order to begin the process of making a film, which will then reveal itself as something already known, indicating the latency of memory and the compulsion to repeat. Yet it is the forgetting that is essential if one is ever to start.

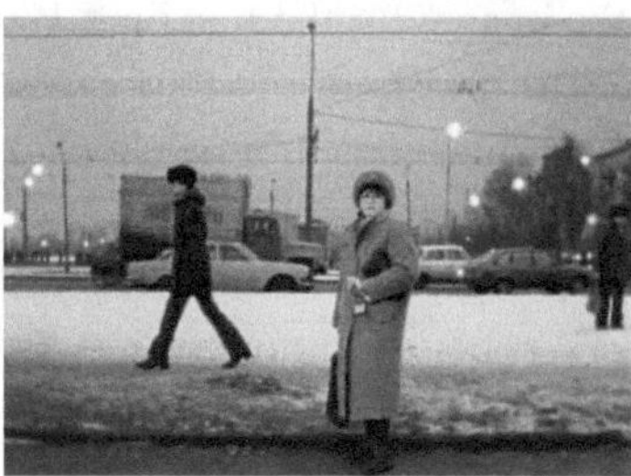

Figure 5. *D'Est* (1993)

Introduction to the Screening of *Là-bas*, Basel, 22 October 2016

Claire Atherton

I learned a lot about editing from studying Chinese philosophy. In Chinese thinking, particularly for the Taoists, efficiency is not planned in advance; it comes from the potential of a situation. That means process and effect are linked, and it also means that different layers of signification appear during the process of creation.

Each time Chantal wanted to make a documentary, she had this same approach. She needed to discover while doing. If she knew too well what she was looking for, she would no longer have the desire to make the film.

When Chantal was asked to make a documentary about Israel, she had some resistance. She said, "No, not me. Chantal and Israel: it seems a little bit too heavy." But it was too late. Something had happened; she was feeling attracted to the idea. So she went there, to Israel, with a camera. Before going, she wrote a lot of notes, but she lost them.

She arrived in the Tel Aviv apartment, and she found herself unable to go out. She looked out her window. One day she made an image, and from that moment on she felt it was not about Chantal and Israel anymore; it was just Chantal filming. Since she couldn't go out, she went on filming from her apartment, and she also did some writing every day. One day she went out, and she filmed on the beach.

When she came back to France, she called me to look at the images with her. She gave me the tapes and her writing, and she said, "Let's see if something is possible." It was always a very powerful moment when we discovered the images for the first time. We wouldn't talk very much. Sometimes we gave names to the images. I usually wrote the names and our impressions in a notebook. I recently found this notebook, so I can tell you some of the names: the plant man, the wife of the plant man, the woman with the Marlboros, the workers, the sea, the workers between the curtains, the yellow building, the neighbor of the plant man, the woman from across the street, the building of the plant man, the neighbor's building, the building with plastic, the son of the woman with the Marlboros, the neighbors on their balcony . . .

When we heard the first phone call in the rushes, we felt there should be other calls, so we recorded them and added them during the editing. We did the same thing with the sounds of everyday life. It wasn't a decision that was made in advance; it came during the process. Chantal was very receptive to chance. For instance, one day I was racing through some footage of a night sequence from the plane, and it occurred to us that the speed created tension. So we decided to use it in the film.

There is one last thing I would like to tell you. One day—I think it was about the fifth day of the edit—Chantal had an appointment and wasn't there. I began to look at the images, and I couldn't connect with them at all. It's not that they were not well filmed; it's just that I wasn't feeling any tension. I began to worry. I started wondering if my response to the images had been linked to Chantal's presence next to me. Then at one point in the rushes, the phone rang, and I heard a man's voice answer and say: "No, Chantal is not here today. I am filming a little bit by myself." I was incredibly relieved. When Chantal came back, I told her what had happened, and she smiled. I think she liked this story.

When a Scene Breaks into Song
Eva Meyer

One might think that Chantal Akerman's *Golden Eighties* (France/ Belgium/Switzerland, 1986) is her attempt to tap into an easygoing genre. She wants to get "away from the camps," which cast a shadow over her life because of her mother's history as a Holocaust survivor. She says: "I felt so trapped that I wanted but [to] breathe. These days I'd rather sing." She longs "for lightness. I've come to a point in my life where I want to be lighthearted."[5] But her gay and colorful film doesn't satisfy the expectations of a musical comedy when it brings up an event that surpasses it: love or the burden of the past, whose repetition forms the series within which this musical comedy unfolds. And we realize that a leap into the future can turn around so far back in time that it leads to the camps after all.

We need song and dance to understand this leap better. If there is an inexplicable event here, it will not be reconstructed. It is transferred to a rhythmic monotony that eludes the piety of memory by generating a collective tension and a collective spell. These do more than disenable the usual cinematic flashbacks of personal memories. They replace them, though without effacing their ramifications in time, which now involve numerous people, breaking down the individual law of causality into false continuities. These hold on to those tensions. They insert themselves into the tensions and carry on working with singing and dancing bodies. They get close to the point where the secrets of memory, of dream, and of time intermingle and where the real and the imaginary become indistinguishable.

Though we are given a story as a narration of memory, that story is punctuated by ruptures regulated by dance and song. These ruptures mutualize the distances and overcome blame cultures. We discover a work of nonrepression that neither talks nor keeps still. Through singing and dancing, *Golden Eighties* passes from the narrative to the spectacular and enters another world, another person's dream or past. This work is not a personal capacity of remembering, nor is it a collective story. It is a transference that divides and loses and recovers itself as an incommensurable or free and indirect relation.

Food or Family?
Mathias Lavin

The difficulty of forgetting in Akerman's cinema can be examined in relation to the representation of food. As a social event, the meal can underline the filmmaker's relationship to a historical and familial heritage, as Maureen Turim points out in "Forgetting to Eat: A Commemoration" in this collection. In this respect, the subtitle of *Histoires d'Amérique* is indeed telling: *Food, Family, and Philosophy*.

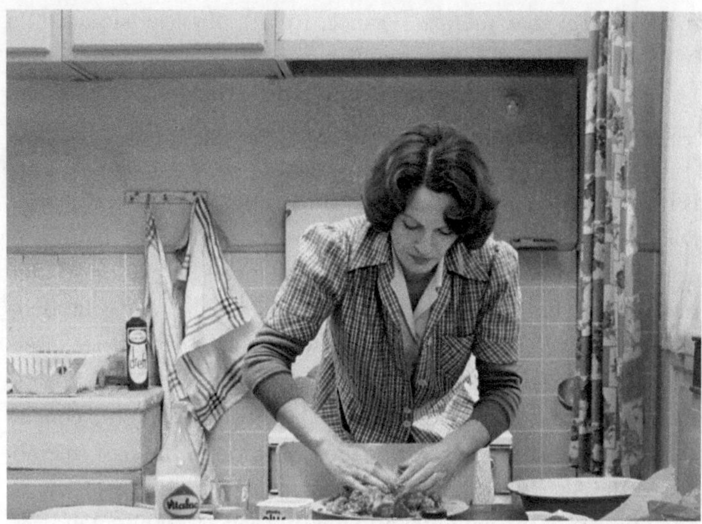

Figure 6. *Jeanne Dielman, 23 quai du Commerce, 1080 Bruxelles* (1975). Courtesy of Janus Films

From *Saute ma ville* (Belgium, 1968) to *No Home Movie* (Belgium/France, 2015), a culinary motif is recurrent: spaghetti with tomato sauce in *Saute ma ville* (the same meal returns in *Portrait d'une jeune fille de la fin des années 60 à Bruxelles* [France, 1993]); steak and fries, sandwiches with butter and cheese or Nutella in *Je tu il elle* (Belgium/France, 1974); potatoes, veal cutlets, and meatloaf in *Jeanne Dielman* (fig. 6); chicken, pizza, and clam soup in *A Couch in New York* (France/Belgium/Germany, 1996); and so on.

Although Akerman's cinema is deeply autobiographical, religious dietary restrictions that would connote her family's Eastern European Jewish origins rarely appear. One exception occurs in *Histoires d'Amérique*, perfectly described by Turim, during the sequence in an outdoor restaurant where (mostly) elderly men tell Jewish jokes. This collective meal also stands out because Akerman's characters often eat alone. The heroine of *Saute ma ville* locks the kitchen door as if she wants to eat in radical isolation. More comically, in *L'Homme à la valise* (France, 1983), the character avoids the man she's hosting and prefers to have breakfast alone. Sometimes the food theme implies the impossibility, sometimes the refusal, to eat. The reason can be economic (the two girls without money in *J'ai faim, j'ai froid* [France, 1984]), physical (stomach flu in *Là-bas* [Belgium/France, 2006]), or more enigmatic (in *Demain on déménage* [France/Belgium, 2004], the protagonist and a man visiting her apartment are unable to eat a piece of chicken).

Food has a profound ambivalence in Akerman's films: it is nutritious and repulsive at the same time. Just think of Jeanne Dielman holding the veal cutlet with the extremities of her fingers as if the meat were a disgusting rag. The meals have a social value in this film, but they occur in silence or melancholic solitude—like in many of Akerman's other works. *No Home Movie* offers another interesting example with its numerous sequences showing Akerman and her mother eating and conversing. But the conclusion confirms the ambivalence: the evocation of the past (memories of the Akerman family reconstructed by the stories, questions, and answers of the daughter and her mother) is less about its preservation than about the beginning of mourning, as time is always lost.

Beyond the Windowpane: *Les Rendez-vous d'Anna*
Ute Holl

The sounds of train wheels hitting rails and of footsteps on hard floors dominate *Les Rendez-vous d'Anna* (France/Belgium/Germany, 1978). A cold light illuminates the images of train stations and searchlights on platforms, a functional light, as in train compartments or hotel rooms near train stations. "How are things in Germany?," the mother of the film's protagonist Anna (Aurore Clément) asks, as they talk in a station restaurant. Strangely, Anna answers with a smile: "There are curtains everywhere, there are tulips on every table, and . . . it is full of Germans." No trouble, no inquietudes. The second time in the film that Anna will smile is at the end when she sings the song of the suicide lovers.

There is no film on Germany in the seventies that is comparable to Akerman's relentless protocol of absence in *Les Rendez-vous d'Anna*. Shot by shot, the film captures the dark side of Germany's new wealth. Symptomatically, in the city of Essen, Anna is

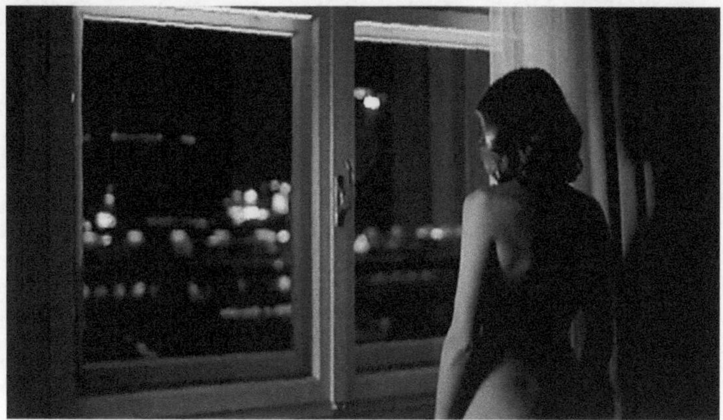

Figure 7. *Les Rendez-vous d'Anna* (1978).
Courtesy of Janus Films

constantly hungry but unable to eat. She cannot participate in this country.

When she enters a hotel room, Anna draws the curtains, and a traveling camera follows her in a horizontal plane. On the other side of the window, there are again tracks and trains. When she opens the windows, the sounds of wheels and screeching brakes fill the room. Anna's movement of opening the curtains will be repeated at nighttime while she stands naked after she has thrown a German man named Heinrich out of her bed and room. Again, she is faced with transportation: with trains moving and people looking away.

Les Rendez-vous d'Anna is a portrait of a country and a people complacently self-absorbed, including perpetrators rehabilitated in a society of good citizens: an ice-cold image of Germany in brownish colors presents the reality of a country that has chosen to ignore the atrocities committed by its population. The film assembles symptoms. In its precision it proves, shot by shot and sound by sound, that the stuff of history was very present in the 1970s: in the shape of the trains, in the texture of the curtains, in the design of coffee cups and wallpaper, in the tulips on the table, and in the constant mentions of good food. As Ivone Margulies shows, Akerman's film can be seen as an account of Jewish experience, battling with speech and voice to counteract history as written by its winners.[6]

In the repeated opening of curtains there is, I feel, another dimension to the film. Akerman has construed an interface, a windowpane, opening toward the cruelties of persecution and murder committed against Jewish communities, families, and people that need to be acknowledged before any form of reconciliation can take place. But the film shows that, in reality, the curtains were not drawn, not in Germany in 1978. A country of refusal and dumbness is portrayed. As is the despair of a filmmaker.

Forgetting to Eat: A Commemoration
Maureen Turim

אַלץ קען דער מענטש פֿאַרגעסן נאָר ניט עסן.
Alts ken der mentsh fargesn nor nit esn.
A person can forget everything but eating.

This Yiddish saying, marking the centrality of eating in Jewish culture, tears at the heart in remembering the films of Chantal Akerman, in commemorating the brave film artist, author of an installation whose title places her inside an empty refrigerator. "Nisht fargesn," the Yiddish for "Do not forget," so close to the German phrase, summons the issues of Jewishness I addressed in my Basel conference presentation that is here elaborated as an essay. Empty refrigerators, forgetting to eat, eating compulsively: immediately these evoke the constellation of eating scenes in Akerman's films that Mathias Lavin addresses as well in his comments on "Food or Family?" in this collection. For example, the compulsive sugar-eating out of a paper bag in *Je tu il elle*'s first section accompanies the performative and conceptual display of writing as an apparent writer's block spreads fragments discarded across the floor. I wrote of this before, in "Personal Pronouncements in Two Akerman Films," and return to it now to rethink this sugar compulsion, this incorporation of reduced nourishment, as cinematic ritual.[7] As I noted in that essay, this scene is echoed in the third segment of the film, as Akerman's character Julie eats jam at the former lover's apartment, an action reminiscent of Marie and the miser confronting each other as she tries to eat his jam from a jar in *Au hasard Balthazar* (dir. Robert Bresson, France/Sweden, 1966).

Food figures repetitively in so many of Akerman's films, such as the food offered by two of the elderly Shoah survivors she interviews in *Dis-moi* (France, 1982), the minutely followed preparation of food in *Jeanne Dielman, 23 quai du commerce, 1080 Bruxelles*, and the kitchen table eating scene in *No Home Movie*. Here in this brief commemoration, I note both the running jokes about eating and the recurrent accounts of the tragedy of starving as depicted in *Histoires d'Amérique*, which bears the English subtitle *Food, Family, and Philosophy*. The monologue scenes, rendered by actors full face to the camera, tell of the dire struggles of immigrants to the US: a man who almost mercy kills his dying wife, only to rethink his action when she gasps for breath, tells us: "And she was hungry, she wanted to eat. And she began to get better." In addition, there is the woman who tells of a period of despair when "her husband couldn't feed" their two children, evoking the absence of food as a dire experience of poor immigrant Jews. Interspersed with these food-laced tragedies are comic dialogues, many also about food, that culminate in a long final sequence set in a restaurant, though staged outdoors like all the other scenes. The philosophy emanating from food stems equally from the comic Jewish humor scenes and from the tales of coping with economic difficulties.

Encapsulated (Hi)Stories
Eva Kuhn

In *Jeanne Dielman, 23 quai du Commerce, 1080 Bruxelles*, there is a tension between, on the one hand, the brilliant superficiality and bold visibility created by the hyperrealistic recording of everyday textures and details (fig. 8) and, on the other, a disturbing opacity caused by the complete absence of classical narrative or explanatory logic. And then there is the long duration of the images, their

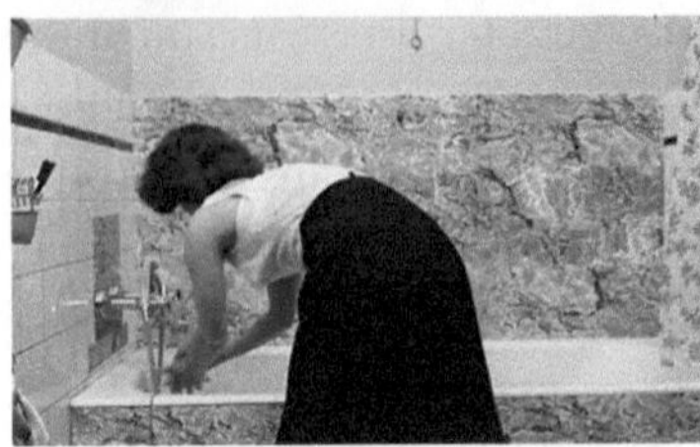

Figure 8. *Jeanne Dielman, 23 quai du Commerce, 1080 Bruxelles* (1975)

insistence on surfaces and on the rhythms of succession that work independently of the underlying story. In this manner, a presence is created that refuses to go away and that seems as if it could break open and escape at any moment.

Akerman's cinematic oeuvre bears witness to a longing for the everyday, which is not a matter of course, as her films clearly show us. Uniform sequences, patterns, recognizable rhythms, long lapses of time, repetitions, and routines characterize their structure and content. The films deal with the disruption of these rhythms and act it out. Things are subtly brought out of balance or the rhythm is interrupted; monotony is gradually derailed or an order abruptly explodes. The reason why remains open.

The mother never reveals much of her story—neither in *Jeanne Dielman* nor when directly confronted by the daughter's little camera in her last and most intimate film, *No Home Movie.* In this film, signs of her dwindling life are intermittently interspersed with images from the desert. In an interview famously held in her pajamas shortly after her stay in Cambodia, Akerman talks about the book of Exodus and the forty years that the Jewish people spent in the desert to cast off the marks of slavery.[8] It's a story about taking one's time to forget. In the case of the concentration camps, some survivors say that three generations are required.

Madame Dielman's history and the history of her neighbor—the histories of all the characters in Akerman's films—are embodied and thus internalized. History is encapsulated in people as experience. Akerman's films discern the symptoms of these experiences on the surfaces of the visible world—on faces, bodies, landscapes, city streets, and building facades. At the same time, her films show us the strength with which people offer resistance to these experiences. The neighbors on the balconies of the building adjacent to her apartment in Tel Aviv summon this resistance to the violence of history—by talking, smoking, sitting, drinking, and watering their plants (*Là-bas*). Or by filming, like the subject, respectively the auteur of these films who expresses the bigger historical picture in forms that are reduced and introverted to the greatest possible degree. This reduction lets us see film as a membrane on which inside and outside, private and public, (auto) biography and world history meet. Film—as a materially concrete, audiovisual perception—turns out to be the interface on which all these oppositions converge.

Endings
Heike Klippel

Like *Saute ma ville* and *Jeanne Dielman, 23 quai du Commerce, 1080 Bruxelles, News from Home* has a very clear ending: New York's slow disappearance in the fog, seen from the ferry leaving Manhattan (fig. 9). The extreme slowness seems to blind us to what happens: the disappearance conceals itself from us, and we are consigned to a state of an eternal too-late, confronted with the unpalatable fact that all our gaze can do at this speed is to compare an after with a remembered before. The gaze necessarily creates artificial differences because it can't keep pace with the fluidity of the change. The constant draw of the water, the ceaseless shrinking and gradual disappearance of what appears to be the only city left in an inhospitable world—all this simulates a sort of painless drowning.

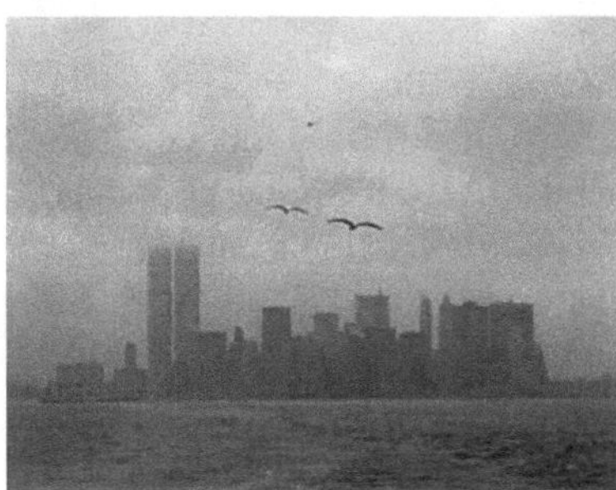

Figure 9. *News from Home* (1976)

As at the ends of *Saute ma ville* and *Jeanne Dielman*, there is a death here, too. It is the result not of a linear development but of the negation of what has gone before. To understand these negations in terms of mortality is to follow Emmanuel Levinas's notion of death as absolute antagonism. For him, death is something so entirely different that it cannot be grasped: the absolute future, the astonishing, always outwits the present. Death "becomes the limit of the subject's manfulness. . . . What is important about the approach of death is that at a certain moment we are no longer *able to be able*. It is exactly thus that the subject loses its very mastery as a subject."[9] But what might this mean for a female subject who has neither potentiality nor mastery to lose? Of what does her Other then consist? Akerman replaces mastery with serial repetition of attempts to take control and, when they fail, of attempts to find compromises. Her films illuminate different kinds of compromise: in *Saute ma ville*, fragmentation and the renunciation of productivity; in *Jeanne Dielman*, an unattainable fulfillment; in *News from Home*, a patient biding of time that seeks to spellbind its object. The figurations of death at the ends of these films throw this seeming passivity into relief and thereby subvert it. Instead of trying to point to some heroic, absolute Other, they stage cessation as an end that knows not whether it should mourn for what happened before or for what was impossible before—for what it has missed.

Notes

1. Nicole Brenez, "Das Pyjama-Interview," *Retrospektive Chantal Akerman*, ed. Astrid Ofner, Claudia Siefen, and Stefan Flach (Vienna: Schüren, 2011), 14.

2. As Alphonso Lingis comments: "Consciousness appears to Levinas as constituted in the horror of the indeterminate. The insomnia that endures the night is the very experience of this horror." Lingis, translator's introduction to Emmanuel Levinas, *Existence and Existents* (The Hague: Martinus Nijhoff, 1978), n.p.

3. Chantal Akerman, *A Family in Brussels* (New York: Dia Art Foundation, 2002), 9–10.

4. Gilles Deleuze, "The Exhausted," trans. Anthony Uhlmann, *Substance* 24, no. 3 (1995): 3.

5. Brenez, "Das Pyjama-Interview," 19.

6. See Ivone Margulies, *Nothing Happens: Chantal Akerman's Hyperrealist Everyday* (Durham, NC: Duke University Press, 1996).

7. Maureen Turim, "Personal Pronouncements in Two Akerman Films: *I . . . You . . . He . . . She* and *Portrait of a Young Girl at the End of the 1960s in Brussels*," in *Identity and Memory: The Films of Chantal Akerman*, ed. Gwendolyn Audrey Foster (Carbondale: Southern Illinois University Press, 2003), 9–26.

8. Brenez, "Das Pyjama-Interview."

9. Emmanuel Levinas, *Time and the Other*, trans. Richard A. Cohen (Pittsburgh, PA: Duquesne University Press, 1987), 74.

Claire Atherton is a film editor born in San Francisco. She was attracted when very young to Taoist philosophy and visual ideograms. In 1986, she started working with Chantal Akerman, which triggered a thirty-year collaboration on Akerman's films and installations. Atherton also works with a wide range of directors and artists.

Ute Holl is professor for media studies and media aesthetics at Basel University. Her research focuses on the history of perception, the epistemology of audiovisual media, a media history of acoustics and electro-acoustics, and experimental film and the wider field of memoryscapes. Publications in the field are *Cinema, Trance, and Cybernetics* (2017) and *The Moses Complex: Freud, Schoenberg, Straub/ Huillet* (2016).

Heike Klippel is professor of film studies at the Braunschweig University of Arts. She coedited *Poisons and Poisoning in Science, Fiction, and Cinema* (2017) and *Film als Idee/Film as Idea* (2016), a bilingual edition of the writings of experimental filmmaker Birgit Hein. She is also coeditor of the feminist film journal *Frauen und Film*.

Eva Kuhn is currently senior lecturer in art history and film studies at the Leuphana University in Lüneburg. From 2008 to 2017, she worked as lecturer at the Institute of Art History at the

University of Basel, Switzerland. She earned her PhD with the thesis "Living—Filming: Jonas Mekas's Cinematic Life Work" (publication forthcoming). Among her recent publications are *Élie Faures Cineplastik oder vom Kino und Bilden der Künste* (2016) and *Im-Mobile Kadragen zwischen Lebenswelt und Kunst – zwei kinematografische Figuren von Chantal Akerman* (2018).

Mathias Lavin is senior lecturer in film studies at the University of Paris 8. He has written several books on Manoel de Oliveira (e.g., *La Parole et le lieu: Le Cinéma selon Manoel de Oliveira* [2008]), as well as a short essay on snow in the cinema ("L'Attrait de la neige" [2015]). He edited with Diane Arnaud *Ozu à présent* (2013) and, with Christa Blümlinger, *Geste filmé, gestes filmiques* (forthcoming).

Alisa Lebow is a film scholar and filmmaker who teaches film studies at University of Sussex. Her most recent project, *Filming Revolution* (2018), is an interactive Web-based inquiry into filmmaking in Egypt since the revolution (www.filmingrevolution.org).

Ivone Margulies is professor of film studies in the Film and Media Studies Department at Hunter College, City University of New York. She is author of *Nothing Happens: Chantal Akerman's Hyperrealist Everyday* (1996), coeditor with B. Ruby Rich of a dossier on Akerman for *Film Quarterly* (Fall 2016), cotranslator with Flora Süssekind of *Uma família em Bruxelas* (2017), editor of *Rites of Realism: Essays on Corporeal Cinema* (2003), and author of *In Person: Reenactment in Postwar and Contemporary Cinema* (2019).

Eva Meyer is a philosopher, writer, and filmmaker based in Berlin. She is the Eberhard Berent Visiting Professor and Distinguished Writer in Residence at New York University. She has written numerous books ranging from *Zählen und Erzählen: Für eine Semiotik des Weiblichen* (1983, reprint 2013) to *Legende sein* (2016). She has also written radio dramas and films with Eran Schaerf, from *In the Habit: A Set Piece* (1997) to *Rehearsing Europe* (forthcoming).

Cécile Tourneur has a doctorate in the history, aesthetics, and science of cinema and the audiovisual from Université Paris 8. She wrote her dissertation about the "voice system" in Jonas Mekas's films through an interdisciplinary approach. She is pursuing research about voice in documentary, and she works as a lecturer in the art center Le Jeu de Paume in Paris.

Maureen Turim is professor of film and media studies in the
Department of English at the University of Florida. She is author
of *The Films of Oshima Nagisa: Images of a Japanese Iconoclast* (1998),
Flashbacks in Film: Memory and History (1989), *Abstraction in Avant-Garde
Films* (1985), and *Desire and Its Renewal in the Cinema* (forthcoming).
She has published over one hundred essays in journals and books,
including on Akerman.

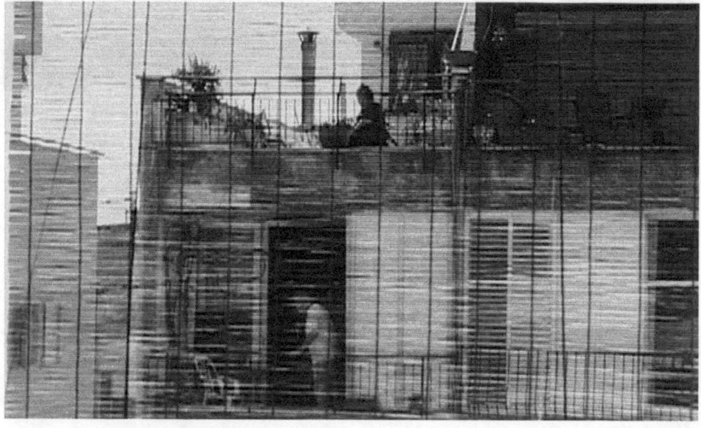

Figure 10. *Là-bas* (2006)

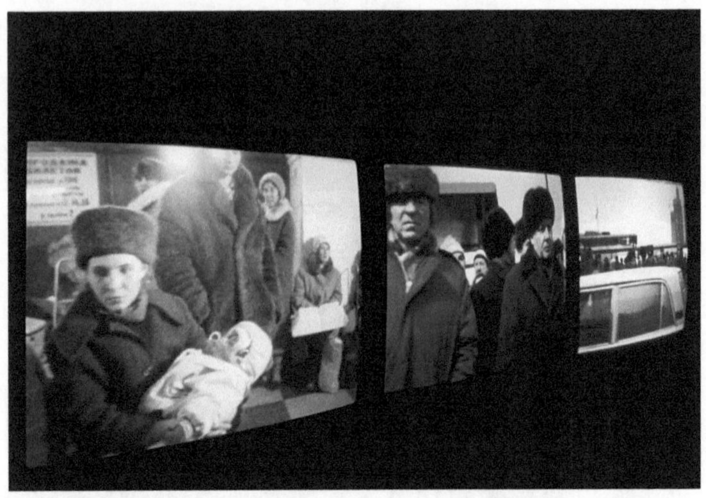

Figure 1. Chantal Akerman, *D'Est, au bord de la fiction*
(*From the East: Bordering on Fiction*) installed at Ambika P3,
University of Westminster. Installation made from the
film *D'Est*, two rooms, 24 + 1 monitors, color, sound, loop.
Photograph by Michael Mazière

Chantal Akerman in London

Michael Mazière

> Curating is not so much the product of curators as it is the
> fruit of the labor of a network of agents. The outcome is a stir-
> ring of smooth surfaces, a specific, multi-layered way of agitat-
> ing environments both inside and outside the white cube. The
> curatorial involves not just representing but presenting and
> testing; it performs something here and now instead of merely
> mapping something from there and then.
> —Maria Lind

Chantal Akerman was one of the first independent filmmakers
to engage with the gallery space in the mid-1990s, expanding
her audience and addressing issues of installation and visual art.
Akerman's work pursued a critical investigation into geography
and identity, space and time, borders, itineraries, identity, and
states of mind.

    Since 2013, Akerman's work has been at the center of a
series of interconnected projects in London involving retrospective
screenings, in-person presentations, symposiums, a major exhibition,
an international conference, and a publication. This Akerman
project, which grew spontaneously, was initiated by A Nos Amours
(curators and filmmakers Adam Roberts and Joanna Hogg), who

Camera Obscura 100, Volume 34, Number 1

DOI 10.1215/02705346-7264196　© 2019 by *Camera Obscura*

Published by Duke University Press

presented an exhaustive retrospective of Akerman's film and video works.[1] More than forty films in twenty-five screenings were programmed at London's Institute of Contemporary Arts over a two-year period from 26 September 2013 to 22 October 2015. Many of the films were translated and subtitled live for English-speaking audiences for the first time and shown in the format most similar to the original. Akerman attended a number of screenings in person to introduce the films and take questions; most screenings were sold out.

Following the screening series and developed to coincide with the premiere of her latest film, Ambika P3 presented the major exhibition *Chantal Akerman: NOW* in its central London underground space from 30 October to 6 December 2015. The exhibition was jointly curated by Ambika P3 (Michael Mazière) and A Nos Amours and presented in association with the Marian Goodman Gallery.[2] Subsequently, the Centre for Research and Education in Arts and Media (CREAM) at the University of Westminster organized a two-day conference to celebrate and critically explore the work and legacy of Chantal Akerman.[3] The conference took place on 4–6 November 2016 and included keynotes by Janet Bergstrom (UCLA), Sandy Flitterman-Lewis (Rutgers University), Parisian filmmaker and critic Dominique Paini, Griselda Pollock (University of Leeds), Adam Roberts, and Corinne Rondeau (University of Nimes). Their papers, including a selection of papers from the conference, and new material, will be published in an issue of the *Moving Image Review and Art Journal* due out in 2019.[4]

These connected manifestations of Akerman's work developed through a combination of serendipity, commitment, and collaboration on the part of all the participants. They were driven by the desire to find new audiences for an important artist who had been in the shadows and to give renewed critical attention to alternative and radical film and video practices overlooked by changes in the economy, politics, and dissemination of the moving image.

The exhibition was born of a meeting between the duo A Nos Amours (who had been curating the retrospective of Akerman's single-screen work), Rosie Thomas (who had directed the

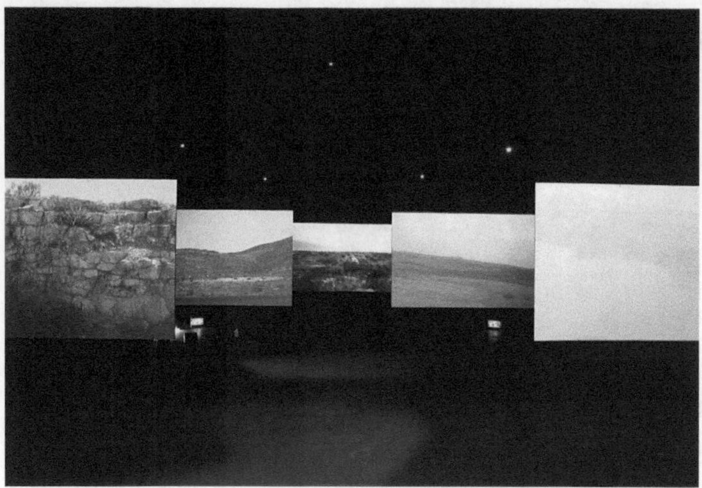

Figure 2. Chantal Akerman, *NOW* installed at Ambika
P3, University of Westminster. Seven-channel, HD video
installation, color, five soundtracks, mono and stereo.
Photograph by Michael Mazière

research group and brokered the meeting), and me (the curator
of the Ambika P3 space). The site of the exhibition, Ambika P3,
has a special significance: it is an unusually large postindustrial
venue, neither a public-funded space nor a commercial gallery but
a public-facing site for experimentation and research under the
auspices of the University of Westminster. Unlike such venues as
museums, galleries, and cinemas, this multidisciplinary, industrial
site enables the exhibitions to operate at arm's length from the
physical boundaries of the white cube and the black box and from
their ideological constraints.[5]

I knew Akerman's early, iconic works of the 1970s, particularly her experimental films *News from Home* (Belgium/France,
1976), *Je tu il elle* (Belgium/France, 1974), and *Hotel Monterey* (Belgium, 1972), and had only recently connected with her later work.
Her installation work was largely unknown in the UK and rarely
shown there. We hoped that Akerman would be interested in
exhibiting with us because of the eclectic nature of our program

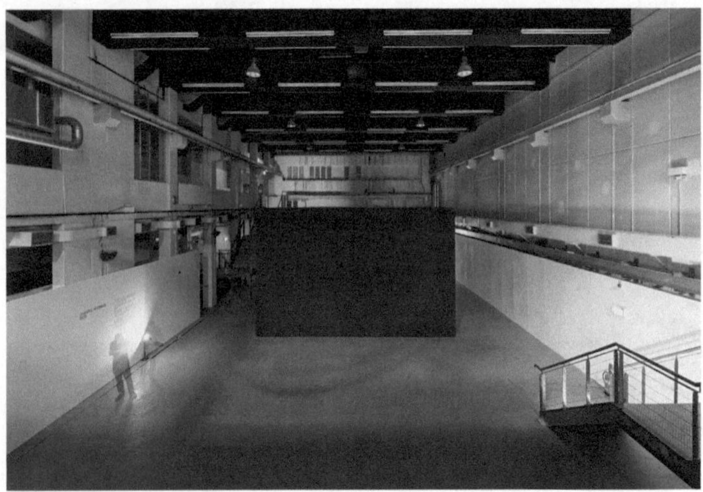

Figure 3. Chantal Akerman, *NOW* installed at Ambika
P3, University of Westminster. Seven-channel, HD Video
installation, color, five soundtracks, mono and stereo.
Photograph by David Freeman

and its reputation for risky innovation, and also because the collaboration had the potential to present a substantial retrospective of her installation work for the first time in the UK.

Following and complementary to the major two-year retrospective of her single-screen works at the Institute of Contemporary Arts, this exhibition was to take the audience through an itinerary of her installation work in a bespoke design, including, as its centerpiece, the UK premiere of a new commission by Marian Goodman Gallery titled *NOW* (2015), a multiprojection work shot in the Middle East. The exhibition would include seven of her nine large-scale installation works, and the opening would coincide with the UK premiere of her new film, *No Home Movie* (Belgium/France, 2015), on 30 October 2015, at Regent Street Cinema, London.

I first met Chantal Akerman in May 2014 at our first production meeting in Ambika P3. For most of the meeting, she talked with great frankness about her personal life and the impact of her mother's recent death. She mixed the political and the personal, disinterested in boundaries as ever. Developing the exhibition was challenging because, first, many works had complex and precise requirements in terms of space, projection, and sound; second, Akerman was living in Paris and was not always accessible; and third, the configuration of *NOW,* which was in development for the Venice Biennale, kept changing.

At our meetings, Carole Billy, the exhibition manager at the Marian Goodman Gallery in Paris, always accompanied Akerman and played an invaluable role as a go-between during the eighteen months of development. Many variations on the layout, design, and selection of works took place over that period—Akerman wanted the audience to travel through her works in the space as she had traveled through the world making them. She had a distinct idea of how each work should be positioned in relation to the next and a specific itinerary in mind for the audience. So, the logics of space, sound, content, and scale were not the only guiding factors in the layout—they all came into play within the framework of her imaginary itinerary. She was forceful yet open to suggestions, new ideas, and strategies for the exhibition.

The curatorial process was collaborative. The curators working on the project had to share knowledge and communicate regularly in order to produce a selection of work and a design of the space that would facilitate the audience's engagement in dense and demanding artworks. The decision to present seven substantial works meant that we had to build a very large, made-to-measure construction to museum standard.

NOW opened at the Venice Biennale in May 2015.[6] After the Venice Biennale, we pursued the development of the Ambika P3 exhibition project with the support of Akerman's gallery and designer. Akerman came back to the gallery on 15 July 2015, and we spent the day finalizing all aspects of the exhibition. I noticed that her hair was cropped short and uneven. She said she had cut it herself. We walked around the Ambika P3 space together and then set up a chair for her—she sat in the middle of the vast bunker.

Akerman's work is very subjective while at the same time consistently in flux, formally and conceptually. The project was developed in a manner that suited Akerman's way of working—that is, not fully conceptualized from the outset but open to a form of process-led production. That type of flexibility is possible only if the curation is approached as it was, as a development and dialogue with the artist. It took time—two years from start to finish.

There were seven works at Ambika P3, but the centerpiece was *NOW*, which consisted of a multichannel video installation with surround sound.[7] *NOW* was different from what we anticipated. It was a larger, more ambitious piece, devoid of people and the many different visual forms and styles Akerman had used in her earlier works. It was a breakthrough work, a departure. That is why we gave the exhibition its name. For this work, Akerman collected images from desert regions, specifically violently contested regions in the Middle East. She aimed to present the current condition of violence and conflict as lived experience. The stillness of much of her work—which is often concerned with interiority, domestic spaces, and forgotten and erased histories—is here replaced by the clamor of war and amplified noise. Upon entry to the exhibition, one was assaulted by a densely layered soundtrack of birds, screams, helicopters, gunshots, explosions, and wind, while on five hanging Perspex screens were projected a suite of films of the empty desert shot from a moving car. It was mesmerizing and hard for the audience. She told me she wanted to transmit "the claustrophobia of war." At the back stood two fake Chinese fish tanks surrounded by colored neon. Maybe they proposed an antithesis to the violence of the installation, but not for long. The densely layered and sometimes overbearing soundtrack operated as the driving narrative and the images functioned as backdrops—she had inverted the conventional hierarchy of sound and image. Other works in the exhibition spanned from 1995 to 2013 and investigated a variety of emotive themes such as the US-Mexico border (*A Voice in the Desert*, 2002), the atom bomb and Hiroshima (*Maniac Summer*, 2009), women reclaiming images of themselves (*In the Mirror*, 2007), the dichotomous relationship between presence and absence (*Maniac Shadows*, 2013), the Eastern bloc countries before the fall of communism (*D'Est, au bord de la fiction*, 1995), and the dark (*Tombée de nuit sur Shanghai*, 2007).

The final design dedicated the main space to *NOW*, which the audience would access last, as Akerman wished. In the lower side of the space we fitted five works, and on the mezzanine we

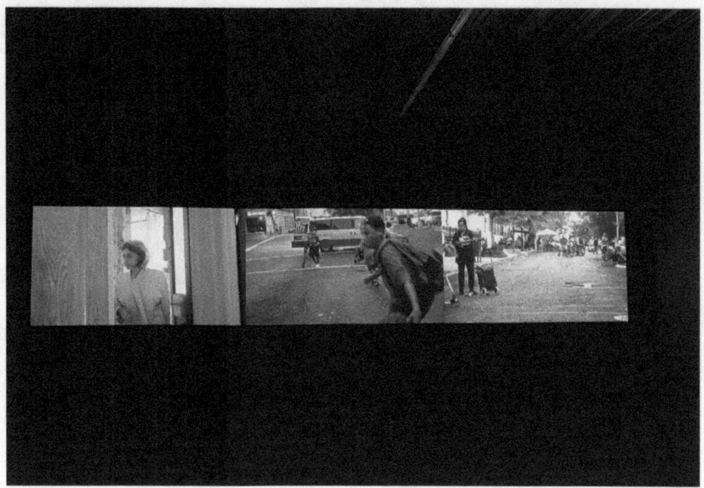

Figure 4. Chantal Akerman, *Maniac Shadows* installed at
Ambika P3, University of Westminster. Three-channel
video installation, color, sound, and a grid of 96 C prints.
Photograph by Michael Mazière

placed her earliest work, *In the Mirror*, excerpted from a 1971 film
with a portrait of a woman looking at her naked body in the mirror
and commenting critically on her body. This design allowed the
audience to have a beginning and end point and, in the lower space,
a more open territory to traverse. The open territory provided the
appropriate nomadic itinerary among a borderless grouping of
works that could be navigated in a nonhierarchical way. The form
of the exhibition was then suited to its function and offered the
audience a way into Akerman's life experiences and art strategies.

Chantal Akerman disappeared on 5 October 2015, just
short of a month before the opening of the exhibition. The immea-
surable tragedy of Akerman's suicide is not a matter for this essay.
Her absence during this crucial preproduction and build leading
to the opening of the exhibition meant that a number of contin-
gencies had to be put in place on short notice. Carole Billy from
Marian Goodman Gallery and Claire Atherton (Akerman's film
editor and collaborator) came on site to advise on construction
details, and Pascal Willekens from Vidi-Square (who had previ-

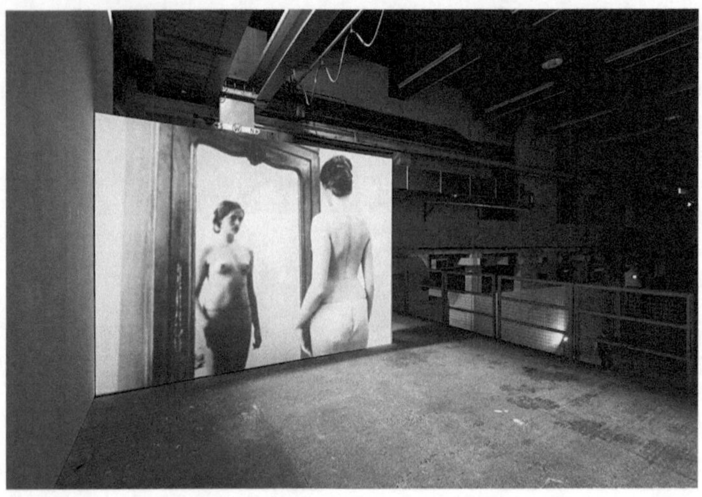

Figure 5. Chantal Akerman, *In the Mirror* installed at
Ambika P3, University of Westminster. Single-channel
video projection with sound (16mm transferred to video).
Photograph by Michael Mazière

ously installed some of the works) also came to help on the build. This was a difficult moment that tested all involved, and it was some compensation to see the public, the press, and our colleagues engage so strongly with Akerman's complex work. The exhibition made visible Akerman's contemporary installation work to a broad UK audience, most of whom knew her for her cinema, and also provided some comfort for the global community as well as her close friends and family.

The project seen in its totality and in its process, with its multiplicity of outputs and the collaborative dedication of the partners, has become a fitting testament to the strength of Akerman's work. For the exhibition, the formal and aesthetic presentation was the result of a flexible and experimental strategy. It was also Akerman's response to the qualities offered by the Ambika P3 space, the openness and flexibility of the structure, and her ability to exploit its industrial site.

In her absence, the exhibition was delivered exactly as we had planned it with her, so that the audiences, the press, and the art world would experience Akerman's rarely seen installation work as she had wished. It was extremely well attended and extensively covered by the international press. Akerman was not a conceptualist; she developed her work through process, always questioning her own decisions and aiming to meet the extraordinarily high standards she set herself for all her works.

Chantal's voice, her face, her body, her life, her past, her ancestral past—all these are, for those of us who have traveled through her work, now imprinted on us forever.[8]

Notes

1. A Nos Amours, founded by Joanna Hogg and Adam Roberts, is a curatorial artist-led initiative launched in 2011 to promote and explore the conditions of film and spectatorship at a critical time of change for the screening and experience of moving images. Hogg is a renowned film director and screenwriter who has won numerous awards for her feature films, including *Archipelago* (UK, 2011) and *Exhibition* (UK, 2014). Roberts has made a distinctive body of film work, in particular with such dancers and choreographers as Sylvie Guillem and Jonathan Burrows, and has been supported by the British Films Institute, the National Lottery, and the UK Film Council.

2. *Chantal Akerman: NOW* was funded by the Arts Council England, Marian Goodman Gallery, and the University of Westminster. Production credits include Mohammed Ali, Claire Atherton, Carole Billy, Heather Blair, Andrew Leslie Heyward, Christian Marti, Christian Newton, Jonathan Samuels, Pascal Willekens, and the Vidi-Square team.

3. CREAM comprises thirty-five researchers and over sixty-five PhD students. The 2014 Research Excellence Framework considers the group the UK's leading research center in art and design, with 95 percent of the research judged as world-leading or internationally excellent.

4. The *Moving Image Review and Art Journal* is an international peer-reviewed scholarly publication devoted to artists' film and video and its contexts. It offers a forum for debates surrounding all forms of artists' moving-image and media artworks: films,

video installations, expanded cinema, video performance, experimental documentaries, animations, and other screen-based works made by artists. The journal aims to consolidate artists' moving images as a distinct area of study that bridges a number of disciplines not limited to but including art, film, and media. The Akerman issue will be the first of our new coeditorship of the journal at CREAM (coeditors Lucy Reynolds and Michael Mazière).

5. Ambika P3 was developed in 2007. Artists who have addressed the site include Anthony McCall (2011), David Hall (2012), Ilya and Emilia Kabakov (2013), Victor Burgin (2013), and Elizabeth Ogilvie (2014), with solo exhibitions, and Jasmina Cibic, Federico Díaz, Lynn Hershman Leeson, Rémy Markowitsch, Lindsay Seers, and Tunga with the group exhibition *Casebooks* (2017).

6. The installation commission *NOW* was exhibited at the Biennale as part of the Arsenale exhibition *All the World's Futures* curated by Okwui Enwezor, which opened on 6 May 2015.

7. Works in the exhibition were *In the Mirror*, single-channel video projection with sound (16mm transferred to video); *A Voice in the Desert*, single-channel video projection with sound; *Maniac Summer*, four-channel video projection, with sound; *Maniac Shadows*, four-channel video projection, two soundtracks, ninety-six images; *Tombée de nuit sur Shanghai*, single-channel video projection with sound and two Chinese lanterns; *D'Est, au bord de la fiction* (*From the East: Bordering on Fiction*), twenty-four monitors and one single monitor, with sound; and *NOW*, seven-channel video projection with surround sound.

8. Joanna Hogg and Adam Roberts, "Chantal Akerman: Extraordinary Artist of the Everyday Who We Will Miss Forever," *Guardian*, 8 October 2015, www.theguardian.com/film/2015/oct/o8/chantal-akerman-feminist-film-maker-died-retrospective.

Michael Mazière is an artist and curator, currently reader in film and video at the University of Westminster. His practice encompasses the production of artworks, the curation of exhibitions, lecturing, and writing about artists' film and video. He is the cofounder and curator of Ambika P3, an experimental research space for international contemporary art, an active member of the Centre for Research and Education in Arts and Media, and coeditor of the *Moving Image Review and Art Journal,* an international peer-reviewed scholarly publication devoted to artists' film and video and its contexts.

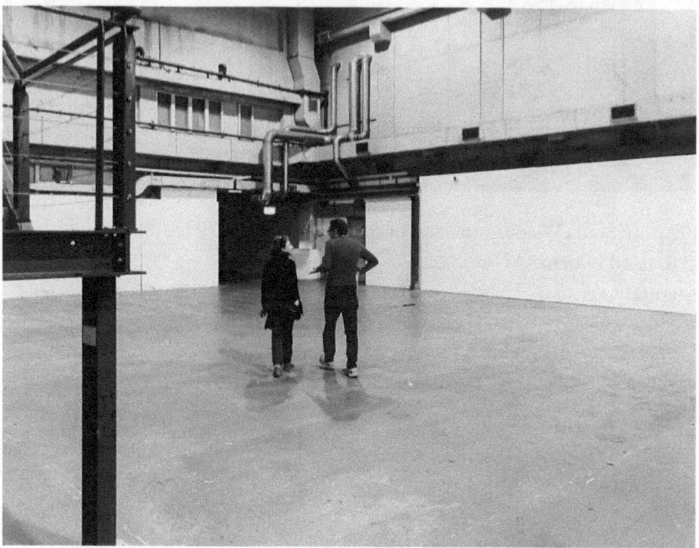

Figure 6. Chantal Akerman and Michael Mazière at Ambika P3, University of Westminster, 2014. Photograph by Joanna Hogg

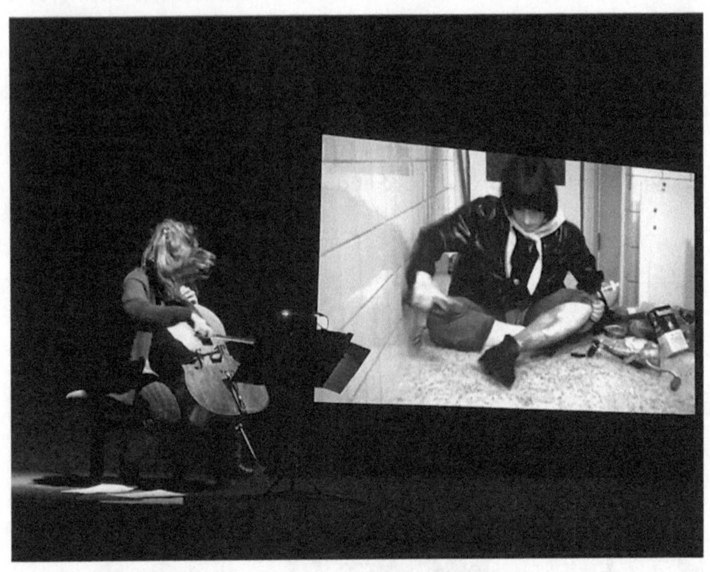

Figure 1. Sonia Wieder-Atherton performing *CHANTAL?* (2018).
© Renaud Bouchard-Gonzalez. Courtesy of Fondation
Chantal Akerman

CHANTAL? A Dialogue with Sonia Wieder-Atherton

Sandra Percival

Sonia Wieder-Atherton's live performance *CHANTAL? Dialogue between a movie, a cello, and a text* (2018) was the culmination of Zena Zezza's Chantal Akerman film and event series in Portland, Oregon (June 2016–May 2017).[1] In *CHANTAL?*, Sonia plays in conversation with Chantal in the director's first film, *Saute ma ville* (*Blow Up My Town*, 1968), interwoven with Chantal's spoken words from her fictional stream-of-consciousness text *A Family in Brussels* (1998) (fig. 1).

    CHANTAL? and this dialogue began with a letter I wrote in July 2016 to cellist and composer Sonia Wieder-Atherton, Chantal Akerman's collaborator and life partner for more than thirty years. I recounted finding Sonia time and again while researching the artist project season *LOOKING, REALLY* LOOKING! *The Films of Chantal Akerman 1968–2015* and its integrated series of performative events.[2] I knew Sonia had a special, inside view of Chantal. I wanted to hear her cello. I extended an invitation to come to Portland. Her short response was, "I am very moved to read your letter. I should come to you."

Camera Obscura 100, Volume 34, Number 1

DOI 10.1215/02705346-7264208   © 2019 by *Camera Obscura*

Published by Duke University Press

Chantal and Sonia collaborated in myriad ways, beginning in 1983, on nearly twenty films, installations, and live performances, while each maintained her own sphere, an artistic pas de deux. This exchange with Sonia about her collaboration with Chantal began in a public conversation at the Oregon Jewish Museum and Center for Holocaust Education on 2 May 2018, held in conjunction with the Portland performances of *CHANTAL?*

Our onstage conversation was structured around clips from Chantal's films. We continued to talk and write for the next two months, between Paris and Portland, working around Sonia's international performance schedule. Her visit, her performances, and our exchanges since 2016 were compelling and filled with emotion; hers is a rarely heard voice among those who speak so knowingly about Chantal Akerman. Beside the filmmaker, for decades, was Sonia. In her own words:

CHANTAL? is deeply inspired by what happened in our two apartments, one above the other, in Rue Henri Chevreau in Paris, France, when I played and Chantal wrote. The images mingled with the words, and the words with the music.

The text that follows combines our onstage interview, our subsequent e-mail correspondence, and my own observations on Chantal and Sonia's collaboration. For publication we organized the dialogue by artwork. My framing texts are followed by Sonia's accounts of how their collaboration shape-shifted over time. Next to the film titles are Chantal's own, pithy descriptions.[3]

We preface with the proviso that memory is our guide. Fact may tell a different story.

Les Années 80 (*The Eighties,* 1983). "Song."

Golden Eighties (1986). "It took five years. *Les Années 80* was a test-run."

Sandra Percival: In a scene from *Les Années 80*, Chantal vigorously and joyfully conducts a recording of Magali Noël singing:

"I'd leave too, I'd drop everything, burn my bridges, I'd walk away naked. Even to Moscow . . . since love is stronger than all." This clip of Chantal opened the Portland conversation as a way to pose the question: who was conducting their collaboration?

Sonia Wieder-Atherton: The scene from *Les Années 80* says a lot about Chantal's physical implication in her work. Chantal always had head, heart, and body functioning together. She loved musical comedy, which shows in *Golden Eighties*, the film that grew out of *Les Années 80*. Chantal loved the idea of performing live on the stage. Sometimes she even said she dreamt of being a rock singer. Her head functioned very fast and very intensely; it had to go and live through her body.

Before discovering my work with the cello, she wasn't interested in classical music. She listened to my interpretations and when she watched me searching for a rhythm, a color, a contrast, or the form of the work, she discovered the emotional power of music. Suddenly it began to enter her universe.

Percival: Chantal wrote the script and all the lyrics of love and longing for *Golden Eighties*, in which Sonia accompanies Delphine Seyrig singing "Cette nuit."

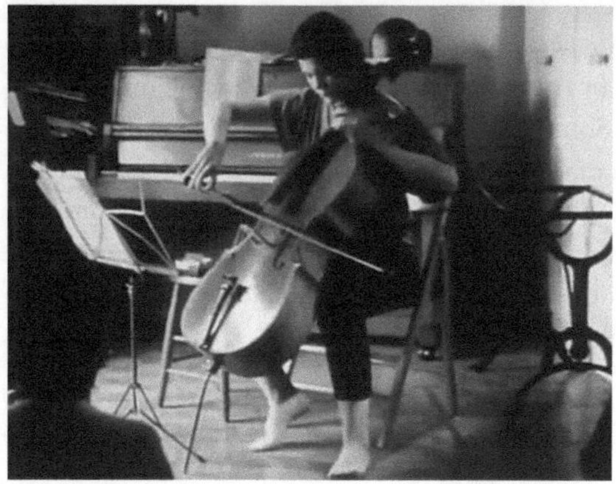

Figure 2. Sonia Wieder-Atherton in *Portrait d'une paresseuse* (1986)

***Portrait d'une paresseuse* (*Sloth,* in *Seven Women, Seven Sins,* 1986).** "Sonia works, I stay in bed."

***Rue Mallet-Stevens* (1986).** "I play at being pilot."

***Trois strophes sur le nom de Sacher* (*Three Stanzas on the Name Sacher,* 1989).** "Sonia's debut."

Percival: Sonia appears playing the cello in several short films by Chantal that we watched to prepare this dialogue. In these, Chantal positioned Sonia within constrained domestic interiors.

Portrait d'une paresseuse is set in a small apartment. In one shot is Chantal, in another, Sonia. In editing that shifts from one to the other, Chantal, in a messy room, procrastinates getting out of bed. Sonia, barefoot and in a T-shirt, busily practices her cello (fig. 2). Chantal slips into her shoes and gets up to smoke a cigarette, a moment to deflect the day.

Rue Mallet-Stevens is filmed within Villa Mallet-Stevens, the house where the French modernist architect Robert Mallet-Stevens lived on the street that bears his name. Sonia appears in a corner near the entrance playing a composition by Henri Dutilleux. A figure (Chantal, the "pilot") lurks around the corner and behind her, smoking and holding flowers wrapped in plastic (fig. 8). The film ends as the bow and a red rose drop together to the floor.

In *Trois strophes sur le nom de Sacher,* Sonia plays three cello solos composed by Dutilleux for the Swiss conductor and impresario Paul Sacher. Sonia plays in a parlor saturated in color as people move in and out of view through the windows behind her. Chantal told Sonia, "Imagine you come home from an evening out, you don't get changed, you hang up your coat and play as though the party was still going on in your imagination."[4] Dutilleux came to this shoot (fig. 3).

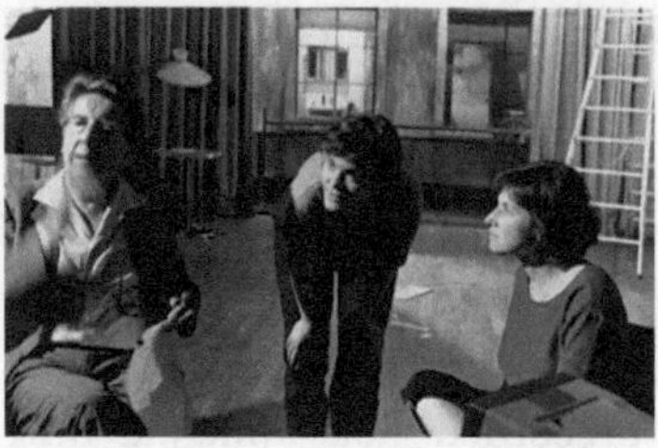

Figure 3. Henri Dutilleux, Sonia Wieder-Atherton, and Chantal Akerman (from left) on the set of *Trois strophes sur le nom de Sacher* (1989). Courtesy of Bertrand van Effenterre, Mallia Films

Histoires d'Amérique (*Food, Family, and Philosophy*, 1988).

"The Jews. (In exile, as usual.)"

Percival: In *Histoires d'Amérique*, the cello is heard but not seen. Chantal's images and stories shaped Sonia's music, and Sonia's research into the singing of the hazzan later enters her repertoire. The film begins with a shot from the Staten Island Ferry across the water to lower Manhattan in the mist and fading light. We hear a blurring of distant voices whispering in Yiddish and other Eastern European languages as lights from the city's skyscrapers draw nearer. Chantal's voice is heard telling the story of a rabbi's prayer, and as her voice fades, a cello begins to play. This clip of the voices and the prayer that repeats through generations began our onstage conversation on how voice and music were structured in *Histoires d'Amérique*.

Wieder-Atherton: After the story of the prayer ends, I play the *Kol Nidre* on the cello, and the rhythm of my phrases follows the movement of the boat. Jewish stories have no name. They change through the different people who tell them, remember them, and tell them again.

Percival: *Histoires d'Amérique* is set outside in an abandoned plot in Brooklyn. There are scattered tables, lights, and umbrellas, there's feasting and dancing. A theatrical scene. Chantal cast a group of largely unknown Jewish actors to perform the stories of first- and second-generation Jewish immigrants directly to the camera.

Wieder-Atherton: I came to see Chantal during the shoot, and she said, "I would like to have the voice of your cello." I began by listening to the singing of great hazzan. I listened to their psalmodies, their improvisations, which were sung with intense expressivity. These songs are usually built in three parts: a prayer at the beginning, then a dance or a lively conversation, even a fight sometimes! And, at the end, back to the prayer. Among them, of course, was *Kol Nidre*. I would discover a song and try to get close to it with my bow, in the breathing of the music making. Chantal and I chose the songs, and then I recorded them while watching the images and hearing the voices of the actors.

One man I would sing with, play the cello with another. I remember the scene where an old man began to sing the Yiddish song "Oyfn pripetshick" [On the Cooking Stove] at the end of his monologue. After the song ends, he raises his head, looks up at the stars, and says, "What a beautiful night!" At that moment, he chose to live; he could have chosen differently. I accompanied him on cello, as if to cradle him from far away—and disappeared when he looked up at the sky.

Working on the music for *Histoires d'Amérique* opened up something, allowing me to understand why I had chosen to study in Moscow. Russia is the place on Earth where the string playing is most vocal. I knew then that somewhere inside myself there was a very strong connection with the art of the hazzan. Through this work with Chantal, I discovered a part of my own story, on my mother's side. But I didn't know it then. Sometimes you understand something of your life looking backward.

D'Est (*From the East,* 1993). "An evocation of war. Implosion."

D'Est, au bord de la fiction (*From the East: Bordering on Fiction,* 1995).

D'Est in Music (*From the East in Music,* 2005).

Percival: Their collaboration on the 1993 film *D'Est* influenced the future work of both Chantal and Sonia. Like *Histoires d'Amérique,* Sonia came to the project after Chantal's filming. *D'Est* is Chantal's first essay film, shot while traveling across Eastern Europe—from the former East Germany, through Czechoslovakia, Hungary, Poland, and across Russia toward

Moscow—just as the Soviet system was about to collapse. There is no narration or dialogue in *D'Est*, but there are voices, discontinuous and never subtitled: the voices of people waiting outside in the cold, in train stations with their belongings, and crowding together at the closed door of an official building. In many scenes, music is heard.

At the Portland event, I shared several clips from the film—a girl in her apartment listening to a record player, an ensemble playing on stage while people gather to dance, and a cellist. I wanted to know from Sonia where the music in the film came from.

Wieder-Atherton: The soundtrack is mostly synchronized sound. I love the scene with the young girl in her pajamas, preparing a little dinner for herself and eating a "buter brod s kolbocoy" [bread and sausage] while listening to music on the radio (fig. 4). The way Chantal films, and the look between her and this young girl. . . . She could be that person, and that person could be Chantal. That's why we experience Chantal's films so deeply.

There are moments when the direct sound is very strong. One is when Natalia Shakhovskaya (my Russian teacher in Moscow) plays the cello, an aria by Boris Tchaikovsky, in the "Mali zal," the mythic concert hall of the Moscow Conservatory where all the great musical interpreters of the world played. Chantal, to whom I had told the story of many people coming to thank their beloved artist by offering a few flowers—the cost of which was often the equivalent of a month's work—recreated that scene to shoot for the film.

Or the dancing scene. It's like a dream piece. In a very

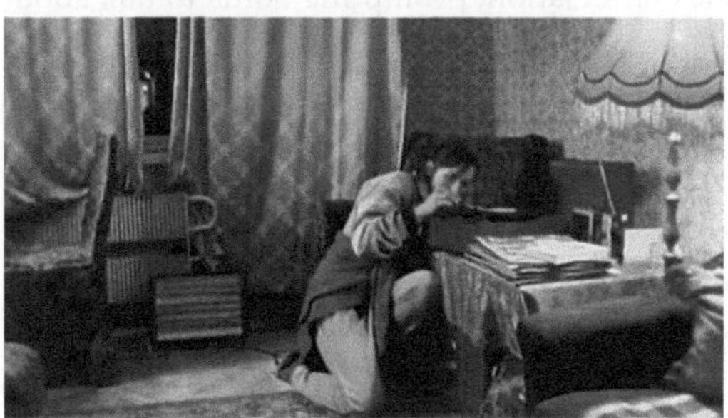

Figure 4. A still from *From the East* (*D'Est*, 1993), a film by Chantal Akerman. Courtesy of Icarus Films

grand hotel in the center of Moscow, some ordinary Russian people, dressed up for a Sunday evening, dance to an orchestra playing "musique de variété" [popular music]. It's very moving; they are so ill at ease in their nice clothes but still really enjoy the moment. The contrast between this gorgeous palace room, where one can only imagine what was going on before the revolution, and people dancing within it—Chantal liked this moment a lot.

We worked together on the music that was added after the film was shot. Like Feodor Chaliapin, the Russian singer, singing the *Massenet Elegy* in a Moscow station. Along with the existing sounds, the overlays of music were more like adding a color.

Percival: In *D'Est*, Sonia's music embraces the poetry of Chantal's cinematography and submits to the sound of the scenes Chantal captured. The film evolved into Chantal's installation work, *D'Est, au bord de la fiction*. In the last of three rooms in which the work was installed, a monitor showed a nighttime image of street lights with a voice-over of Chantal reading in Hebrew and English. The text quotes the Second Commandment's prohibition against the making of graven images and connects images in *D'Est* with "old images of evacuation, of walking in the snow with packages toward an unknown place."[5] While Chantal reads, Sonia's cello begins playing, again the *Kol Nidre*.

Sonia's live performance, *D'Est in Music*, evolved more than a decade later. Sonia scored the music of Russian composers over the ambient voices and sounds of the film, shifting *D'Est* from the big screen to the live stage. Images of *D'Est in Music* were projected in our public conversation, prompting Sonia to talk about how her work transformed the film.

Wieder-Atherton: The film *D'Est* haunted me. I wanted to add the music that the people seen in the film might have had in their heads. My idea was to project fragments of the film onto a large black tulle veil and to position myself on cello, and Laurent Cabasso on piano, barely lit, behind this transparent screen to give the impression that we were part of the film, performing within its scenes. The audience thus sees excerpts from *D'Est* in another dimension on stage (fig. 5). The first scene I worked on

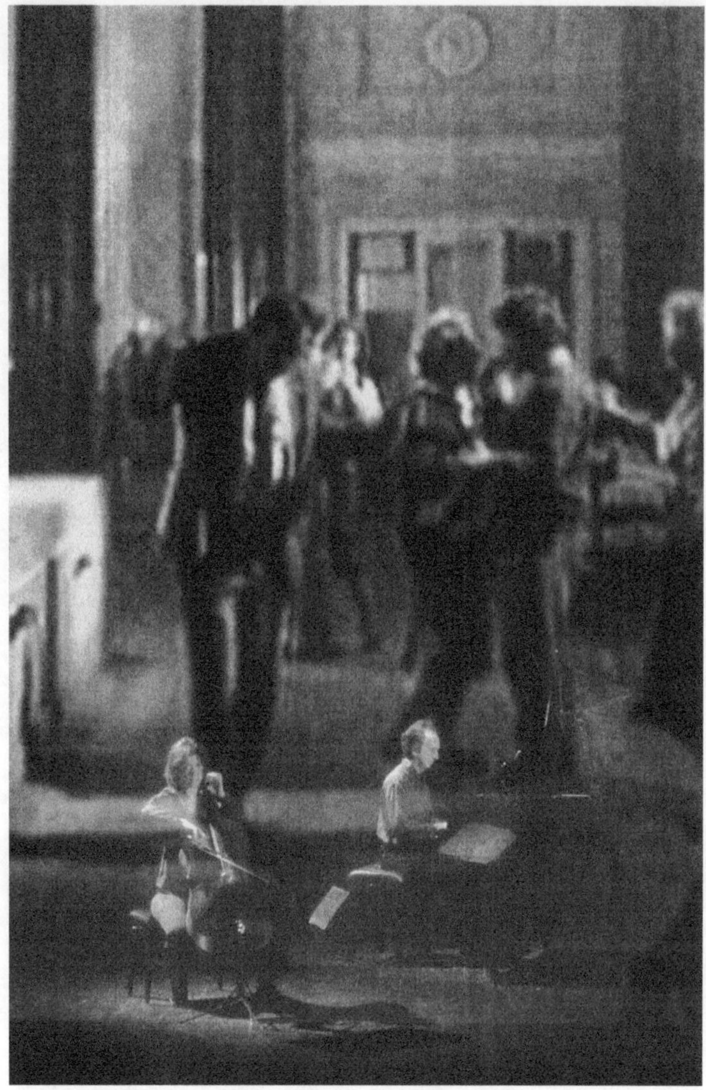

Figure 5. Sonia Wieder-Atherton performing in *D'Est in Music* (2005). Courtesy of Fondation Chantal Akerman

is where Chantal follows the cars in the yellow lights of Moscow. Alfred Schnittke's sonata emphasizes the menacing edge of Stalinist architecture, the yellow light from lampposts in streets and station lobbies. When I chose Sergei Rachmaninov's sonata, I had in mind the people waiting, or trudging along snow-covered streets, who are mute in the film. And yet, for life ultimately winning out, I play Sergei Prokofiev's adagio for the people dancing in a dream, at times in step, then out again.

After I finished I told Chantal, "Come and see it." She came and said, "I want to be part of it." And she was. She produced a new edit of the film. She loved it so much that when we performed it together, she would kick out the lighting man and play with the light—"whoosh," "whoosh!" Suddenly it would be light in the white marble hall of Kievsky Station in Moscow, and then again, outside, in the dark. Chantal followed the music with her eyes. She was painting.

Avec Sonia Wieder-Atherton (_With Sonia Wieder-Atherton_, 2002). "Sonia again."

À l'Est avec Sonia Wieder-Atherton (_In the East with S.W.A._, 2009). "Sonia again."

Percival: Chantal and Sonia's shared passion for the live stage in _D'Est in Music_ is seen in _Avec Sonia Wieder-Atherton_ and _À l'Est avec Sonia Wieder-Atherton_.[6] These films reveal a collaboration of equals, merging cinematography, cello, and a repertoire originating in _Histoires d'Amérique_ and _D'Est_.

The forty-one-minute _Avec Sonia Wieder-Atherton_ opens with a blue light, moon, and stars cast over the stage with Sonia playing _Jewish Prayer_. The film ends with Franz Schubert's _Litany for the Feast of All Souls_ (1816). Chantal's voice opens the film:

They say that Sonia Wieder-Atherton chose the cello because it is a string instrument whose sound she can make last a long time. _It's true._ . . . They also say that stages seem too narrow when she comes on them. _It's true._

The staging in *Avec Sonia Wieder-Atherton* is minimal: Sonia sitting on a chair with her cello and a music stand on a parquet floor. Sonia occupies the center of the frame, but Chantal narrows the space, filming her as the sides of the room close in. In another shot, Chantal's frame becomes two-dimensional, filling a portion of the black surround with a grainy portrait of Sonia on cello. The camera then reveals two projections side by side in the black surround as first a grand piano, then two cellos, join Sonia.

Wieder-Atherton: Chantal and I chose a program that would fit the parameters of the producer, ARTE France. The films could not be too long, and they had to have a specific musical program. The constraints made it like a game with a set of strict rules from which a sense of freedom would nonetheless emerge. Being filmed by Chantal is like living in the frame for the duration of the film, even though there are moments when you want to break out and escape. I remember Chantal telling me that she would film from far away at the beginning as if she dare not come closer. She inserted a game to play with the musicians, playing with the frames, adding more and more musicians, and daring them to escape from each other. Her almost immobile perspective allowed time to unfold. It could not do otherwise; that time is the music.

Percival: The second film, *À l'Est avec Sonia Wieder-Atherton*, draws directly from *D'Est* but is conceived entirely as a musicscape, staged and filmed live in a Warsaw radio studio with the Warsaw Symphony accompanying. Sonia is poised on an elliptical stage with tall bamboo poles rising in groves on the edges: a chaotic assemblage of music stands, black light stands of varying heights piercing upward, and planes of black tulle dividing the cellist and other musicians. In one scene we revel with Alexander Tcherepnin's *Tartar Dance*; the cello and wind instruments play; one interrupts the other as the tempo increases, until they end in unison. In the silence before the clapping begins, we hear the moving of chairs and the frame freezes. In our conversation, I asked Sonia how she would describe this musicscape.

Wieder-Atherton: The music, *Songs From Slavic Lands*, sits at the crossroads of where cultures converge. The musicians and songs come from Russia, Czechoslovakia, Hungary, Moravia, Slovakia, and more. It does not have a geographic or a formal logic. It goes from tragic singing to a lullaby, from a short love song to a longer form, from a lied telling a dream to a frantic dance. The musicians move us across terrains of the mind—Leoš Janáček's *Moravian Folksongs*, Zoltán Kodály's *Rondo Magyar*, Prokofiev's *Field of the Dead*, Ernst von Dohnányi's *Ruralia hungarica*, and Bohuslav Martinů's *Variations on a Slovak Folksong*. The languages and accents hold the history of their people. Music says what it is impossible to describe. There are two challenges: one is remembering their language, and the other is speaking what has been forbidden.

Percival: In *Avec Sonia Wieder-Atherton*, Sonia begins to tell her own story: "I was born in San Francisco, and the house where we lived in Berkeley had an upright piano. I spent my time at the piano, tapping away, looking for sounds." For this dialogue, I asked Sonia to tell me more, as we already know so much about Chantal in her own voice.

Wieder-Atherton: I was eight when we moved to France. My strongest memories of the States are linked to sounds from my childhood; I remember the different ways of talking in the North and South. My father, who was American teaching American studies at New York University, left everything to follow my mother's desire to return to France, where she later taught philosophy.

My mother was born a Romanian Jew in Bucharest. Her family escaped Romania just in time, and after a year living in Palestine, they arrived in Lebanon, where they stayed during the war. They left Lebanon for France when she was about eighteen. My mother never talked about her past, about Judaism, or her parents. Something in the transmission was broken, as it is for so many Jews. She wanted to forget. The only person who knew about her life before France was Delphine Seyrig, who was like a sister to my mother.

When I worked on the Jewish liturgical music for *Histoires d'Amérique*, I discovered how the story of my mother and her Judaism were deeply inside me. There is a family secret about why my grandmother, Florica, stopped playing the piano—she had even played professionally—but my grandmother would never mention music. After learning this part of my own story, I decided to add "Wieder," my grandparents' name, to my name, to be connected with them and with their story, full of blanks.

It is through Delphine that I met Chantal in 1983. I would practice, and she would sleep. It was a time in Chantal's life when she needed to sleep a lot; she woke up slowly to the sounds of the cello. And that connection never ended. Chantal had a very close relationship with my brother Marc, who appears in *Rue Mallet-Stevens*. Claire, my sister, became her editor and a close collaborator. The story continues . . .

Maniac Shadows (2013).

Ma mère rit (My Mother Laughs, 2013).

Odyssey for Cello and Imaginary Choir (Sonia Wieder-Atherton, 2013).

Percival: In 2013, changes in Chantal's world are revealed in her confessional book *Ma mère rit*. From a staged reading of an excerpt from this text at The Kitchen in New York, Chantal produced a moving-image self-portrait as part of her installation *Maniac Shadows* (fig. 6). Chantal invited Sonia to be part of *Maniac Shadows* with a live performance of her new work, *Odyssey for Cello and Imaginary Choir*. While now traveling in different directions, Chantal's and Sonia's paths continually converged.

As part of Chantal's artist project season in Portland, we restaged her performance reading of the excerpt from *Ma mère rit*. In our onstage conversation, I asked Sonia to tell me more about her performance and how Chantal was part of the *Odyssey*.

Wieder-Atherton: My *Odyssey* is a series of adventures in the course of which I face up to the wind, the waves, chaos, the storm, tears, a

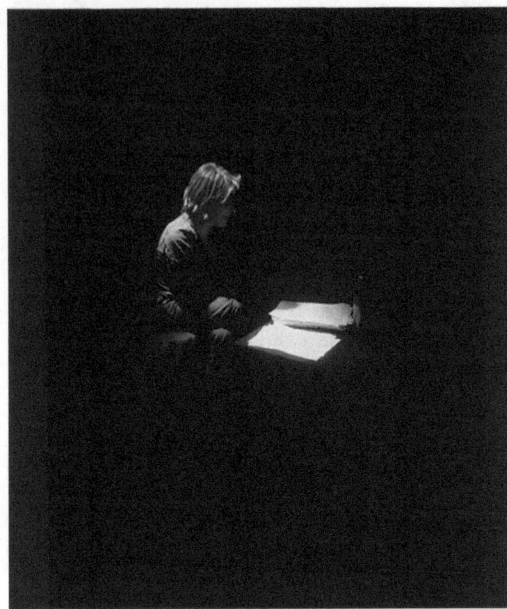

Figure 6. Chantal Akerman, installation view of *My Mother Laughs* in *Maniac Shadows* (2013), The Kitchen. Courtesy of The Kitchen. Photo by Jason Mandella

choir. The voice is the voice of my cello. I realized that to become part of this story, I had to be stripped of all my familiar props—no harmony, no timbre, not even another presence. Hence the idea of a soundtrack.

I set out on the long task of gathering a wide range of sounds from different sources: film sounds from Pasolini, Rossellini's *Stromboli*, Akerman. I began to work on this raw material, mixing, distorting, superimposing sounds. Creating a scenario of sound. Then I was ready to bring back the music. At The Kitchen, I performed this matrix as *Songs from the Mediterranean*, the final piece in a triptych that began with *Jewish Songs* and *Songs from the East*. The music, performed in a setting that evoked a landscape baked by the scorching sun, included an Arabic Andalusian song, a psalm of Egyptian origin, a Corsican lullaby. Chantal wanted to film this performance in the desert (fig. 7).

Chantal knew about my work on the soundtrack for *Odyssey for Cello and Imaginary Choir*. She knew that I was collecting a lot of sounds, and she would give me ideas. She said, "Oh, take the

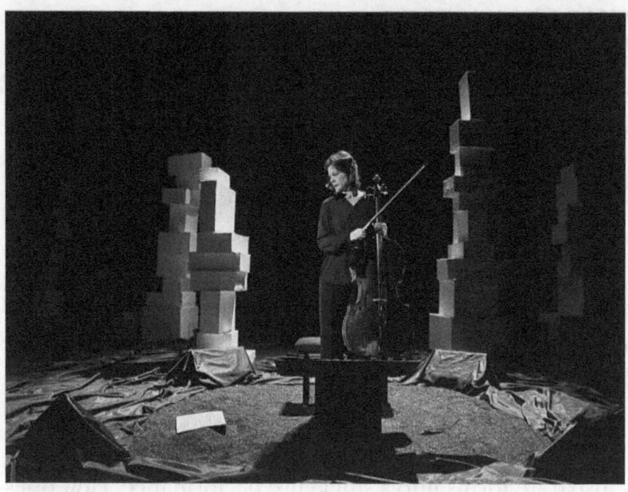

Figure 7. Sonia Wieder-Atherton, *Odyssey for Cello and Imaginary Choir*, 20 April 2013, The Kitchen. Photo © Paula Court

sea from *La Captive*," and "Take the steps from this film," and she would give me all her films and say, "Take all the sounds you want." The cello infiltrated her images more and more; she even took a track of music I performed and played it in reverse. Our universes were communicating all the time, like an uninterrupted movement of sounds, texts, images, and ideas.

Percival: Performing *Odyssey*, Sonia has taken journeys afar to places like Portugal, Greece, India, Italy, Israel, and the US. Her chapters of *Odyssey* offer sanctuary and bear witness through the voices and dreams of writers such as Aharon Appelfeld, children in schools and refugee camps, women making tea, a priest, or untouchables. Chantal was elsewhere, interviewing witnesses and hearing stories in Jasper, Texas, and on the border between Arizona and Mexico. Chantal captured sounds in the landscapes she traveled, sounds that evoked fear and flight, chaos and war, for what would become her last work, *NOW*.[7]

CHANTAL? Dialogue between a movie, a cello, and a text (2018).

Percival: *CHANTAL?* marries the intuitive and visionary minds that Sonia and Chantal have each brought to their work. When I met Sonia in person in Paris at the end of 2017, we finalized plans for the US premiere of *CHANTAL?* The work premiered in Paris and Brussels in early April 2018, in productions with Aurore Clément reading from Chantal's autobiographical text *Une famille à Bruxelles* on one side of a screen showing Chantal's first film, *Saute ma ville,* while Sonia played on the other side.[8] *CHANTAL?* was presented with Sonia alone onstage in late April and early May in Los Angeles, Seattle, and Portland. With *CHANTAL?,* Sonia merges disparate forms into a single live performance. How does Sonia, and how do we, now talk to *CHANTAL?*

Wieder-Atherton: La Ferme du Buisson asked me to participate in the exhibition *Maniac Shadows* in Noisiel, France, in 2017. I said I would walk around the space. I entered a little upstairs room where *Saute ma ville* would be shown "en boucle"—in a loop, time after time. I wanted to remain there, to be with Chantal and my cello.

At the beginning I was shy. Little by little I began to talk with Chantal. I would listen to Chantal reading, over and over. It sounded like a prayer. I wanted to play along with her, her every move, her silences, her dancing at once burlesque and deadly serious, her anxiety, as she is humming little tunes. Tracking her, surprising her, surprising myself at each step.

CHANTAL? begins with Béla Bartók's Sonata for Solo Violin, transcribed here for cello. This is followed by a child's voice singing softly at first and then getting louder: Chantal's voice in *Saute ma ville.* Janáček's *Moravian Poem* and *Traditional Jewish Prayer* are pieces that Chantal liked above all. *New York Quartet* reminds me of *A Couch in New York.* The cadenza from Prokofiev's Symphony-Concerto, Op. 125, for cello has a dramaturgic power that demands a tremendous physical energy.

After the explosion at the end of the film, Chantal's voice

reading *A Family in Brussels* gently slips its way between the notes and the images. A sequence of colors, dances, virtuosity, folk tunes, deep songs—Bartók's last piece has the strength to be with the eighteen-year-old Chantal. The third time the film is shown, it is silent. Only at the end does the voice of Chantal come back, as if the past and the present were walking together, hand in hand. The screen is big, facing Chantal. . . . I sit on the side, partly in the frame. I look at Chantal.

Percival: At the end of *CHANTAL?*, I felt a presence and an absence come together. Chantal's voice reading from *A Family in Brussels* makes it seem as if she is in the room speaking to us, called forth by the cello and Sonia's presence, a presence whose notes when silent are seeking Chantal's words. I recalled Chantal's last voice-over in *Avec Sonia Wieder-Atherton*:

[They say that Sonia] seizes us, takes us along with her, so far away, so powerfully, to yet unknown places, sometimes dark, others light, ancient and new, in a mixture of pleasure and tension. They also say that she's had an atypical career, with an atypical repertoire. That's what they say about her. But she searches, she keeps searching, she pushes forward, she moves on, she keeps looking. She searches for an opening, for a sound, for a spark. The spark of life. *This too, is true.*

Over a thirty-year odyssey, cellist and filmmaker were not merely soloists; they were conducting together. Movingly, Sonia concluded our public conversation in Portland with these words:

Wieder-Atherton: There were always exchanges, especially early in the morning, Chantal's favorite time. We talked about what we were doing all the time, and that's why it's hard to figure out who, what, and when. We were very close in the way we thought. Chantal opened a huge world to me, through who she was. This is still growing in me, so rich, strong, and fragile at the same time. And through the form of her work, how she builds form. You see it in her exhibitions—she always knew how to put something in that would break the thing that was too perfect.

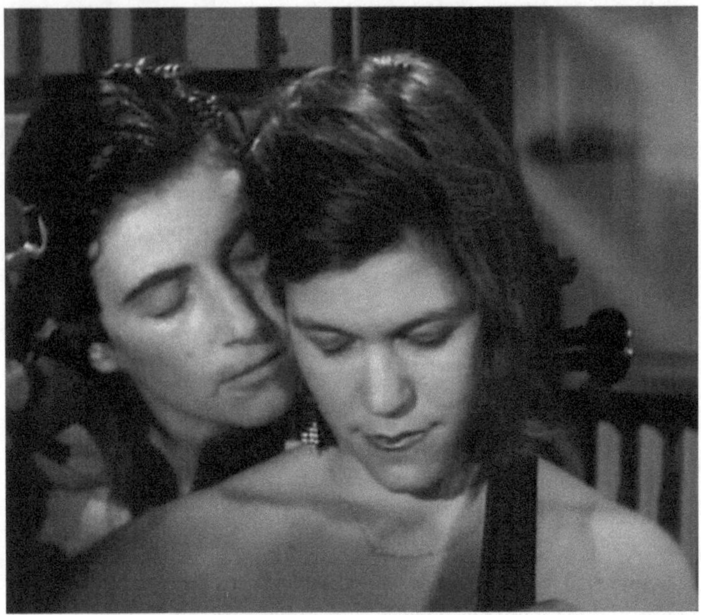

Figure 8. Chantal Akerman and Sonia Wieder-Atherton in
Rue Mallet-Stevens (1986). Courtesy of Fondation Chantal
Akerman

Perfection is so sought after, but perfection is not life. She knew instinctively what she liked, what she didn't like, when she wanted to stay silent, and when she was ready to say something. She didn't want people to ask her too many questions, because then she would have to explain things that she didn't know or didn't want to know yet. There was a process to go through that was not easy for her; it meant that Chantal was quite uneasy, like a cat that doesn't like to be held too tight. So when someone would say to Chantal, "Well, what is it you want to do with that?" Chantal would say, "No, please, just shhh."

Notes

1. Founded and curated by Sandra Percival, Zena Zezza is a contemporary art project in Portland, Oregon. Zena Zezza features individual artists in a durational artist project season

that includes an exhibition and an interrelated series of public programs, with artists and leading thinkers, on the ideas and influences within each artist's practice. *LOOKING, REALLY LOOKING! The Films of Chantal Akerman 1968–2015* (June 2016–May 2017) featured a nonchronological survey of thirty-five films, copresented in collaboration with the Northwest Film Center. Zena Zezza's series of discursive and performative events included *Errant Soul: From East to West and In-Between*, with Luis Croquer and Marat Grinberg; *Chantal Akerman: La Passion de l'intime/An Intimate Passion*, with Bérénice Reynaud; *Studio Visit: 90.3 FM*, a radio program on music in Chantal Akerman's films with Sandra Percival and Abigail Susik; *The wind crosses the brown land, unheard.*, with Laura Fried and Kyss Jean-Mary; and *Ma mère rit* (*My Mother Laughs*), a restaging of Akerman's performance reading at The Kitchen, directed and acted by Grace Carter. Recordings of these events can be found at zenazezza.org.

2. *A Nos Amours: Chantal Akerman Retrospective* at the Institute of Contemporary Art, London (2014–15), along with Adam Roberts's writings for A Nos Amours, the Institute of Contemporary Art, and the *Huffington Post* blog, served as a filmography and description source.

3. The brief quotes beside the titles of Akerman's works are her own, drawn from Nicole Brenez, "Chantal Akerman: The Pajama Interview," originally conducted at the Vienna International Film Festival in 2011 and reprinted in the online journal *Lola*, no. 2 (June 2012), www.lolajournal.com/2/pajama.html. Included with editors' permission.

4. "Trois strophes sur le nom de Sacher by Chantal Akerman," Movingimage.US/images/enews/AMatterOfVisibility _ProgramNote.pdf (accessed 22 June 2018).

5. "Audio Recording in the Third Room, Read by Chantal Akerman," transcript provided by the Jewish Museum, New York, 1997.

6. *Chantal Akerman Films Sonia Wieder-Atherton* (DVD set and booklet; Naïve, 2011).

7. *NOW* (2015), Chantal Akerman's last installation work shown at the 2017 Venice Biennale, and in the collection of the Jewish Museum, New York.

8. Chantal Akerman, *Une famille à Bruxelles* (Paris: L'Arche, 1998). The English-edition artist book includes a two-CD recording: *A Family in Brussels/Chantal Akerman* (New York: Dia Art Foundation, 2002).

Sandra Percival is founding director and curator of Zena Zezza, a contemporary art project in Portland, Oregon, where she has curated artist project seasons with the work and films of Josiah McElheny, Anthony McCall, Stan Douglas, and Chantal Akerman. Presented in collaboration with academic institutions such as Reed College and Pacific Northwest College of the Arts, an integrated series of events with art historians, writers, and leading thinkers brings new perspectives and scholarship to each artist's practice. Percival curated exhibitions of Pae White and Frances Stark at Mills College Art Museum (2009–11) and, when in London (1991–2005), she commissioned new work with Tacita Dean, Marie José Burki, Roni Horn, Constance DeJong, Adrian Paci, and Pipilotti Rist. She was adjunct professor in the Curatorial Practice Program at California College of the Arts (2005–9).

Sonia Wieder-Atherton is a composer and cellist based in Paris who at the age of nineteen went to Moscow, where she studied with Natalia Shakhovskaya at the Tchaikovsky Conservatory. At twenty-five she returned to France, where she won the Rostropovich Cello Competition. She has premiered works of composers and has played with prestigious orchestras. She has instigated projects combining musical and visual experiences: *Songs from Slavic Lands*, a journey through Mitteleuropa; *Vita*, the story of Angioletta-Angel via Monteverdi and Scelsi; *Odyssey for Cello and Imaginary Choir*; *Little Girl Blue, from Nina Simone*; *The Night Dances*, with Charlotte Rampling; and Marguerite Duras's *Navire Night* with Fanny Ardant. In 2011 she received the Bernheim Foundation Award, and in 2015 she was named Chevalier de l'Ordre des Arts et des Lettres.

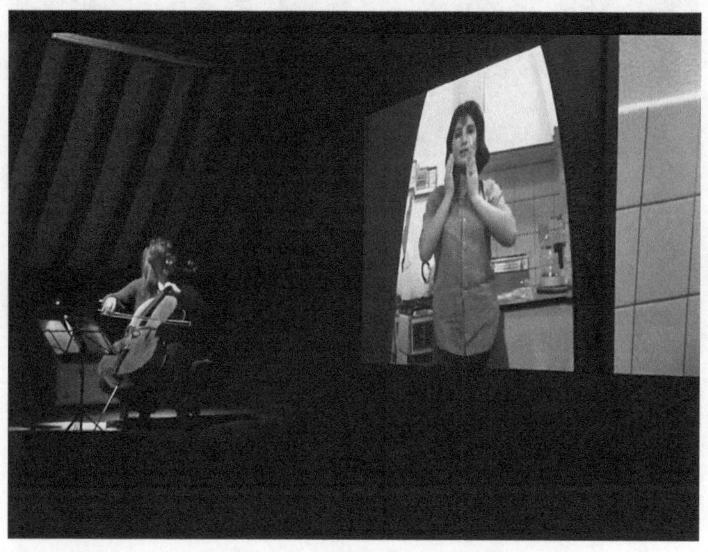

Figure 9. Sonia Wieder-Atherton performing *CHANTAL?* (2018).
© Renaud Bouchard-Gonzalez. Courtesy of Fondation
Chantal Akerman

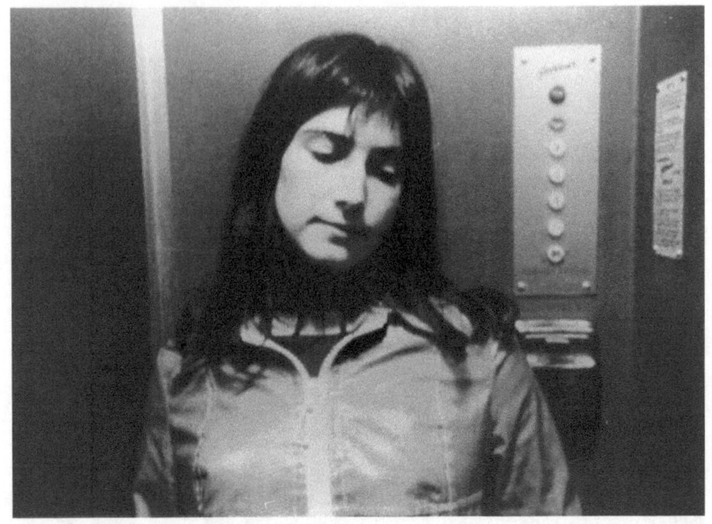

Figure 1. *Je tu il elle* (Belgium/France, 1974).
Courtesy of Janus Films

Chantal Akerman Filmography

A definitive catalog of Akerman's works is being undertaken by the Chantal Akerman Foundation and the Cinematek–Royal Belgian Film Archive. This filmography, compiled by Claire Atherton from published sources, is as complete and correct as possible.[1]

Saute ma ville (*Blow Up My Town*)
1968, Belgium
Written and directed by Chantal Akerman
Cinematography by René Fruchter
Editing by Geneviève Luciani
35mm, 13 minutes, B&W

L'Enfant aimé ou Je joue à être une femme mariée
    (*The Beloved Child, or I Play at Being a Married Woman*)
1971, Belgium
Written and directed by Chantal Akerman
Featuring Claire Wauthion, Chantal Akerman, and Daphna
    Merzer
16mm, 35 minutes, B&W

La Chambre (*The Room*)
1972, Belgium, shot in New York
Written and directed by Chantal Akerman
Cinematography by Babette Mangolte

Camera Obscura 100, Volume 34, Number 1
DOI 10.1215/02705346-7264220   © 2019 by *Camera Obscura*
Published by Duke University Press

Editing by Geneviève Luciani

16mm, silent, 11 minutes, color

Akerman later made a version with sound, now lost.

A transcript is available in Chantal Akerman, "Two Rooms,
    Monologues, Imaginaries, as Seen through Their Texts,"
    trans. Mark Cohn, ed. Ivone Marguiles, *Film Quarterly* 70, no.
    1 (2016): 70–78. See also Chantal Akerman, "La Chambre,"
    in *Bande(s) à part, Tome 25: Chantal Akerman*, ed. Dominique
    Bax and Cyril Béghin (Paris: Bande(s) à part Festival de
    Cinema à Bobigny, Le Magic Cinéma, 2014), 36–41.

Hotel Monterey

1972, Belgium, shot in New York

Written and directed by Chantal Akerman

Cinematography by Babette Mangolte

Editing by Geneviève Luciani

16mm, silent, 63 minutes, color

Le 15/8

1973, Belgium

Written and directed by Chantal Akerman and Samy
    Szlingerbaum

Cinematography and editing by Chantal Akerman and Samy
    Szlingerbaum

Featuring Chris Myllykoski

16mm, 42 minutes, B&W

Hanging Out Yonkers (uncompleted)

1973, Belgium, shot in New York

Written and directed by Chantal Akerman

Cinematography by Babette Mangolte

16mm, color

Je tu il elle (*I, You, He, She*)

1974, Belgium/France

Written and directed by Chantal Akerman

Cinematography by Bénédicte Delesalle

Editing by Luc Freché

Sound by Alain Pierre and Samy Szlingerbaum
Featuring Chantal Akerman, Niels Arestrup, and Claire
     Wauthion
35mm, 90 minutes, B&W

Jeanne Dielman, 23 quai du Commerce, 1080 Bruxelles
1975, Belgium/France
Written and directed by Chantal Akerman
Cinematography by Babette Mangolte
Editing by Patricia Canino
Featuring Delphine Seyrig, Jan Decorte, and Henri Storck
Produced by Evelyne Paul and Marilyn Watelet
35mm, 200 minutes, color

News from Home
1976, Belgium/France
Written and directed by Chantal Akerman
Cinematography by Babette Mangolte
Editing by Francine Sandberg
Sound by Dominique Dalmasso
Produced by Marilyn Watelet and Alain Dahan
16mm, 89 minutes, color

Les Rendez-vous d'Anna (*The Meetings of Anna*)
1978, Belgium/France/Germany
Written and directed by Chantal Akerman
Cinematography by Jean Penzer
Editing by Francine Sandberg
Sound by Henri Morelle
Featuring Aurore Clément, Helmut Griem, Magali Noël, Lea
     Massari, and Hanns Zischler
Produced by Marilyn Watelet and Alain Dahan
35mm, 127 minutes, color

Aujourd'hui, dis-moi/Dis-moi (*Tell Me*)
1982, France
Written and directed by Chantal Akerman
Cinematography by Maurice Perrimond

Editing by Francine Sandberg
Sound by Xavier Vauthrin
16mm, 45 minutes, color

Hôtel des Acacias
1982, France
Made by students at the Institut National Supérieur des Arts
    du Spectacle et des Techniques de Diffusion under the
    direction of Chantal Akerman
Cinematography by Michel Houssiau
Editing by Suzy Rossberg
Sound by Henri Morelle
Format unknown, 40 minutes, color

Toute une nuit (*All Night Long*)
1982, Belgium/France
Written and directed by Chantal Akerman
Cinematography by Caroline Champetier
Editing by Luc Barnier
Sound by Ricardo Castro
Produced by Marilyn Watelet and Nicole Filipo
35mm, 90 minutes, color

Les Années 80 (*The Eighties*)
1983, France/Belgium
Directed by Chantal Akerman
Written by Jean Gruault and Chantal Akerman
Cinematography by Michel Houssiau and Luc Benhamou
Sound by Marc Mallinus, Daniel Dehays, and Henri Morelle
Editing by Nadine Keseman and Francine Sandberg
Produced by Marilyn Watelet
35mm and video, 79 minutes, color

"Un jour Pina a demandé . . ." (*On Tour with Pina Bausch*)
1983, France/Belgium
Directed by Chantal Akerman
Cinematography by Babette Mangolte and Luc Benhamou

Editing by Dominique Forgue and Patrick Mimouni
Sound by Jean Minondo
Produced by Alain Plagne
16mm, 57 minutes, color

L'Homme à la valise (*The Man with the Suitcase*)
1983, France
Written and directed by Chantal Akerman
Cinematography by Maurice Perrimont
Editing by Francine Sandberg
Sound by Jean-Claude Brisson
Featuring Chantal Akerman and Jeffrey Kime
16mm, 61 minutes, color

Family Business
1984, UK
Written and directed by Chantal Akerman
Cinematography by Luc Benhamou
Editing by Patrick Mimouni
Music by Marc Hérouet
Featuring Aurore Clément, Chantal Akerman, Marilyn Watelet,
    and Leslie Vandermeulen
16mm, 18 minutes, color

J'ai faim, j'ai froid (*I'm Hungry, I'm Cold*)
    in *Paris vu par, 20 ans après* (*Paris Seen By, 20 Years Later*)
1984, France
Written and directed by Chantal Akerman
Cinematography by Luc Benhamou
Editing by Francine Sandberg
Sound by François de Morant and Jean-Paul Loublier
35mm, 12 minutes, B&W

Lettre d'une cinéaste: Chantal Akerman
    (*Letter from a Filmmaker: Chantal Akerman*)
1984, France
Written and directed by Chantal Akerman

Cinematography by Luc Benhamou
Music by Marc Hérouet
Featuring Aurore Clément and Chantal Akerman
Video, 8 minutes, color

Autour d'un marteau (*The Hammer*)
1986, France
Directed by Chantal Akerman
Cinematography by Claire Atherton
Sound by Alix Comte
Editing by Claire Atherton
Video, 4 minutes, color

Rue Mallet-Stevens
1986, Belgium
Directed by Chantal Akerman
Cinematography by Claire Atherton and Luc Benhamou
Sound by Alix Comte
Editing by Claire Atherton
Video, 7 minutes, color

Golden Eighties/Window Shopping
1986, France/Belgium/Switzerland
Directed by Chantal Akerman
Script by Chantal Akerman, Jean Gruault, Leora Barish, Henry
    Bean, and Pascal Bonitzer
Cinematography by Gilberto Azevedo and Luc Benhamou
Editing by Francine Sandberg
Sound by Henri Morelle and Michel Rejas
Produced by Martine Marignac and Mailyn Watelet
Featuring Myriam Boyer, John Berry, Delphine Seyrig, Nicolas
    Tronc, Lio, Pascale Salkin, Fanny Cottençon, Charles
    Denner, and Jean-François Balmer
35mm, 96 minutes, color

Letters Home
1986, France
Directed by Chantal Akerman

Play by Rose Leiman Goldemberg from the correspondence
    between Sylvia Plath and her mother
Cinematography by Luc Benhamou
Editing by Claire Atherton
Sound by Alix Comte
Featuring Delphine Seyrig and Coralie Seyrig
Video, 104 minutes, color

Portrait d'une paresseuse/La Paresse in *Sept femmes, sept péchés*
    (*Sloth* in *Seven Women, Seven Sins*)
1986, France/Austria/Belgium/US/West Germany
Directed by Chantal Akerman
Editing by Claire Atherton
Featuring Chantal Akerman and Sonia Wieder-Atherton
16mm, 14 minutes, color

Histoires d'Amérique: Food, Family, and Philosophy
1988, France/Belgium
Written and directed by Chantal Akerman
Cinematography by Luc Benhamou and Claire Atherton
Editing by Patrick Mimouni
Sound by Alix Comte
Music by Sonia Wieder-Atherton
Featuring Maurice Brenner, Carl Don, David Buntzman, Judith
    Malina, Eszter Balint, Dean Jackson, and Roy Nathanson
Produced by Marilyn Watelet and Bertrand Van Effenterre
35mm, 92 minutes, color

Les Trois dernières sonates de Franz Schubert
    (*Franz Schubert's Last Three Sonatas*)
1989, France
Written and directed by Chantal Akerman
Cinematography by Jean Monsigny
Editing by Francine Sandberg
Sound by Xavier Vauthrin
Featuring Alfred Brendel
Video, 49 minutes, color

Trois strophes sur le nom de Sacher (*Three Stanzas on the Name Sacher*)
1989, France
Directed by Chantal Akerman
Violoncello by Sonia Wieder-Atherton
Cinematography by Raymond Fromont
Editing by Rose Legrand
Sound by Nicolas Joly
Video, 12 minutes, color

Pour Febe Elisabeth Velasquez, El Salvador in *Contre l'oubli*
    (*For Febe Elisabeth Velasquez, El Salvador* in *Against Oblivion*)
1991, France/Belgium/Switzerland
Written and directed by Chantal Akerman
Cinematography by Jean Monsigny
Music by Mino Cenelu
Featuring Catherine Deneuve and Sonia Wieder-Atherton
Video, 3 minutes, color

Nuit et jour (*Night and Day*)
1991, France/Belgium/Switzerland
Written and directed by Chantal Akerman
Cinematography by Jean-Claude Neckelbrouck
Editing by Francine Sandberg
Sound by Alix Comte
Music by Marc Hérouet and Sonia Wieder-Atherton
Produced by Pierre Wallon, Marilyn Watelet, Martine Marignac,
    and Maurice Tinchant
35mm, 90 minutes, color

Le Déménagement (*Moving In*)
1993, France
Written and directed by Chantal Akerman
Cinematography by Raymond Fromont
Sound by Alix Comte
Editing by Rudi Maerten
Produced by Sophie Goupil
Featuring Sami Frey
35mm, 42 minutes, color

D'Est (From the East)
1993, France/Belgium
Directed by Chantal Akerman
Cinematography by Raymond Fromont
Editing by Claire Atherton
Sound by Pierre Mertens and Thomas Gauder
Produced by Helena Van Dantzig and Marilyn Watelet
16mm, 110 minutes, color

Portrait d'une jeune fille de la fin des années 60 à Bruxelles
    (Portrait of a Young Girl at the End of the 1960s in Brussels)
1993, France
Written and directed by Chantal Akerman
Cinematography by Raymond Fromont
Sound by Pierre Mertens
Editing by Martine Lebon
Featuring Circé Lethem and Julien Rassam
Super 16mm, 60 minutes, color

Un divan à New York (A Couch in New York)
1996, France/Belgium/Germany
Directed by Chantal Akerman
Written by Chantal Akerman and Jean-Louis Benoît
Cinematography by Dietrich Lohmann
Editing by Claire Atherton
Sound by Gérard Lamps and Pierre Mertens
Music by Sonia Wieder-Atherton
Featuring William Hurt, Juliette Binoche, Richard Jenkins, and
    Matthew Burton
Produced by Diana Elbaum, Régine Konckier, and Jean-Luc
    Ormières
35mm, 105 minutes, color

Chantal Akerman par Chantal Akerman
    (Chantal Akerman by Chantal Akerman)
1996, France
Directed by Chantal Akerman
Cinematography by Raymond Fromont

Editing by Claire Atherton
Sound by Xavier Vauthrin
Produced by Xavier Carniaux, Thierry Garrel, and Claude
    Guisard
Video, 63 minutes, color

Le Jour où . . . (The Day When . . .)
1997, Switzerland
Written and directed by Chantal Akerman
Cinematography by Raymond Fromont
Editing by Claire Atherton
Sound by Nicolas Lefebvre
35mm, 7 minutes, color

Sud (South)
1999, France/Belgium
Directed by Chantal Akerman
Cinematography by Raymond Fromont
Editing by Claire Atherton
Sound by Thierry de Halleux
Produced by Xavier Carniaux and Marilyn Watelet
Video, 70 minutes, color

La Captive (The Captive)
2000, France/Belgium
Directed by Chantal Akerman
Written by Chantal Akerman and Eric de Kuyper
Cinematography by Sabine Lancelin
Editing by Claire Atherton
Sound by Thierry de Halleux
Featuring Stanislas Mehrar and Sylvie Testud
Produced by Paulo Branco and Antoine Beau
35mm, 107 minutes, color

De l'autre côté (From the Other Side)
2002, Belgium
Directed by Chantal Akerman

Photography by Raymond Fromont, Robert Fenz, and Chantal
    Akerman
Editing by Claire Atherton
Sound by Pierre Mertens
Produced by Marilyn Watelet and Xavier Carniaux
Video and 16mm, 102 minutes, color

Avec Sonia Wieder-Atherton (*With Sonia Wieder-Atherton*)
2002, France
Directed by Chantal Akerman
Cinematography by Sabine Lancelin
Sound by Pierre-Antoine Signoret
Editing by Claire Atherton
Video, 52 minutes, color

Demain on déménage (*Tomorrow We Move*)
2004, France/Belgium
Directed by Chantal Akerman
Written by Chantal Akerman and Eric de Kuyper
Cinematography by Sabine Lancelin
Editing by Claire Atherton
Sound by Pierre Mertens
Musical direction by Sonia Wieder-Atherton
Featuring Sylvie Testud, Aurore Clément, Jean-Pierre Marielle,
    Lucas Belvaux, Dominique Reymond, Natacha Régnier, Elsa
    Zylberstein, and Gilles Privat
Produced by Marilyn Watelet and Paulo Branco
35mm, 110 minutes, color

Là-bas (*Down There*)
2006, Belgium/France
Directed by Chantal Akerman
Cinematography by Chantal Akerman and Robert Fenz
Editing by Claire Atherton
Video, 78 minutes, color

Tombée de nuit sur Shanghai, in *L'État du monde*
     (*Nightfall in Shanghai,* in *The State of the World*)
2007, France
Direction and cinematography Chantal Akerman
Editing by Claire Atherton
Video, 15 minutes, color

À l'Est avec Sonia Wieder-Atherton
     (*In the East with Sonia Wieder-Atherton*)
2009, France
Directed by Chantal Akerman
Cinematography by Sabine Lancelin
Sound by Pierre-Antoine Signoret
Editing by Claire Atherton
Video, 52 minutes, color

La Folie Almayer (*Almayer's Folly*)
2011, France/Belgium
Written and directed by Chantal Akerman
Adapted from *Almayer's Folly* by Joseph Conrad (1895)
Cinematography by Raymond Fromont
Editing by Claire Atherton
Sound by Pierre Mertens
Produced by Patrick Quinet, Chantal Akerman, and Paulo
     Branco
35mm, 127 minutes, color

No Home Movie
2015, France/Belgium
Direction and cinematography by Chantal Akerman
Editing by Claire Atherton
Produced by Chantal Akerman and Serge Zeïtoun
Video, 115 minutes, Color

Note

1. Sources consulted include *Chantal Akerman, Monographie* (Bobigny, France: Ciné-Festivals/Magic Cinéma, 2014); *Chantal Akerman: Autoportrait en cinéaste* (Paris: Editions du Centre Georges Pompidou/Editions Cahiers du cinéma, 2004); and Nicole Brenez, "Chantal Akerman: The Pajama Interview," trans. David Phelps, originally conducted for the Vienna International Film Festival in 2011, *Lola* 2 (June 2012), www.lolajournal.com /2/pajama.html.

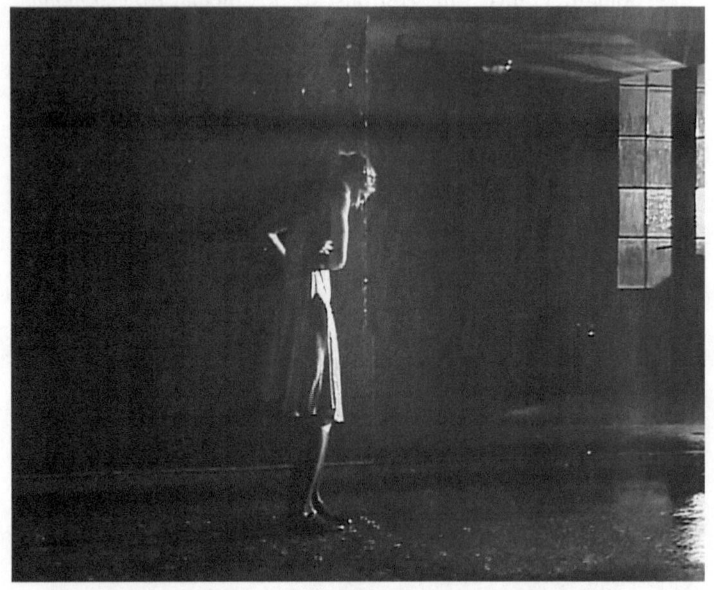

Figure 1. *Femmes d'Anvers en Novembre* (2011). Courtesy of
Fondation Chantal Akerman and Marian Goodman Gallery.
Photograph by Claire Atherton

List of Installations by Chantal Akerman

All works directed by Chantal Akerman with editing and spatialization for image and sound by Claire Atherton.

D'Est, au bord de la fiction (*From the East: Bordering on Fiction*)
1995
Video installation with twenty-five monitors in two adjacent
    rooms
Twenty-four monitors on pedestals (eight triptychs) and one
    single monitor (called "the twenty-fifth image")
With sound
Based on *D'Est* (1993)

Vingt-cinquième écran (*Twenty-fifth Screen*)
1995
Single monitor video installation
With sound
25th monitor of the installation *D'Est, au bord de la Fiction*

Selfportrait/Autobiography: A Work in Progress
1998
Video installation with six monitors arranged in a pyramid, and
    three chairs

Camera Obscura 100, Volume 34, Number 1
DOI 10.1215/02705346-7264232   © 2019 by *Camera Obscura*
Published by Duke University Press

With sound

Made with images and sounds from *D'Est, au bord de la fiction* (1995), *Jeanne Dielman, 23 quai du Commerce, 1080 Bruxelles* (1975), *Hotel Monterey* (1972), and *Toute une nuit* (1982) and the sound of Chantal's voice reading *Une famille à Bruxelles* (1998)

Woman Sitting after Killing

2001

Video installation with seven monitors

With sound

Made from the last sequence of *Jeanne Dielman, 23 quai du Commerce, 1080 Bruxelles*

From the Other Side

2002

Video installation with nineteen monitors and one projection in three adjacent rooms

One monitor in the first room; eighteen monitors on pedestals (six triptychs) in the second room; one projection in the third room

With sound

Based on *De l'autre côté* (2002)

From the Other Side; Fragments of an installation

2002

Video installation in two parts (one monitor and one projection)

With sound

Made out of the film *De l'autre côté*

A Voice in the Desert

2002

Installation with one projection

With sound

Third room of the installation *From the Other Side*

Marcher à côté de ses lacets dans un frigidaire vide
  (*Walking Next to One's Shoelaces in an Empty Fridge*)
2004
Installation with one spiral and multiple projections in two
  adjacent rooms
A text projected on a spiral screen in the first room, a silent
  projection on a floating tulle screen with a projection of a
  B&W diptych on the wall in the second room
With sound

In the Mirror
2007
Installation with one projection
With sound
Made from *L'Enfant aimé ou Je joue à être une femme mariée* (1971)

Je, tu, il, elle, l'installation
2007
Installation with three projections
With sound
Made from *Je tu il elle* (1974)

Femmes d'Anvers en Novembre (*Women from Antwerp in November*)
2008
Installation with multiple projections on two walls of the same
  room
One group of five projections in color and B&W, one single B&W
  square projection
Silent
Cinematography by Raymond Fromont

Maniac Summer
2009
Installation with multiple projections on three walls
One color projection on the left, two color and B&W diptychs in
  the center, one B&W projection on the right
With sound

An adjacent room may include the projection "My Mother
 Laughs, prelude," a video of Chantal reading in English from
 Ma mère rit (2013)

Tombée de nuit sur Shanghai (*Nightfall in Shanghai*)
2009
Installation with one video projection and two Chinese aquarium
 lamps
With sound
Made from *Nightfall in Shanghai* (2007)

La Chambre
2012
Installation with one video projection or five monitors
Silent
Made from *La Chambre* (1972)

Maniac Shadows
2012
Installation with multiple projections on three walls and a wall of
 photos
One triptych on the center wall and two shadows on the side
 walls
With sound
An adjacent room may include the projection "My Mother
 Laughs, prelude," a video of Chantal reading in English from
 Ma mère rit (2013)

My Mother Laughs Prelude
2012
Single projection video installation
With sound

De la mèr(e) au desert (*From the Mother to the Desert*)
2014
Installation with three projections
With sound

NOW

2015

Installation with multiple projections, Chinese aquarium lamps,
   and fluorescent lamp tubes

Five projections on acrylic screens, two projections on the floor

Seven mono and stereo sound channels distributed around the
   room

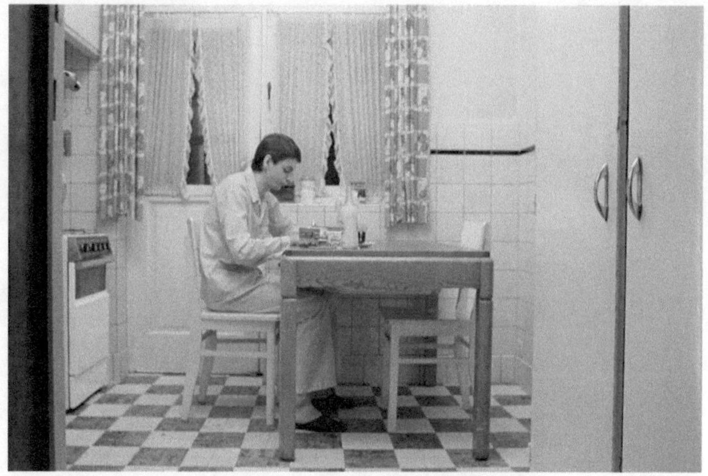

Figure 2. *Jeanne Dielman, 23 quai du Commerce, 1080 Bruxelles*
(1975). Courtesy of Janus Films